Praise for

"In today's age of flimsy comic-book characters passing for superheroes, it is life-affirming—hell, it's vital—to recall the red-blooded humanity James Jones poured into his 1951 National Book Award-winning *From Here to Eternity*. How the semi-autobiographical novel made its way before an eager public provides much of the spine of M. J. Moore's enlightening *Star-Crossed Lovers* . . . but the narrative offers so much more. At its core is an iconoclastic love story that provides further ammunition to Jones's recurring theme of the individual versus society—all of which Moore soundly spells out in engaging and impressively researched detail."

~ **STEPHEN M. SILVERMAN**, author of *David Lean*; *The Catskills: Its History and How It Changed America*; and *Dancing on the Ceiling: Stanley Donen and His Movies*

"You have an enviable ability to diffuse each paragraph with an extraordinary amount of information—and still retain lightness."

~ **KENNETH SLAWENSKI**, author of *J. D. Salinger: A Life*

"Oh, to be young and a writer and finding your way with an exotic older woman! M. J. Moore's *Star-Crossed Lovers* is an incredible tale of James Jones, his novel *From Here to Eternity*, and the years he spent under the spell of his lover, Lowney Handy. Indispensable!"

~ **LUCIAN K. TRUSCOTT IV**, author of *Dress Gray*, *Heart of War*, and other novels; *Village Voice* staff writer; Class of '69 West Point graduate

"I did read *Star-Crossed Lovers* with great interest. Fascinating story—kept my interest throughout. My congratulations to you . . ."

~ **OLIVER STONE**, Academy Award-winning writer/director of "Platoon," "Born on the Fourth of July," "JFK," and other films; author of the novel *A Child's Night Dream* and the memoir *Chasing the Light*; and Purple Heart veteran of the U.S. Army's 25th Infantry Division

Star-Crossed Lovers

STAR-CROSSED LOVERS

James Jones, Lowney Handy, and the Birth of *From Here to Eternity*

M. J. MOORE

 Heliotrope Books
New York

Other Books by M. J. Moore:

For Paris, With Love & Squalor

Mario Puzo: An American Writer's Quest

ISBN 978-1-956474-21-3 paperback
978-1-956474-20-6 eBook

Cover Design by M. J. Moore and Naomi Rosenblatt
Typeset by Heliotrope Books

Unless otherwise credited, all photos are public domain from varied online archives.

In memory of Joan Didion Dunne
and John Gregory Dunne, with gratitude . . .

and for Mary Tierney, with love and appreciation.

CONTENTS

INTRODUCTION

Star-Crossed Lovers is the story of two unique individuals: James Jones had a mercurial personality; Mrs. Lowney Handy was as idiosyncratic as her name (which rhymes with Tony). Both of them were volatile. Gifted, stubborn, and intense. Sometimes volcanic.

Novelist James Jones, in his youth, is this story's "through line"—up to a tipping point. The moment Lowney Handy appears, Jones's life becomes a shared narrative. Together, with devoted assistance from others, they made a significant contribution not just to American letters, but to world literature: the National Book Award-winning *From Here to Eternity.*

When they met on the weekend of his 22nd birthday in 1943, Jones was an AWOL combat veteran, plagued by an alcoholic upbringing compounded by Post-Traumatic Stress Disorder (PTSD). He'd survived the attack on Pearl Harbor; and he'd been wounded at Guadalcanal in the war against Japan. Jones was an embittered, hard-drinking, angry young man. She was a creative, spiritual, self-educated maverick devoted to helping troubled renegades.

Meeting 39-year-old Lowney Handy (childless, with a boldly unconventional marriage) in 1943 was more than lucky for Jones. It was a life-transforming benediction, especially by the time she turned forty in April 1944.

Lowney Handy advocated for Jones's "medical discharge" in the summer of '44, when the Army was prepared to court-martial him. It was Lowney and her husband with whom Jones lived full-time, at their mutual invitation; and Jones often traveled with Lowney as she (more than anyone else) coaxed out of him what became *From Here to Eternity*, between 1946 and 1950. Expanding their shared vision of life, they inaugurated a unique writers' colony, legally incorporated in the State of Illinois on September 21st, 1951. Supported annually almost wholly by Jones's earnings from *Eternity* (in 1952 alone, he gave $65,000 to the Handy Writers' Colony), dozens of writers attended the Colony in the 1950s. Aside from writing priorities, Lowney and Jones practiced Yoga, meditation, breathing exercises, and macrobiotic diets; they studied Hinduism, Buddhism, and American Transcendentalism. And from 1943–1957, they sustained their tempestuous, trans-generational love affair.

In this book, James Jones's youth unfolds, from childhood to the Army, setting the stage—until he collides with Lowney Handy, as he did in November 1943.

Then, it becomes the Jones and Lowney story; with critical allies ranging from her husband, Harry Handy, to the dean of American book editors: Maxwell Perkins at Scribners in New York.

Art and alcoholism, war and PTSD, Max Perkins's and Scribners's, visions of The Great American Novel, an open marriage in small-town Illinois, plus immersions in studies of the religions of India and the Far East—all that (and more) induced *From Here to Eternity*, which exploded like a nova in 1951.

Challenging questions arise. For example, how did Jones's anti-authority, profane, blistering portrait of the U.S. Army win the National Book Award not only at the height of the McCarthy Era, but at the peak of the Korean War in 1952? Has any other debut novel ever conquered our culture in such a way? The novel *From Here to Eternity* was both critically acclaimed *and* a blockbuster popular success, despite evocations of adultery, binge-drinking, prostitution, homophobia, anti-Semitism, hazing in the military, hypocrites hiding behind officers' rhetoric, and racism polluting the ranks and society at large. Oddly, *Eternity's* phenomenal success dovetailed with Eisenhower's election to the presidency, defying cliches about America in the 1950s being an uptight society of Silent Generation "squares."

This is the true-life love story of Lowney Handy and James Jones, with its mythological, fateful arc. After he married Gloria Mosolino in 1957, the remainder of James Jones's life and career became another story, and belongs properly to another book. The Jones and Lowney odyssey is exceptional in literary history.

She was an eccentric small-town autodidact driven by creative zeal and fueled by her blazing non-conformist streak. He was a distressed ex-GI (flat broke, without prospects, damaged by war) who obsessed over his hunger for a writer's life. Some of their unpublished letters are in the Handy Writers' Colony collection at the University of Illinois (Springfield). Quotations from their letters enhance this book.

In the early life of author James Jones, all roads led to Lowney Handy. And Jones's unorthodox long-term love affair between 1943 and 1957 with a childless, married, older woman (17 years his senior) in downstate Illinois . . . that is the ultimate focus of *Star-Crossed Lovers ~ James Jones, Lowney Handy, and the Birth of* From Here to Eternity.

1
EARLY STRUGGLES

The last words he was supposed to have said were, "I've left you all well-provided-for." The Crash was not long in coming.
~ James Jones, "The Ice-Cream Headache"

When author James Jones wrote short stories based on his childhood, he often exhumed conflicts and anecdotes illustrating his parents' distress.

In his story "Just Like the Girl," Jones dramatizes upsetting incidents that he experienced before he was ten years old. His alter ego in the story is John Slade. Similar to how Hemingway deployed his youthful doppelganger, Nick Adams, in a number of short stories, the character of John Slade serves as a stand-in for Jones; allowing the author to discharge a large amount of autobiographical grief through the crises endured by his protagonist. Tense family despair and rage are palpable.

The livid mother in "Just Like the Girl" is convinced that her alcoholic husband is having affairs. She makes no secret of her suspicions and fear. Most of all, she leans on her young son, and confides her dread quite inappropriately. Finally, she creates a new level of mother-to-son tension when ordering the boy to hide in the backseat of her husband's car, on the assumption that when he drives off after dinner, the husband will surely be en route to an assignation with a floozy. Persuading her younger son to spy on his father, whom she assumes will later return home drunk, is not the worst thing to happen in this story. What's worse is that the mother conveys her requests in a way that causes young John Slade to think that he *must* do her bidding, to prove his son's love for her.

It is a story so stark in its evocation of childhood despair that one editor, in particular, recoiled. Jones remembered: "I once showed ["Just Like the Girl"] to a newspaper editor in my hometown of Robinson, Illinois, who had known and admired my mother. The strange, guilty, upset, almost disbelieving look on his face when he handed it back, which seemed to say: 'Even if it's true, why *do* it?' was worth to me all the effort I put into writing it."

One answer to the question—"Why *do* it?"—is deceptively simple, yet it's the key to understanding the lifelong odyssey James Jones undertook as a postwar author. To answer that question in one word: *Honesty.*

That was, at bottom, Jones's ultimate intention as a writer. Whether composing a chapter to one of his capacious novels or writing a short story, crafting a passage for his nonfiction World War II chronicle or noting details about America's exodus from Vietnam (which he covered for *The New York Times Magazine* in 1973), he held to a rigorous code of narrative integrity; always writing as honestly as possible.

Poet, novelist, and biographer George Garrett, in his 1984 book *James Jones*, writes that "Jones was always a truth seeker and a truth teller. [He] has left a good record of his own mixed feelings about himself and his youth. If we turn to the evidence of the John Slade stories published in *The Ice-Cream Headache*, stories Jones claimed as autobiographical and that tend to conform to the known details of his youth even while adding more information, we discover other characteristics and other forces at work within him . . . we are presented with a more complete picture than anywhere else of the family, a 'Faulknerian' family. In letters, in interviews, and in some of the best of the stories collected in *The Ice-Cream Headache and Other Stories*, there is strong evidence of the conflicts and contradictions . . ."

Jones had despondent parents. His small-town dentist father, Ramon, was an alcoholic whose unsteady hands caused some patients to seek treatment elsewhere. And Jones's mother, Ada (once considered a great beauty in her youth, prior to marriage and motherhood) suffered from diabetes exacerbated by depression and obesity. Ramon and Ada named their first child George, but he was always called Jeff. Born in 1910, Jeff had no siblings until James Jones was born on November 6, 1921; followed by the birth of Mary Ann Jones in 1925.

Worn down by life's disappointments, both Ada and Ramon were melancholy.

Jones's memories of his youth were visceral. Describing himself as a child, he highlighted that he was "a shy kid with glasses." Such a casual remark conveyed something more about why Jones felt awkward and insecure as a young boy.

Having an alcoholic father who is unhappily married to a woman plagued by chronic discontent could make any child feel anxious, worried, and perhaps guilty for lacking the capacity to make the parents happy. But in Jones's case, his poor vision and the serious need for glasses in his youth set him on the path that led to his career. Conversing once with interviewer Leslie Hanscom, for a piece entitled "The Writer Speaks," Jones confirmed this. Inquiring about how Jones segued from soldiering to writing, Hanscom said: "You're somebody who appears to be designed by nature to exert physical strength. Yet you have undertaken to pursue the four-eyed profession of writing. What happened?" Jones replied that the trajectory of his life was, indeed, partly the result of being " . . . as you said, four-eyed. I think it was because I had to wear glasses when I was little."

Jones's poor vision as a child was matched by his physical frailty. A small boy, his short stature was exacerbated by the way his large ears stuck out on a head that seemed too big for his body. Unlike his older brother Jeff, who filled out early and had natural gifts as an athlete, Jones was never able to achieve any real competence in team sports, although he tried in every way to engage in athletics as a means of demonstrating his feisty spirit. Plus his courage. As often as not, he tried too hard and that usually resulted in more frustration for a gawky boy, whose own father kidded about him. Ramon joked that with his large head and big jug ears, Jones resembled an automobile with both its doors wide open. Jones felt that he always had to compensate for a slight physique, small hands, and eyeglasses. Perhaps to rebel against the idea that he was compromised by wearing glasses, he vigorously participated in everything all the other neighborhood boys were up to: snowball fights, war games, different sports, and plenty of pranks.

At home, Ramon taught both of his sons the rudiments of boxing. Rather than take it easy, Ramon punched hard enough to knock Jones down. And instead of complaining or crying out, Jones reacted with vehemence. He determined early on that the best strategy was to fight as aggressively as he could, no matter what.

* * *

With her older son Jeff gaining his independence more and more as the 1920s reached their end and with her only daughter, Mary Ann, receiving the favored treatment that's sometimes enjoyed by the baby in the family, Jones as a middle child caught the brunt of Ada's worsening moods. Once, as a neighbor looked on, Ada smacked Jones harshly across the face. The impact of such a blow to a sensitive child can be devastating. And there were other blows, as well: Jones was whacked with broomsticks and at times chained to a backyard post, so he would not roam while Ada did chores.

One of the earliest photographs of James Jones shows him riding a tricycle. His oversize head and wire-rimmed glasses are highlighted by the way his jaw is thrust forward. He steers the tricycle like a race car, with a posture and an attitude that signifies determination. Childhood friends recalled, many decades later, how speedily and relentlessly Jones rode down the sidewalks of Robinson on his red tricycle, darting past anyone and everyone in his path.

And yet, another side of young James Jones emerged before he entered high school. As is often the case with children who absorb the antagonism and turmoil exuded by combative parents, Jones cultivated the solitary side of his personality. There was an attic in his home and he often retreated up there to play with a variety of toys, especially traditional sets of toy soldiers and figures of Arthurian knights. More than toys, however, there was the paramount presence of books.

Ramon Jones knew that his father (a prominent local attorney) self-published a small book called *The Trials of Christ: Were They Legal?* in 1922. Patriarch George W. Jones composed that book to present compelling legal arguments proving that the Roman authorities flouted their own laws in persecuting Jesus. Throughout Ramon and Ada's home, stacks of books were shelved. Jones was known in the neighborhood for asking any guest who visited the house to read to him; and he amazed visitors by complaining when a passage was omitted. Jones's extraordinary memory was a feature of his personality that never diminished. He had vast powers of recall throughout his life.

A Carnegie Library near Jones's boyhood home, and its staff, had a tremendous impact on the growth of the future author. In addition to furnishing an inventory of books that filled his imagination with visions of heroic adventures, the library provided him with a safe, quiet sanctuary within which his mind and spirit were unencumbered. In the library, all domestic strife dissolved.

Early on he obsessed over P. C. Wren's war trilogy *Beau Geste, Beau Sabreur* and *Beau Ideal.* Jones once said that he had re-read each of those French Foreign Legion narratives "at least twenty times; and I knew all of their characters; and each character's big scenes."

One librarian, Vera Newlin, became a teacher and guide for Jones. She retained all her life a vivid singular memory of when she first encountered him: "As a little boy coming over to the library," she explained to interviewer J. Michael Lennon. "He was always very eager to get there." When asked how old he was at the time of their initial encounter, Vera Newlin said: "Oh, riding a tricycle! My first memory of Jim is on a tricycle riding back and forth in the neighborhood. And he always had his jaw stuck out like he was just expecting somebody to hit it."

It was not too long before young Jones's exceptional curiosity and precocious intelligence were apprehended by Vera Newlin. She shepherded him through the children's library, time after time, helping to introduce him to writers and stories that are that were enshrined as so-called "boys' books": *Kidnapped* and *Treasure Island* and other works by Robert Louis Stevenson; the stories of Rudyard Kipling (whose lines of poetry would later provide Jones with titles and epigrams for *From Here to Eternity, The Thin Red Line,* and *Go to the Widow-Maker*); the novels of Charles Dickens, and others. Vera Newlin quietly exempted Jones from the rules and regulations separating the adult shelves from the children's inventory in the basement; and the shy, quiet, bespectacled boy was allowed to not just browse but to check out almost any title available. "He had a number of exceptions made for him," Vera recalled. "You couldn't help but like him. You could get aggravated at him, but you would like him. "

Vera Newlin ascertained some of Jones's boyhood distress while mentoring the bookish youngster in the Carnegie Library throughout his early years in Robinson: "His mother was older than I was, but we played cards in the same circle. She was a complainer. I shouldn't say that. But she was. He had a feeling that his mother liked his older brother much better than she liked him. And then there was the sister. Jim felt like he was the outcast." When reflecting on the favoritism that she detected in the dynamics of the Jones family, Vera concluded: "Jim always had a feeling, I think, that his [parents] didn't like him as well as they did the other kids." The rapport between Jones and Vera, the instructive reference librarian, was highly beneficial.

Annis Skaggs Fleming was a fellow student with whom Jones became friends at Lincoln Grade School. She clearly recalled the way Jones was allied with Vera Newlin, whom she remembered as " . . . a lovely person. Strict. She kept a good library and you could go there to study; you could go there to explore. And she gave him directions [about] books he should read. She kept telling him: 'Now Jim, you should read this; you should read that.' And he followed. And he kept up!"

Ruminating many years later on the earliest part of his life, Jones spoke warmly of the Carnegie Library, concluding: "It had a great deal more to do with my becoming a writer than I had any concept of at the time I was reading there." One of Jones's future allies, fellow author James Baldwin (who was also born with the name James Jones, but then renamed Baldwin after his mother remarried), experienced a similar rite of passage due to his immersions in the Public Library in Harlem.

What Baldwin recalled about that library's effect on him resembles what Jones had experienced. In the documentary film *The Price of the Ticket*, Baldwin says:

You think your pain and your heartbreak are unprecedented in the history of the world. But then you read. It was books that taught me [that] the things that tormented me the most were the very things that connected me to all the people that were alive; who had ever been alive. I went to the 135th Street library at least three or four times a week. And I read everything there; I mean every single book in that library. In some blind and instinctive way, I knew that what was happening in those books was also happening all around me. And I was trying to make a connection between the books, and the life I saw, and the life I lived. I didn't know how I would use my mind or even if I could. But that was the only thing I had to use.

Books fed Jones's hunger for imaginative diversion and vivid dramatic engagement. As he progressed through elementary school, his passion for reading remained his main defense against the distress of his increasingly unhappy home.

* * *

The summer of 1929 was a particularly unhappy time. George W. Jones, the autocratic, temperamentally frightful paternal grandfather whom Jones adored and whom Ada resented and before whom Ramon always felt shrunken and feckless, died at the age of seventy-one. The loss of this towering figure of stability, success, and fiscal potency was ominous. The following October, between so-called "Black Thursday" (October 24, 1929) and "Black Tuesday" (October 29, 1929), the stock market imploded. Robinson's first casualties were those whose big money had been fast acquired after oil was discovered on private properties, like the farm land owned by George W. Jones. For the Jones family, the fallout from the stock market crash worsened badly over time.

Another nagging problem at the start of the Great Depression was that clients for Ramon's dental practice were fewer. This diminished Ramon's income a great deal, which increased Ada's anger, bitterness, and contempt.

She became a more forbidding figure to her second son, whose older brother Jeff had parlayed his excellent high school grades, athletic prowess, and yearbook status as Most Popular Student into a successful getaway from the toxic Jones home. Jeff had already left for college before the death of his grandfather or the collapse of the stock market in 1929, and he was twenty-four years old when James Jones entered eighth grade in the fall of 1934. Jeff was spared the worst of his family's tumultuous convulsions, which worsened in the early 1930s as the Samuel Insull Utilities Investment Company collapsed, devastating over one million shareholders. It was with Insull's seemingly invincible stock that George W. Jones invested (on behalf of his heirs) all the profits from his law practice and oil earnings.

Everything was wiped out. Dividends, stock portfolios, trust funds, and annuities dissolved overnight. The family fortune was lost. The heirs of George W. Jones were suddenly without any financial cushion. Their social status nosedived.

In those same years, Ramon's dental practice continued shrinking. He took to bartering with patients, instead of turning them away. But bartering was hardly a substitute for a positive cash flow, and the deepening Depression years shredded what remained of the little confidence and self-esteem Ramon had ever had.

It was necessary now for Jones to wake daily, always before dawn, and earn money delivering newspapers. By the time Jones was a seasoned newspaper carrier, his behavior in school and in public was increasingly belligerent. Cantankerous at times. Obnoxious in some ways and rude in others.

In his final years at Lincoln Grade School, it became clear that Jones wouldn't follow in the much-admired footsteps of his older brother, Jeff, whom the yearbooks celebrated as being the most popular of students; also for his athletic achievements and school spirit. Going to the opposite extreme, Jones would later tell his brother that his own personal goal at Robinson High School was to succeed at being "considered [the] class prick."

He also entered adolescence with an entirely different home life than Jeff had known in the family's better days. Jones later wrote to his editor at Scribners about the contradictory perspectives the two brothers cultivated as young men: "[Jeff] grew up before our family lost its money and its social position, whereas I came along 12 years later and was forced to fight for my pride from the first time I entered school."

One of his high school yearbooks highlighted his reputation for brawling and for dozing off in classes by describing him as "a scrapper" and "a napper."

Even in an era that did not consider "putting up your dukes" taboo, Jones had a titanic reputation for raising hell. On one occasion, he lost control and ended a fight on the street by shoving a boy through a plate-glass window.

Mortified by his act, he was confused and petrified. He immediately ran to the downtown bowling alley, where he knew he could find his father. By this time, with his dental practice floundering and his dependence on booze increasing badly, Ramon Jones was spending more time imbibing than he was at the office. But on this occasion, Jones recalled that he still came through in a protective, loving way.

Jones explained to his father what had just happened. And later he recounted that although his father "was half [drunk], he got right up and went back across the street with me and took the whole thing on his shoulders and got it straightened out. I'll never forget that. It's a fine thing for a boy to have someone who is rather like a rock to his small intellect, someone who will always be there when needed."

One healthy means by which Jones channeled his aggression in those years was in boxing. Having learned the rudiments of the sport from his father at home, Jones was well prepared to accept the invitation of Si Seligman to train for the Golden Gloves competitions in Terre Haute, Indiana (40 miles east of Robinson).

Si Seligman owned and operated the newsstand on the Square downtown where Jones appeared on his bike at five o'clock every morning. He earned Seligman's trust because he held the job for years. The job's toughest requirement was to arrive every morning before sunrise, in order to sort out the newspapers from Chicago, Indianapolis, Robinson, and Terre Haute. In all those years on the job, Jones was never late and never missed a day, despite the frigid Illinois winters.

Si Seligman inevitably observed Jones's steadfastness, and he recruited him to box with every intention of entering him in Golden Gloves bouts. Seligman was a coach figure whom the local boys respected.

Jones enjoyed his first Golden Gloves fight in neighboring Terre Haute, winning solidly be decision. In a subsequent bout, he surprised the judges and Si Seligman by not really trying all that hard. He seemed to let the other fighter win by default. When asked about why he let himself slide, Jones said that he didn't really feel like hurting the other guy. Perhaps he was just exhausted. The yearbook's quip about Jones being "a scrapper" and "a napper" made light of his dozing in mid-day classes. But his daily job at the newsstand impelled him to rise at four-thirty, in order to bike downtown by five in the morning. Sleep deprivation must have been onerous.

Jones was bored in most of his classes and by nearly all of his teachers. His own reading habits remained encyclopedic and robust, while rote learning anesthetized him. The strict protocols of classroom behavior in the 1930s—sitting passively and taking notes while the teacher lectured up front—did not capture his imagination.

Most distressing in Jones's life as a high school student was the insecurity of the family's finances, as the Great Depression metastasized. Following the collapse of the Chicago-based Insull company (a utilities empire), it was necessary for Ramon and Ada to sell their house on Main Street. They become renters. More than once in the first half of the 1930s the Jones family had to relocate (making very public moves in a small-town where everybody gossiped) to another rental property; each time to a house that that was a bit smaller, a little shabbier, on a street that was more run down than the one last one. This decline in fortunes devastated the status-conscious Ada, and ensured that Ramon drank even more, while his dental practice gradually diminished.

If Jones as a teen suffered any symptoms of depression amid such tension, then everything was worsened by the hormonal hurricanes endured by boys of fifteen and sixteen and seventeen.

*   *   *

Just before Jones began his sophomore year at Robinson High School, he surely saw the August 10, 1936, *TIME* Magazine that featured on its cover a writer who in that season was commanding the attention of the world: John Dos Passos. It would have been inconceivable for Si Seligman's newsstand on the Square in downtown Robinson not to stock *TIME* (soon to be joined by its successful sister publication: *LIFE*). Those magazines were windows onto the world. And if Jones read merely the first two paragraphs of *TIME*'s cover story on John Dos Passos, he may very well have had his first inkling of how powerfully engaged with his contemporary world an American author could be. *TIME* proclaimed:

Old history is in books and new on front pages. Yet neither tells the whole story of a people, a period, a place. Behind the extraordinary news in the papers, the decisive events described by historians, lies a mass of anonymous, miscellaneous human happenings, comprising the routine stuff of daily living. This is private history, and, though it rarely gets into public history, it outweighs soldiers and statesmen, battles and booms, in the final balance of time.

To relate these minutiae of contemporary experience to the broad sweep of historical developments has been the task, for the past ten years, of a novelist named John Roderigo Dos Passos. Last week Author Dos Passos, 40, offered readers a novel called "The Big Money" that stood midway between history and fiction, the last of a series of three books that constitute a private, unofficial history of the U. S. from 1900 to 1929.

TIME's cover story on John Dos Passos highlighted not just the completion of the innovative author's *U.S.A.* trilogy, but also the notion of a living novelist being at the center of American culture. Other articles in *TIME* (and *LIFE*) described a world hell-bent on another global war, one that would affect James Jones as profoundly as the Great War affected John Dos Passos. Meantime, Jones was at war with himself.

There was no one with whom he could share his thoughts about the demise of his family. Guidance counselors were not in vogue in that era, so at Robinson High School he did not have a confidante. His mother's Christian Science bromides did not in any way comfort him. Ramon's lack of stability worsened through the years and though he might rise to the challenge of the occasional crisis, in general he had become a pathetic figure. No priest or doctor or clergy of any kind was relevant, and though there were a few teachers who now and then noted Jones's potential, he was so indifferent to his studies (most of the time) that he was, by and large, tolerated; yet not truly comprehended or attended to. He craved authentic attention.

A ferocious desire to escape Robinson rose up in Jones as a teenager. His vivid imagination was rarely invited to express itself in coursework at school, but that did not prevent him from using that imagination to vent in his own way. Fueling his dreams were the shame, insecurity, rage, and confusion he felt about his own life.

Money was not just tight in Jones's household; it was scarcely available. Brand new clothes were rarely bought and the prospects of any future financial recovery were remote. Jones's moodiness and his behavior revealed his furious discontent.

His anger led to a new awareness of the importance of repressing his feelings—shielding both himself and others from the volcanic emotions he felt. He vowed to master the ability "never to tell anyone the truth about any of the things that were important to me." In his future writings, this trait would be personified, again and again, by his male and female protagonists; many of whom struggle with the issues of either repressing one's private thoughts or harboring secrets.

With so many legendary stories committed to memory (Jones never lost his appetite for books, not even at the peak of his tumultuous adolescence) and reams of heroic narratives re-read continuously, it is no surprise that the teenager who was an autodidact in World Literature would day-dream so feverishly about escaping from Robinson. On more than one occasion, he literally tried to do so.

"I would sneak off and take refuge in my secret ambition to run away and join the Foreign Legion as an adventurer," Jones later admitted, wryly alluding to his endless preoccupation with the *Beau Geste* trilogy.

When not immersed in his imagination, Jones sometimes tried to walk off into the sunset in his own way. On one occasion, he headed due north in an effort to walk his way to Chicago. He was two miles down the road when he was retrieved and returned to Robinson. His escape was deferred.

Mediocre grades defined Jones throughout high school. His report cards were mostly splattered with Cs and Ds. Only in two English classes did Jones come alive, and in one case it was an issue of having a crush on his teacher.

"I was of course in love with her," Jones fondly reminisced, when speaking of the twenty-four-year-old woman who was his English instructor during freshman year. "She liked me, and loyally set out to make a reader of me, only to find that with the exceptions of Shakespeare and Joyce, I had very nearly read as much as she had (including Hemingway and Fitzgerald) without knowing any of these people were 'writers,' simply because my father had the books around." The attractive teacher had been taken in as a lodger by Ada Jones (a common practice in hard times), and Jones's libido was galvanized: "I would hang around the upstairs hall," he confessed, "trying to catch a flash of thigh or panties or breast. She was very nice about this though I'm sure it embarrassed her."

Less than a decade later, Jones's life would be forever transformed by another older woman with whom he would experience a profound and complicated rapport.

Another dimension of Jones's passion was evoked throughout his junior year, when Harriet Hodges, his English 3A teacher, regularly asked her students to engage in vigorous discussions about literature. This was the first time Jones experienced the opportunity in class to express any personal reactions or emotional responses to assigned readings. He had a knack for effectively reading literature aloud (a gift that later made his Caedmon Spoken Arts album superb) and in Hodges's English class, Jones spent his junior year vividly participating, and also thriving as a class leader.

"I was at a peculiar stage of my life," Jones later explained, "where I was getting a great charge and a great emotional release out of writing openly fictional themes (always derivative of some book I'd just read, naturally) for her English class. Attacked in class by what I now realize were several jealous straight-A plodders, I was defended by this lady who told me to keep right on and added that all writing was not necessarily the cataloging of summer vacations." Once again, an intelligent and sympathetic older woman affirmed Jones, and by doing so inspired him greatly.

*   *   *

His senior year of high school (1938–1939) unfolded against a national and international backdrop of one grim historic milestone after another. Throughout 1938, Hitler was in the news with morbid frequency. The Third Reich cast its shadows everywhere. In the January 2, 1939, issue of *TIME* magazine, the Man of the Year was announced. It was hardly an occasion for celebration, as *TIME* reluctantly noted:

He had torn the Treaty of Versailles to shreds. He had rearmed Germany to the teeth—or as close to the teeth as he was able. He had stolen Austria before the eyes of a horrified and apparently impotent world.

All these events were shocking to nations which had defeated Germany on the battlefield only 20 years before, but nothing so terrified the world as the ruthless, methodical, Nazi-directed events which during late summer and early autumn threatened a world war over Czechoslovakia. When without loss of blood he reduced Czechoslovakia to a German puppet state, forced a drastic revision of Europe's defensive alliances, and won a free hand for himself in Eastern Europe by getting a "hands-off" promise from powerful Britain (and later France), Adolf Hitler without doubt became 1938's Man of the Year.

To imagine Jones in his senior year of high school is to see a young man who in no way felt at home with standard classroom protocols, looking out upon a world that was spiraling toward another international conflagration. With the exceptions of the two English classes he'd enjoyed, high school was a wasteland for Jones. He collected Cs and Ds in his senior year, and later concluded that his speedy, accurate typing skills of 55 words per minute were "probably the only thing of value I garnered out of my high school career." If he had any fond memories of the activities he signed up for along the way (he tried the Latin Club; sang in the Mixed Chorus; played trombone in the band; and also performed in an operetta), Jones never said so publicly. But his typing skills proved invaluable.

Equally invaluable was his ability to apprehend "the truth of Imagination," as poet John Keats eloquently put it.

No matter how disconsolate Jones was about his family's lack of money or the fact that after selling their home on Walnut Street and renting on King Street, they had to finally settle for leasing a drab house on the aptly named Ash Street (adjacent to the local railroad tracks), he was always able to lose himself in the many books that fed his fervid inner hunger for drama, heroics, and intoxicating stories.

Other intoxicants were absorbed as Jones's cigarette smoking and drinking patterns took hold. He was a heavy smoker and two-fisted boozer most of his life.

Girlfriends of any lasting significance were not part of Jones's adolescence in Robinson, although his admittedly colossal sexual appetite kicked in at that time. In certain stories featuring his narrative alter ego, John Slade, the theme of chronic sexual frustration is both overt and covert. Once again, his mother was his nemesis. Ada's religiosity was merely one reason why she was incapable of being Jones's ally.

When she caught Jones masturbating on one occasion, she ranted about his sinful ways and warned that if he continued, he'd acquire a black hand. She caught him again, and shortly thereafter used shoe polish to paint his hand black in his sleep. In every way she seemed to be overwhelmed by the world at large all around her.

By the time his high school years were almost behind him, Jones's view of his mother was anything but affirmative. As his father once tried to converse with Ada about some issue of substance, Jones recalled that her only concern was "flipping through pages of a magazine with a placid bored air."

Her readings in Christian Science did not enliven her or manage to uplift her. She seemed to her second son to have resigned herself to being one who "drinks coffee and smokes and just sits around," usually saying "Nothing!" when asked what was on her mind. The fiscal insecurity of the family scarcely improved in the 1930s, and Ada's reaction to their chronic financial stress was to yield to her own ennui; she behaved as though numb.

Jones believed she had nothing whatsoever to give to the two children still at home with her. Ada was, he later growled, "totally selfish, totally self-centered, and totally whining and full of self-pity." He once wrote with blistering disdain: "She was basically stupid in the very lowest sense of the word. Whether she had any intelligence to begin with and later lost it or let it atrophy, I don't know. But she certainly showed no intelligence or sensitivity or sympathy toward Mary Ann and me, not from the first moment I can remember her." As the father of two children later in his life, Jones parented in ways that were the polar opposite of Ada.

*   *   *

His 1939 senior yearbook comically expressed surprise that "Jim Jones" made it to graduation at all. They humorously assumed he had no future. Then, as if his high school years required a slapstick Hollywood ending, there occurred on the night of Jones's graduation an accident symbolizing his hard luck. He volunteered to solve a wiring problem in the skylight area, way high up above the auditorium seats, which were slowly filling up with family and friends gathering that night in June 1939, for Robinson High School's commencement. The Class of '39 was the last graduating class prior to the outbreak of war in Europe the following September.

It was the end of an era. And Jones crashed through the skylight and landed thirty feet below, smashing onto a row of metal folding chairs. No bones were shattered, though he was seriously banged up. He had to borrow a crutch in order to walk through the ceremony.

After graduation, Jones went on the road in his own maverick way. He visited older brother Jeff in Findlay, Ohio, where Jeff had a job with the Ohio Oil Company; briefly Jones worked in construction by day, while at night he and Jeff hashed out the possibility of writing a novel together. Jones then hitchhiked his way to Canada, thumbing for rides and hopping freight cars and bumming along like a Steinbeck character. When his effort to enlist in Canada's military failed, he went home.

He was still only 17. Less than a week after he turned 18 on November 6, 1939, he enlisted in the United States Army, in the twilight time of what was then still called the Regular Army. The Selective Service System would not begin drafting American civilians until 1940. Jones didn't enlist because he had a military vocation.

There was no family money to pay for university studies, and his sub-par grades in high school were on the record. Scholarships? Not a chance. But enlisting ensured that he'd be sustained inside an organization that would feed him, clothe him, and by and large take care of him. Enlisting made practical sense. Completely.

He couldn't have known this yet, but by joining the peacetime Army on November 10, 1939, James Jones crossed a threshold that ensured his destiny as an artist.

He then left home, never to see his parents again.

2
YOU'RE IN THE ARMY NOW!

Dad gave me three bucks when I left Robinson.
~ James Jones,
(written to his brother Jeff)

After James Jones left home by stepping aboard the Illinois Central railroad train in Robinson, shortly after his enlistment, he wrote to his brother Jeff, describing their parents as "receding before [his] grasp like a mist." Ramon and Ada Jones had escorted their younger son to the local train depot, to offer their farewell.

"Maybe I'll never see them again," Jones added. But having "watched Mother and Dad grow smaller" as the Illinois Central commenced its journey to Chanute Field in Rantoul, Illinois, Jones held his emotions in check and "went back into the train and sat in on a Blackjack game."

If another soldier had a deck of cards as his talisman, Jones had dice. In the first days and weeks of his Army experience, exhibiting his flair for self-reliance as well as for making new acquaintances when he truly had to, Jones used his skills at shooting craps to guarantee he'd not be wholly dependent on the Army for every little thing. This savvy aspect of young Jones's persona is crucial.

Ramon Jones's last offering to his soldier-to-be son was three single dollar bills. If Ramon could have spared more, he would have. In 1939, newspapers cost pennies and an adult ticket to the movies was a dime. Three dollars was not a gross pittance. But it was a pittance.

Nonetheless, Jones resolved two issues simultaneously—one was his reluctance to mingle with others; and the other was his resistance to the idea of being fiscally up against it. Doubtless his economically strained home life for so many years had established in him the conviction that no matter what, he should not allow himself to be without money. He bluntly admitted in a letter to Jeff: "If I didn't have my dice, I don't know what I'd do."

Quickly, Jones got to work. He entered that Blackjack game with the three bucks he'd received from his father as a parting gift. By the time the recruits arrived one hundred miles north of Robinson at Chanute Field in Rantoul, his three bucks had become seven dollars. He broke the ice with his new peers by playing cards or rolling the dice. To Jeff, he wrote: "After four days at Chanute Field, I left for New York with $18, not counting what I'd spent, which was quite a bit. Since then my bankroll has never been less than $6 and as high as $27. With that money I haven't needed to draw any canteen checks, so my pay will be that much higher. Also, I can buy my meals at the Post Restaurant, when the food is too rotten to stomach."

In those first four days at Chanute Field, Jones and the other recruits were put through their paces as each man took the required Oath of Allegiance before receiving physical exams and mental tests; followed by the allocation of basic supplies (spare clothes, in addition to a regulation uniform; a knapsack and a mess kit); and of course the all-important mode of identification and information gruffly referred to as "dog tags": on which each GI's serial number, blood type, name, and religion were stamped. Debarking for Fort Slocum, New York, he was now GI # 6915544.

* * *

When he arrived at Fort Slocum on November 24, 1939, Jones had yet to be assigned to a regiment. Before he finally received such orders, his time was spent in the company of other unassigned recruits performing an endless array of tedious, laborious chores. The men were ordered to do everything from standard kitchen police duties to hauling garbage; they spent hours picking up scraps of debris or other windblown items found on the landscape. Jones mentioned in a letter to Jeff that he was "working in the Post Exchange heaving beer kegs and cases of pop. I get all the stuff I want to eat while I'm working. Also, it ought to make a man of me."

The preoccupation with food was hardly incidental. Jones's domestic background in Robinson may have been a story of upscale comforts reduced to lower-middle-class limitations, but he had still known much comfort and abundance compared to what the Army considered acceptable. On Thanksgiving Day 1939, Jones's breakfast consisted of one tiny box (a manufacturer's sample) of cereal, plus a mere half-pint of milk, along with a butter pat (limited to one per man). The main dish was a piece of toast that was slathered in leftovers from the prior night's dinner. Between the toast (which Jones remembered as "rubbery") and the slop ladled upon it, he noted that "the stomach-churning dish [is] rather aptly described by the soldier's word for it: shit on a shingle."

All the more reason his dice were of paramount importance. Wherever he went in those early Army days, Jones's ability to hustle with his dice allowed him to care for himself when possible. This applied to more than nutritional matters. In terms of his physical well-being, the money he acquired through playing craps or Blackjack made certain outings possible. In a sarcastic update to his brother Jeff, he wrote: "I can engage in the sports at the Y.M.C.A. building where in spite of their undoubted self-sacrifice for the soldier's soul, one has to pay to do *anything*."

Jones soon spent a week in the base hospital at Fort Slocum. He had already noticed, back at Chanute Field in Rantoul, a burning discharge when he urinated. But he waited until he was long gone from Illinois before reporting such a personal problem to his superiors. Then he spent several days and nights in the company of soldiers being treated for gonorrhea, and his prodigious embarrassment and shame at being in their company lent him some of the essential narrative details that he outlined to his brother Jeff (who also yearned to write) for their projected, never-to-be-written *Studs Lonigan*-type novel.

Jones admitted to his Army doctors that he had engaged in sexual intercourse approximately five weeks earlier, before leaving Robinson for Rantoul's Chanute Field. It's possible that he had paid a visit to one of the well-known and affordable brothels in Terre Haute, Indiana. Only 40 miles away from Robinson, Terre Haute had a red-light district allowing for saloons and bordellos and small-time gambling in what was commonly referred to as a "wide-open town." It's likely that Jones's trouble derived from a brothel; not from a local Robinson girl.

Much to his own relief, he reported to Jeff: "They took a microscopic test of the discharge and my urine. They couldn't find any gonorrhea germs, but as the symptoms were the same, I was put under observation. While under observation I had a chance to observe the men who had the 'clap' as it is called in the army."

Those days and nights in close quarters with the seemingly amoral, rough-hewn men who "stand around a long sink and treat themselves with solutions" branded Jones's self-esteem with a pulverizing, acidic impact: "I was so humiliated and ashamed at the aspect of being in the ward with those guys." Fortunately, his symptoms cleared up and he was quickly returned to Fort Slocum's routines. The one positive aspect of his quarantine was winning again at Blackjack. Jones had entered the base hospital with twelve dollars, but he left it with twenty-three.

Apprehending the class warfare that percolated throughout the Army's realm, Jones noted that something as random as an afternoon out at the movies was, in effect, a further reminder of the caste system that now placed him at the bottom.

The only time Jones was in the same domain as girls or women while he was at Fort Slocum was when he went to see a movie, and (he explained to Jeff) the rules were rigid: "There the officers' children, who are the only girls on the island, sit in the balcony. We common herd sit in the 'pit' as the rabble did in Shakespeare's day also." Author John Gregory Dunne later noted in his memoir *Harp*: "Therein lies the subversive brilliance of *From Here to Eternity*. James Jones clearly understood that an army is predicated on class hatred; patriotism is only a convenient piety."

Those initiatory weeks at Fort Slocum ended after less than a single month. On December 18, 1939, Jones and hundreds of other soldiers shipped out on the Army transport ship U. S. GRANT, slowly destined for active duty at Hickam Field, close to Pearl Harbor in Hawaii.

Two weeks later, after sailing via the Panama Canal and docking briefly in California, an Army band greeted the arriving troops with Sousa marches; and the band was complemented by dancing "hula girls," swaying like Hawaiian goddesses. The new arrivals were presented with traditional Hawaiian "leis" by the dancers.

Whatever pleasure Jones took in the sight of the bronze-skinned, bare-armed, hip swiveling hula girls was short-lived. His time in the ensuing weeks and months was given over to the daily drills, hikes, marches, and the constant tasks with which the Army structured recruits' daily lives. From reveille to taps, Jones and his fellow soldiers rarely had relaxation time to enjoy the extraordinarily salubrious weather; although Jones noticed it, after enduring a lifetime of Illinois winters.

However, the comfortable delight provided by the daily sunshine and ocean-swept breezes of Hawaii were more than offset by the hardheaded, shrill-voiced, ass-kicking hourly commands of the sergeants who became at this time the masters of Jones's universe. Although he did enjoy the percussive rhythms and the precision required to execute precisely the intricate patterns of close-order drill, there was little else about Jones's continued training that appealed to him. Ironically, the experience tapped into his sense of being a cut above many of those in his midst. By possessing a high school diploma, Jones was doubtless at the top of the list, regarding education attained, amid hard-luck Regular Army recruits.

But it was not necessarily his peers who caused his internal sense of frustrated anger. It was the men giving the orders—they were the bane of his existence. In a note sent to his brother, an astute medley of insights was spelled out by Jones:

"I," he explained to Jeff, "who am better bred than any of these moronic sergeants, am ordered around by them as if I were a robot, constructed to do their bidding. But I can see their point of view. Nine out of every ten men in this army have no more brains than a three year old. The only way they can learn the manual and the drill commands is by constant repetitions. It is pounded into their skulls until it is enveloped by the subconscious mind. The tenth man cannot be excepted. He must be treated the same as the others, even if in time he becomes like them."

There was little danger of Jones becoming dull of mind or in any way dimwitted.

In the middle of 1940, his innate gift as a loner impelled him to find his way to the base library. Considering how his youth was anchored (to some degree) by the abundant stacks and the serene privacy of the Carnegie Library in Robinson, it's no surprise that he frequently visited the Post Library facility available at Hickam Field.

Years later, when he warranted an entry in *Twentieth Century Authors*, Jones wrote an autobiographical note summing up how the U. S. Army's library transformed his life: "I stumbled upon the works of Thomas Wolfe, and his home life seemed so similar to my own, his feelings about himself so similar to mine about myself, that I realized I had been a writer all my life without knowing it or having written."

The timing of Jones's discovery of the works of Thomas Wolfe was serendipitous. If his earlier visions of authoring a book (in league with his brother Jeff) had been serious, but not serious enough to compel him to identify himself as "a writer," then the life-enhancing experience of reading books by Wolfe (who at that time was a larger-than-life figure in contemporary American letters) was a turning point. After he spent untold numbers of hours in mid-1940 reading everything then published by Thomas Wolfe, the reluctant soldier who now envisioned a life as a writer began composing poetry, writing short stories, and drafting articles. Despite each effort being rejected by the editors and publications to whom they were sent, Jones did not stop. He persisted. Much as Wolfe had when he labored in obscurity throughout the 1920s, writing alone, living on hope; all of which Wolfe chronicled in his novels.

*   *   *

In 1940, the year in which he would turn 19, Jones found that his inner life of emotions, grief, and self-awareness was excavated with powerful force by the experience of reading Wolfe's pages. The author had died in 1938, due to a brain tumor that had been undetected too long. When he died, two mammoth novels about a young male hero named Eugene Gant (*Look Homeward, Angel* and *Of Time and the River*) were immensely popular. Shortly after his death in 1938, two more prodigious novels were published, having been pieced together (from thousands of handwritten, unnumbered, unlined pages) and edited to capitalize on his now growing legend: *The Web and the Rock* and *You Can't Go Home Again* (tracing anew the lifelong quest of a young male American from the South: this time dubbed George Webber) added to Wolfe's aura.

Because of the exceedingly in-depth scenes of family tumult and dramatic conflict involving a younger son and his unhappy, forever-distressed, overwhelmed mother and her inability to find any peace or calm within the family's realm, Jones could not help but read in Wolfe's novels what seemed like a recapitulation of the Jones saga.

If Wolfe's family-centered miseries and boyhood memories provided the substance for the bulk of *Look Homeward, Angel* and *Of Time and the River* (which track Eugene Gant's growth from the cradle to college), then the final two novels (published posthumously) lured Jones out of the past and perhaps straight into his still unknown future.

Later in *The Web and the Rock* and most poignantly in *You Can't Go Home Again*, Wolfe wrote reams upon reams of colorful, long-winded, dramatically intricate, and deeply autobiographical episodes about the two main individuals who in his own life had done all that anyone could do to help him achieve his destiny. Their names were changed in the novels, but as surely as "George Webber" was based on Thomas Wolfe, many readers correctly surmised that legendary editor Maxwell Perkins was the model for "Foxhall Edwards"; and the character of "Esther Jack" derived from a true-life married older woman who had been Wolfe's patron, lover, surrogate mother, and all-purpose ally during his years of struggle: Aline Bernstein.

Even if a fortune teller with the most remarkable gift of perspicacity had been available, Jones probably would not have believed that a few years hence his own struggles would similarly be absorbed by an older married woman who would serve as his patron, lover, surrogate mother, and all-purpose ally. Nor would he likely believe (probably not in his wildest dreams) that Thomas Wolfe's editor, Maxwell Perkins, who was immortalized as "Foxhall Edwards" and routinely reported on as the man who edited Ernest Hemingway's books (and had also done the same for F. Scott Fitzgerald) would quietly put young James Jones on the path to literary fame.

*   *   *

Loneliness burdened Jones's life in 1940, even though he was surrounded almost always by fellow soldiers, with rigorous training schedules and hours of drill and organized maneuvers on the agenda. Nonetheless, even in the midst of the busily structured regimen of his Army Air Corps days at Hickam Field, he tended to set himself apart. Never having mingled well at Lincoln Grade School or at Robinson High School, he was used to being perceived as "a loner." Despite his gambling gifts (which were more or less necessary to keep him in pocket money, while at the same time not encumbering his $21-per-month Army pay), he remained ill at ease with most social interactions. He was not chatty or eager to be accepted as one of the guys. He maintained a distance that some saw as aloof from others. But that had been his personal style for a long time, as he reminded his brother Jeff, in a letter explaining his newfound fascination with Thomas Wolfe:

"I, too, like Wolfe, have felt myself different from other kids, especially while I was in high school: I never seemed to mix with the other kids;

I didn't think at all like they did; I never ran around with the gang of boys that were the elite of the campus, nor did I run around with the gang that envied them and disliked them, and ganged together in a sort of mutual protection . . . Even at home they didn't see things the way I did. Don't think I'm a victim of an inferiority complex or an aesthete, who is always complaining he is misunderstood, because I'm not. I don't feel sorry for myself. I've gotten so that I like my own company. I can understand me far better than anyone I know."

Another major factor in Jones's chronic loneliness (aside from his tendency to cut himself off from others) was the lack of any significant relationship with a steady girlfriend. His new life in the Army made such a traditional pursuit quite unrealistic in most respects. Romance was not anything that conveniently fit in with the ways in which his hours, days, weeks and months were scheduled and designed to accord with his duties.

* * *

Until he made his drastic decision in September 1940 to request transfer into the Infantry, Jones's typing skills and impressive IQ continually found him functioning in a bureaucratic capacity. He was ordered to enroll in clerical school, considered to be among the most tedious and undesirable of duties. But he had no choice at the time.

Although considered demeaning, the clerical school posting provided certain benefits to Jones. For starters, his schedule was structured in a way that resembled a college program more than a Spartan military agenda. Free time was a daily benefit that he put to good use, as he read more and more of Thomas Wolfe and continued to sketch his own original writings. Jones began the habit of keeping a small notebook in his pocket, which he'd rapidly grab and write in whenever he had ideas, phrases or sentences that he wished to record. And he tried writing in a variety of genres: autobiographical notes; short stories, experiments in poetry.

In addition to having more time to himself as the mundane courses for clerical school proceeded (with Jones's speedy, accurate typing and high-caliber literacy, the clerical training scarcely challenged him), there was one other noteworthy element.

To attend clerical school, Jones had been transferred to Wheeler Field, smack dab in the middle of Oahu. It was not Wheeler Field, though, that mesmerized him.

Wheeler was merely a small base for the Army Air Corps. What captured his attention was the spit-polished, gung-ho, high-energy activity at nearby Schofield Barracks, which was adjacent to Wheeler Field. As the summer of 1940 went by, and Jones plodded through his bookkeeping, typing and filing classes, the soundtrack of Schofield Barracks was in the air. And Jones was listening.

* * *

He also kept writing. Taking his older brother into his confidence, as always, Jones invited Jeff in one letter to see an example of the monumental effort he was making to reinvent himself as a young man with a writer's identity. Jones prefaced his soliloquy by admitting to Jeff: "I don't want to go all melodramatic on you. I'm afraid you'll laugh at me. Here's . . . one of the things I wrote a while back."

But since he had been in the army, he had come to understand his ungraspable longing and his phantasmal and belly-shrinking dissatisfaction: there were such things he wanted to be, to do, to write. He wanted to be the voice that shrieked out the agony of frustration and lostness and despair and loneliness, that all men feel, yet cannot understand; the voice that rolled forth the booming, intoxicating laughter of men's joy; the voice that richly purred men's love of good hot food and spicy strong drink; men's love of thick, moist, pungent tobacco smoke on a full belly; men's love of woman: voluptuous, throaty voiced, silken-thighed, and sensual.

"I suppose that sounds an awful lot like Wolfe," Jones admitted. "But if it does, it's exactly the way I feel. You know, there's really nobody I can talk to with[out] being afraid of being laughed at, not even you. Right now I'm afraid that you'll laugh when you read this; or worse, feel sorry for me and pity me, because I'm an idealistic, romantic kid, who doesn't know what in hell he's talking about."

Indeed, it all sounded "an awful lot like Wolfe." The passage highlighted by Jones as "one of the things I wrote a while back" is in some ways a remarkable facsimile of the ultra-rhythmic, well-paced, and lushly rhetorical paragraphs that Wolfe often inserted into the middle of a chapter. Reviewers had oftentimes referred to such interpolations as "Wolfean chants." Clearly Jones was listening to the Wolfean echoes in his own nascent writer's voice, when he wasn't listening to the marching cadences and the bellowing of sergeants, just across the way.

In the middle of the summer of 1940, Jones began visiting Schofield Barracks.

3
G. I. BLUES & PEARL HARBOR

I remember thinking with a sense of the profoundest awe that none of our lives would ever be the same, that a social, even a cultural watershed had been crossed which we could never go back over, and I wondered how many of us would survive to see the end results. I wondered if I would. I had just turned twenty, the month before.
~ James Jones, *WWII*

When Jones transferred to Schofield Barracks in September 1940, it marked the beginning of a new phase of Army life for him. For starters, he had to once again go through a full-throttle six-week course in basic training. This time, however, it was a no-holds-barred, all-out, Regular Army regimen of basic training. The routines he'd waltzed through at Chanute Field and Fort Slocum were not comparable to what he was now immersed in. Quickly, and with gusto, Jones fell on in.

His new life differed drastically from his lighter load at Wheeler Field or his rotating assignments at Hickam Field, because he now lived among 146 men in close quarters. F Company was housed within Quadrangle D of Schofield Barracks. There Jones and all the others shared a crowded dormitory with open corridors, communal latrines, and common shower areas. Privacy was impossible and his amenities were limited to a single locker, along with his footlocker—which had to be placed with precision at the end of his regulation rack of a bed.

Yet the privations and the physical rigors were attractive to him. "I love to drill with a rifle," he wrote to his brother Jeff. "And for six weeks, that's about all I'll do. I'll learn the proper way to kill a man with a bayonet, and at the same time, learn how to keep him from killing me. I'll learn how to roll a pack so it will stay high on my back and not cut my shoulder blades, when I go on thirty or forty mile hikes . . . I'll learn the proper way to shoot a .30 cal., 1903 type army rifle, also how to shoot the Garand M-1 rifle, which you've been reading about so much lately. Things like that are the reason I joined the army." Externally, he was thriving.

*   *   *

One particular ritual touched Jones's soul: the nighttime playing of "Taps." At eleven o'clock each night, the bugler's long, pure, clear tones echoed all across the quadrangle. The men had to be silent. It was lights-out time. Day was done.

He did his level best after that month and a half to try yet again through athletics to find a niche. It did not work. As was the case in high school, team sports were not Jones's forte. So even though each company at Schofield Barracks had intramural squads in football, softball, baseball, basketball, and track, Jones had no luck amid so many superior jocks. He was still smaller than most of his peers, and his lack of experience as a team player was a detriment. When he again auditioned his boxing skills with high hopes of making the cut, he was swiftly reminded (by way of too many fast knockdowns) that he was confronting guys who were stronger, bigger, tougher, and much more experienced than he was. Still, he kept trying.

It was while practicing scrimmages with his company's football team that Jones injured his ankle. He toughed it out for the remainder of basic training and did not draw attention to himself. Later, that ankle injury would dog him again in a combat situation, and ironically enough contribute to Jones's survival of World War II.

Appendicitis flared up shortly after Jones ended basic training rerun, and the newly appointed rifleman had surgery at the base hospital on December 16, 1940.

Granted a full month to rest and recuperate after his appendectomy, Jones buried himself once again in books. With his exterior life on hold for four weeks, he took the time to reflect, to write, and most of all to focus on his tumultuous inner life.

The intensity of his ambition to be a writer had not abated. But Jones was deeply conflicted by the internal push-and-pull and the contradictions that he felt inside of himself. Jones was tormented: "I hate myself and my dreams and hopes," he confessed to Jeff in a letter. "I laugh at my attempts to write. And yet I cannot change. I must succeed. To be a nonentity would crack my brain and rend my heart asunder. It is all or nothing. And yet I wish that I were different, a little man with small ambitions and easily satisfied."

With no teacher to guide him or mentor to show the way, Jones began sending some of his writing "over the transom" to popular magazines like *Esquire*. He had sent copies of one story to both his father and to Jeff, and Ramon was encouraging, even after *Esquire* had passed on the story. "I think you have real ability," he told his younger son, and he then offered an astute assessment about language issues, which in future years would loom large in the breakthrough novel of his second son's career: "I think you rely too heavily on profanity and obscenity, and while I know that is the way soldiers would think and speak, it is not primarily for them the story was written, but for prospective readers."

* * *

Ramon also wrote three words of warning on the outside of an envelope for a letter he sent to Jones in March 1941: "Bad news, Jim." That letter told Jones about the death of his fifty-two-year-old mother, who had died of congestive heart failure and the complications of diabetes. Jones was dumbstruck by the news. He read and re-read Ramon's lamentations. But he did not to speak of this to anyone. Instead, he put in a request for a three-day pass and when it was granted, he took off for Honolulu.

Nobody knew him there. He did not have to explain anything. Jones got drunk for three days in a row, and spent each night brooding and boozing until he passed out. Ramon had written to him on March 3, one day after Ada's death, so by the time Jones received his father's grieving letter, his mother had been waked and buried.

Ramon explained that there would be a funeral at the local Presbyterian church, and a smattering of Christian Science benedictions would be included. Ada was to wear a dress made of white lace. There would be hymns and ceremonial gloss. It was a *fait accompli* when Jones read his father's words. Ada was already entombed.

Jones was now a motherless nineteen-year-old soldier stationed five thousand miles from home. Whatever pride he felt months earlier, when completing basic training at Schofield Barracks, was now superseded by the shocking news of his mother's demise; and the resurgence of his moodiness as he pondered his chronic hunger to write.

He assessed himself with bracing clarity: "I'm working in the dark all the time. Whenever I do write something, that black forbidding doubt is in me, making me wonder if I'm just some damned egotistical fool, or if I really have that spark of genius it takes to be a really great author like Wolfe. If only I had some way of knowing. If only some authority that knew would tell [me] I was good and had promise, then I'd be all right, but as it is, I'm always full of that fear that maybe I'm not any good. Sometimes I get so damned low I feel like blowing my brains out. That's no shit, it's the straight dope." Despite his doubts, Jones continued to write, to read, and to nurture his private dream.

One year after his appendectomy, the reflective days and languorous weeks of convalescence with which Jones concluded 1940 must have seemed (in retrospect) like a four-week day dream featuring beloved books, clean sheets, quiet hours, and unencumbered thoughts. With warm baths, plenty of soap, hot food, and attentive nurses included.

Contrarily, 1941 ended for Jones—as it ended for all Americans—with the Japanese attack on Pearl Harbor and America's full-fledged entry into World War II. For the vast majority of Americans on the morning of December 7, 1941, the violently surprising and catastrophically pulverizing sneak attack at America's premier naval installation was a faraway disaster reported on the radio.

To James Jones, it was a life-threatening event exploding all around him, moment by moment, one month after his twentieth birthday. When later reflecting on that day's convulsions, he highlighted the surreal essence of the experience. He and his comrades "had known that the war would start somehow," but they "never really believed that [we] would be right in the midst of it with an excellent chance of getting killed."

And yet, there they found themselves—"right in the middle of the start of a war that [would] make history." Shifting tenses to the second person to try to get at the heart of the paradox, Jones wrote: "You know it's true, but you don't believe it anyway."

*   *   *

Merely four weeks past his 20th birthday, Jones immediately recognized—he not only apprehended but he fully comprehended in the shock, dismay, and fear of the moment—that he and his generation had been plunged into a crucible. It was a life-transforming crisis not just for the aspiring author, but for those all around him.

Like everyone else who survived the sneak attack on Pearl Harbor, Hickam Field, Schofield Barracks and Wheeler Field, Jones's December 7th resembled a near-death experience. Although neither wounded nor disabled by the strafing, shrapnel, and bombs exploding around him, he nonetheless was at the center of an ongoing fiasco that left everyone in his realm stupefied by its complete surprise. Jones knew that for his generation, Pearl Harbor was the point of no return. In his text for WWII, he recalled his initial sense of inner certainty about the enormity of that day's events:

"There was never any question about the beginning of World War II for the United States. Pearl Harbor began it crisply and decisively and without discussion.

"Absolutely nobody was prepared for it. Some 2,400 men were dead; half that many wounded."

Ordered to assume his experienced role as a company clerk, Jones spent that Sunday as a "runner" on behalf of officers who were hamstrung between panic and fearful disorientation all day, bringing messages back and forth—again and again—from one commander to another; running back and forth—even as the attack and its ancillary dangers detonated in his midst—over and again; running here, there, and back and forth across the quads; crisscrossing the entirety of Schofield Barracks and in his capacity as courier, delivering up-to-the-minute orders, memos, notes, alerts, and varied proclamations of emergency.

In the late afternoon on December 7th, the primary fear and the paramount concern of commanders at Pearl Harbor, Hickam Field, Schofield Barracks, and Wheeler Field was that a land invasion by Japanese forces was imminent. A follow-up amphibious assault made tactical sense. Logic dictated that such an all-out aerial sneak attack—so brilliantly effectuated and so shockingly choreographed—had to be the harbinger of an aggressively audacious land invasion. Strictly a matter of time, so they thought.

By nightfall on December 7th, Jones's F Company (in league with other elements of the Twenty-fifth Infantry Division) was ordered to make its way by mechanized caravan along the winding roads with their steep curves and sudden declines, arriving hours later at twilight time on the beaches where invasion was expected.

Non-stop activities were soon underway. Everyone was focused on establishing defensive positions as quickly as possible. The men spent arduous hours carpeting the beaches with barbed wire; the manipulation and arrangement of which are tedious and exhausting procedures.

What was most expected with the rising sun on Monday morning was a massively arrayed aggregation of Japanese naval vessels with the sole intention of landing not just tens of thousands of combat troops on the shores of Oahu, but perhaps more than a hundred thousand well-trained infantrymen. The colossal numbers the Imperial Japanese war machine had deployed to devastate China were well-known.

All through the night (as would be the case on subsequent nights), waiting was the status quo. Waiting and wondering. The troops were forced to be as still as statues. Abnormally quiet. Having no choice whatsoever except to stay in static positions on the beach, inside pillboxes, or in remote outposts. Everyone waited.

Nobody could rest with ease. No one could know at what moment or during which hour or within how many minutes there might be yet another aerial attack, designed to soften up the beaches and intimidate (if not annihilate) the defenders, whom the Japanese had to assume would put up an honorable fight. They were now in a situation where as they waited for anything to happen, there was little they could do. Other than silently ponder the distinct possibility of sudden death.

While waiting for something—at any moment—to erupt or explode, Jones and his fellow soldiers had to accommodate grim blackout protocols (which made even the lighting of a cigarette taboo); they had to wait and brood in the interminable hours of the darkest phases of the night; mulling over their unknown fates.

Personal crises throughout 1942 also had a profound impact and a tremendous influence on Jones's evolution as a soldier and a writer.

* * *

Once again, bad news came to Jones in the form of a letter from the Midwest. This time his older brother Jeff served as the messenger. Only three months after the attack on Pearl Harbor and the overnight transformation of the Hawaiian islands into wartime garrisons (where martial law, curfews, and blackouts were now the norm), this latest jolt to Jones's system came in the mail in mid-March.

Jeff Jones told his younger brother that their father had committed suicide back home in Robinson, Illinois, on Wednesday, March 11.

On that day, at the nadir of his psychological, emotional, spiritual, and alcoholic disintegration in the aftermath of his wife Ada's death one year earlier, Dr. Ramon Jones decided that he'd had enough.

According to the Page 1 story on March 12, 1942, in the *Robinson Daily News*, his first shot missed:

"Dr. Jones was apparently seated in a rocking chair in the back room of his office when he fired the automatic into the back of his head. The first shell misfired, and was ejected, being found lying in front of the chair on the floor. He apparently laid [sic] in the chair for sometime, indicated by his blood soaked coat on the back of the chair. It was then thought that he regained consciousness to take a handkerchief from his pocket, which was found in his hand, before he fell forward to the floor and attempted to make his way to the couch on the other side of the office. His body was found beside the couch."

The second shot gruesomely succeeded. Ramon Jones had managed to shoot himself in the back of the head. It was in that tragic posture of personal defeat that his youngest child, daughter Mary Ann, discovered him with the detritus of his brains bloodily seeping out of his wound. She had followed her usual routine of walking to his office after finishing classes at Robinson High School. The depths of Ramon's despair can be ascertained by the fact that he knew she would find him.

A second story in the *Robinson Argus* on March 19 reported that a number of townspeople claimed to have encountered Ramon Jones on the morning of March 11, but his drunken condition indicated that he was "not in condition to do business." The *Argus* then recapped the story in brief: "Dr. Jones, 55 years of age, was found lying on the floor in a back room of his offices over the Oakley-Kroger store on the south side of the square shortly after 4:30 o'clock on Wednesday afternoon by his daughter, Mary Ann, 17, who had just come home from school."

When Jones read his older brother's letter and pondered this news, he realized that he was neither shocked nor really surprised. In a lengthy letter written to Jeff on Sunday, March 22, 1942, Jones offered an impromptu defense of Ramon's choice:

"I have been expecting Dad to do that for quite a while. I don't know why, call it a premonition if you will, but it didn't surprise me to hear that he had killed himself. I was talking to him one time up at the office and he told me then, 'Well . . . if the time ever comes, when I'm sucked clear under the muck up to my ears, and I know that the net profit isn't worth the cost, I wouldn't hesitate to kill myself. When a man can't see anything to gain in putting up with living, which at best, is a pretty dismal affair, the thing for him to do is get out. And don't ever let anybody tell you it takes more guts to go on living that to kill yourself, because it doesn't; and those who say it does say so because they know in their hearts that they'd never have the guts.' I'm rather proud he went out that way, instead of hanging on and hanging on, wanting to be out, but held back because of his fear of death."

Other information gradually came to light, and Jones better understood the context within which Ramon Jones ended his life. Throughout February, in an effort to regain his self-respect and perhaps recapture a sense of standing in the community, Ramon Jones had tried and failed to re-enlist in the U. S. Army. "My physical condition is excellent," he wrote in an inquiry that he sent on February 25, 1942; and without supporting his claim at all (it was inconceivable that his physical health was "excellent") he quickly added: "and all I ask is a chance." Ramon Jones posted his letter with fuzzy-headed imprecision to the "Commanding Officer/Illinois Military Area," but nothing happened.

Brooding decades later, in his 1974 book *Viet Journal*, Jones (at age 52) included a passage on Ramon's demise:

"The Army turned him down. Cold. They didn't even want him as a dentist. He was . . . at the time, a known alcoholic, a mediocre vet of World War I, and a failure at his profession of dentist. He wrote me a rather despairing letter about it. I read it, wondering how he could imagine the Army would want him for anything. Later I would speculate often whether that turndown by the Army had not been such a slap in the face that it helped awaken him to what he was, what he had become, and he could not stand to face it. I loved my father, and I hated to see it end like that. He deserved a better fate."

During that summer season of more waiting and endless wondering, when there was a period of limbo for Jones's 25th Infantry Division, as they awaited orders that would not materialize until later in the autumn (although training and maneuvers were always underway), Jones was granted permission to attend college courses at the University of Hawaii.

In a letter to his 17-year-old sister Mary Ann that Jones wrote on May 20, 1942, he expressed his happiness about this decision to try college studies: "I have even arranged to go to the summer session at the University of Hawaii. It will be hard, but I think I will be able to make it, because I will be studying things I want to study. It is fixed so that one day a week I will get off to go to the University."

4
SUMMER '42 & JANUARY '43

I was reminded of a little scene I'd witnessed the day I was hit. I had arrived at the regimental aid station with my face all covered in blood, and the first person I saw was our old regimental surgeon with a cigar butt in his teeth . . . he said, 'Hello, Jonesie. Getting more material for that book of yours you're gonna write'?
~ James Jones, *WWII*

Buoyed by his love of reading and his conviction that being a writer was his paramount reason to live (with the looming image of novelist Thomas Wolfe always on his mind), Jones enrolled in one of Professor Laura Schwartz's composition courses; he also signed up for a class in American literature taught by Professor Carl Stroven. With both teachers he established a strong rapport due to their unanimous appreciation for good writing and great books. His work was superior to the submissions of average students.

Both Schwartz and Stroven were seasoned college professors who admired and encouraged Jones's passionate, visceral need to be rhetorically expressive. They were impressed by his papers, which fulfilled the requirements of their assignments while also displaying the young soldier's solid command of language and structure. Jones also articulated ideas. Big ideas. Serious ideas. Clearly he was not a callow young man. In fact, beyond being above average, they believed Jones was gifted.

One of his assignments in English 262 was to grapple with questions regarding Stephen Crane's classic novella, *The Red Badge of Courage*.

It was then already a matter of classroom lore that Crane's *Red Badge of Courage*—the single most famous and perennially durable fiction to evoke a soldier's experience in America's Civil War—was authored by a man who not only did not fight in it, but who was born after the war. Crane's prodigious research as a working journalist (compounded by his superlative imagination and his gifts as a storyteller) allowed him to compose the short novel in a matter of weeks. Crane produced what was commonly taught as the one indisputable Civil War classic; the narrative and its very title were part and parcel of Americana.

That did not stop Jones from making a strong argument that Crane was wrong.

Jones's college paper about *The Red Badge of Courage* reveals the extent to which his experience as an eyewitness at Pearl Harbor had seeped into his consciousness.

Now, less than a year after December 7, 1941, he assessed, recapitulated, and reconsidered his witnessing of the attack so that he could successfully produce paragraphs anatomizing how Pearl Harbor served as a counterpoint to Crane's presentation of cowardice and courage.

Jones wove a mature essay out of his English class assignment: "The plot of Stephen Crane's novel . . . centers about the mental and physical reactions of a central character, Henry Fleming, to the various stimuli of war," he wrote. "The whole plot hinges upon the fact that the boy feels he is a coward when he runs in the midst of his first battle." Jones then elaborated: "From my own experience and from what I have learned through talking to other soldiers and reading about the thing, the circumstances responsible for Henry's flight are almost exactly the opposite to what I believe would cause flight."

This debut essay that Jones wrote for English 262 concludes in a cinematic cross-cutting style, with specific passages of Crane's novella contrasted by more of Jones's detailed recollections of how he and his fellow soldiers reacted to their baptism of fire in ways that were far different from Stephen Crane's Civil War protagonist.

* * *

This dual life Jones led as a soldier and a student in the summer of '42 granted him a sense of balance in that anxious season of grim uncertainty about his future. Prior to attending those two university English classes, only Jones's solitary reading and writing provided outlets for his inner life as a fledgling artist.

The ambitious young writer both wanted and needed to appreciate something other than the arduous physicality and the psychologically aggressive elements that predominated in the realm of soldiers being trained for imminent combat.

Those courses in writing and literature allowed Jones to enter vertically into his private thoughts, feelings, and hidden fears. He was a sensitive human being (although impelled by circumstances to muster a facade of bravado and tough-guy posing most of the time) and he had vowed to learn the art of mastering how words could be arranged in such effective ways that on the page, at least, life could be understood.

The yearning author intuitively sensed that in a universe where others might argue that life had no meaning, the power of language and his own ability to write could, quite literally, give meaning to *his* life. Perhaps even save it.

As the child of a suicidal father, Jones knew that a meaningless life could be fatal.

At the same time, he continued to prove himself as competent and reliable at the rituals and requirements of soldiering, though he knew the training protocols and the keyed-up drills were hardly sufficient to the daunting tasks that lay ahead. He elaborated on this in *WWII*, which was published in 1975:

"Quite suddenly in mid-September we got orders to move back to Schofield Barracks for a period of reorganization and intensive training. While we were at Schofield, whenever we had a free minute, which was seldom, we did what we had done all the past six months. We wondered, and we waited. Our training was neither intensive nor complete, and we knew it. But then these were the early days of the war. And perhaps it was impossible to really train a man for combat, without putting him actually in it."

*   *   *

The second half of 1942 were also months during which Jones's deeply frustrated need for female companionship, and his chronic searching for real love (instead of periodic visits to brothels) continued to torment him. He yearned for a loyal, smart, sexually energized girlfriend. His inability to find such a partner dogged him as summer gave way to autumn, just as it had dogged him for several years.

Since 1940, there were a series of young women that Jones thought enough about to make references to in his letters to his brother Jeff. Now there were female students at the University of Hawaii who caught his eye and with whom he tried to establish a dating relationship—always in the hope of finding an impassioned, erotically carnivorous, female version of himself.

Many years later, in *To Reach Eternity: The Letters of James Jones*, editor George Hendrick sympathetically noted: "On campus, he met several girls with whom he tried to form romantic entanglements, but he was not successful. He was like a stock character in the movies: the confidant of a beautiful woman but not her lover."

Jones needed a sexually adventurous woman who could match his own admittedly incendiary libido. He always seemed aware of the degree to which his powerful sex drive made him feel a constant deprivation in terms of physical well-being. But he had yet to meet a woman who shared his ardor, and so his sexual frustration was routinely sky-high in an era emphasizing boundaries. Irritably, nearly three years after his enlistment, he still lived in a realm that was rife with frustration on every level.

Summing up his chronic discontent in a bold letter to his sister Mary Ann, he wrote: "We are continuing in the same corrupt, ignorant, monotonous rut that I have been I since joining the army. We must suffer the same indignities, the same favoritism, the same graft and red tape." Later in life, he rued the fact that in the barracks he "literally could not find the privacy to masturbate even in the latrines."

All the more reason that Jones told Mary Ann: "I wish I was a dog. Dogs just eat, and sleep and bark."

Jones may have intended his throwaway remark about a dog's life to induce from Mary Ann a momentary grin or perhaps a cynical smirk. However, there is no doubt that when time permitted, he needed to vent his feelings of hopelessness, futility, anger, resentment, and even a worrisome shade of worthlessness. His interior life was always in turmoil.

Having already plowed through the Post Library as well as the resources at the University of Hawaii, reading everything he could find by Thomas Wolfe, John Dos Passos, James T. Farrell, John Steinbeck, F. Scott Fitzgerald, and Ernest Hemingway, it is likely that Jones already appreciated that he and Hemingway shared an uncanny slew of background elements. Both were the sons of Victorian, religiously zealous, overbearing mothers; and both were not just Illinois boys who came of age in small-town milieus (Robinson for Jones; Oak Park for Hemingway) but they were the academically indifferent sons of medical professionals—Hemingway's father, a medical doctor, did not have the drinking problem that made Dr. Ramon Jones's dental practice impecunious in downstate Illinois. But Dr. Hemingway and Dr. Jones were both perceived by their sons as henpecked husbands; and in the end, they shared the same horrendous suicidal fate. Hemingway's father also shot himself to death. It would be the subject of war, and how they wrote about men at war, that in the distant future forever divided the two writers in years to come.

Although he had survived the attack on Pearl Harbor, Jones had yet to engage in any kind of conventional battleground experience. Yet his innate moodiness was surely exacerbated by his visceral awareness that soon enough he would face that crucible.

In one year between March 1941 and March 1942, there had been three shattering episodes that jolted young Jones's life: His mother's death in March '41, followed by the debacle at Pearl Harbor in December of that year; compounded by his father's death in March of 1942.

There was no language at that time giving voice to the diagnosis that is now well known as Post-Traumatic Stress Disorder (PTSD), but even before he endured combat's extremities, Jones was a prime candidate for PTSD, although he had yet to ship out to the South Pacific.

When he was allowed the solitude and the time required to write at the peak of his emerging powers in 1942, he articulated with an extraordinary eloquence just how Wolfe-like were his own personal visions, as he brooded in the shadows of the war. He was pensive when writing these words to his brother Jeff:

"Sometimes the air is awfully clear here. You can look off to sea and see the soft, warm, raggedy roof of clouds stretching on and on and on. It almost seems as if you can look right on into eternity. The wind was blowing and the sun shone thru the leaves and dappled all the ground with light and shadow. Last nite I was down at the beach over the hill, standing on the sand at the water's edge, watching the sunset. A crab ran up a couple of feet in front of me and stopped there, and I stepped on it and smashed it in the sand for I do not like them. The sea rolled up and covered up the crab and my footprint. When it rolled back in its ceaseless motion, the sharp out-lines of my foot-print were gone, and the crab was completely covered. Then the sea rolled up again and back again. In a little while there was no mark upon the sand at all and the crab was nowhere to be seen. The sea rolled on, timeless in its vastness, and did not seem to care that a crab had been killed here. I thought to myself, that life is like the sea, brutal and relentless. It can't go back. It can't stand still. Therefore it must go forward. It plays the percentage. It is governed by a law of Nature. What does it matter, if some little crab or human being is smashed upon the rocks? It can't be bothered. It can't go back. It can't stand still. Therefore it must go forward, and woe be unto those who think they may defeat it. For life, just like the sea, has never lost a battle yet. Perhaps it has been thwarted for a time, but it always comes back in the last quarter to score again, for the game has no final whistle. It ends only when you quit or cannot fight some more."

An annotation by scholar and editor George Hendrick in *To Reach Eternity: The Letters of James Jones* points out that "the key words in the titles of Jones's first and last published novels: **eternity** and **whistle**" are to be found in that one paragraph.

* * *

On December 6, 1942, Jones's F Company of the Twenty-Fifth Infantry Division of the U. S. Army was ordered to make final preparations to ship out. By the end of December, he and thousands of his fellow GIs were crossing the Pacific.

America had now been in the war for one year. But Jones had already been in the Army for three years. The first anniversary of the attack on Pearl Harbor had just occurred earlier that month. And as the minutes, hours, and days unfolded over the two-and-a-half weeks it took to reach their destination, Jones's awareness of the imminence of New Year's Day, 1943, was tempered by his knowledge of all that had happened to make

1942 a pivotal year of milestones and turning points.

The turnaround began in June 1942, when trailblazing advances in code breaking aided Admiral Chester Nimitz in such prodigious ways, that his outnumbered American fleet was able at Midway Island to stun the Japanese with a naval defeat. Then came Guadalcanal. In *1942: The Year That Tried Men's Souls*, Winston Groom outlined the six-month battle to secure Guadalcanal:

"The importance of the Battle for Guadalcanal can hardly be overstated. First it stopped the huge Japanese Pacific offensive in its tracks. It helped make Australia safe from Japanese air attacks on its sea-lanes of communication and supply. And, finally, it confirmed for the American public and its fighting troops that the Japanese army was not the invincible machine they had been led to believe."

Admiral Tanaka, architect of the Tokyo Express, summed it up later: "There is no question that Japan's doom was sealed with the closing of the struggle for Guadalcanal."

*   *   *

"My own part in all of this was relatively undistinguished," Jones once insisted:

"I fought as an infantry corporal in a rifle company in a regiment of the Twenty-fifth, part of the time as an assistant squad leader, part of the time attached to the company headquarters. I went where I was told to go, and did what I was told to do, but no more. I was scared shitless just about all of the time."

There was plenty to be scared about. Everything at Guadalcanal was paid for in blood; and though the Japanese were on the defensive by the time Jones entered combat, their "Bushido" warrior code was intact (making any idea of surrender taboo; mandating that one fight to the death or opt for suicide in lieu of capture).

Even after it was clear that a military defeat was inevitable, the Japanese refused to engage in a conventional withdrawal or retreat. They fought on grimly, retaining bunkered positions on the island's outermost redoubts. In his 1975 book *WWII ~ A Chronicle of Soldiering*, Jones pondered the Americans who were injured:

"Something strange seems to happen when a man is hit. There is an almost alchemic change in him, and in others' relationship to him. Assuming he isn't killed outright, and is only wounded, it is as though he passed through some veil isolating him, and has entered some new realm where the others, the unwounded, cannot follow. He has become a different person, and the others treat him differently."

Suddenly, Jones was one of those casualties.

His division was in the third day of a fight for a unique complex of strategic hills dubbed "The Galloping Horse" (due to visual shapes as seen on the graphics of their maps). Then it all happened quickly: "I was wounded in the head through no volition of my own, by a random mortar shell, spent a week in the hospital, and came back to my unit after the fight and joined them for the relatively little that was left of the campaign. I was shipped out after the campaign for an injured ankle that had to be operated on."

Although not a combat injury, that ankle was now Jones's million-dollar wound.

*   *   *

On January 28, 1943, roughly two weeks after being wounded, Jones summed up as best he could (despite the military censorship he knew was in force) the details of his situation in a letter to his brother Jeff.

Jones's compassion quickly came across by telling Jeff: "I'm writing this more or less to set your mind at ease concerning me. I've inquired around here as to what a guy is able to write, and—as per usual—I've found that there's not a helluva lot to say that won't be censored." He reassured his brother, who was the "next of kin" the War Department alerted by telegram regarding Jones being wounded in battle:

"It's apparently OK for me to tell you that I've been wounded and have just been released from a Base Hospital in the South Pacific. I wasn't hit very badly—a piece of shrapnel went thru my helmet and cut a nice little hole in the back of my head. It didn't fracture the skull and is healed up nicely now." Just as succinctly, and with a storyteller's passion for precise details, Jones went on to muse explain about both his missing helmet and his lifelong nemesis: eyeglasses.

"I don't know what happened to my helmet; the shell landed close to me and when I came to, the helmet was gone. The concussion together with the fragment that hit me must have broken the chinstrap and torn it off my head. It also blew my glasses off my face. I never saw them again, either, but I imagine they are smashed to hell. If I hadn't been lying in a hole I'd dug with my hands and helmet, that shell would probably have finished me off. The hole was only six or eight inches deep, but that makes an awful lot of difference."

Jones was seriously destabilized by his visual infirmity: "I'm not much good without glasses," he explained:

"It bothers you a lot to know you can't see well and that any minute some sniper you should have been able to see but couldn't is liable to cut you down. The glasses don't help a lot either; you have to keep wiping sweat off of them every five minutes, and after a couple of days you don't have rags or handkerchiefs clean enuf to wipe them without leaving them badly smeared. That surprised me quite a bit, because I hadn't [thought] wearing glasses would make much difference. But it does, a helluva lot: the knowledge that you can't see well bothers the shit out of you—especially when you can't make more than one misstep. I leaned a lot of other things, too."

Jones noted the vast difference between reading about combat adventures, as opposed to finding oneself in a war. The discrepancies stunned him.

"I found that reading books about other people fighting wars is adventurous, but when you are doing the fighting, it's a helluva lot different. When you read a book like *All Quiet [on the Western Front]* you understand what the hero is going thru and sympathize with him. Even when he gets killed at the end of the book you sympathize, and in sympathizing, you feel a sadness you enjoy," Jones stated. "But all that time while you are putting yourself into the hero's place you still have the knowledge that after the hero dies you still will be around to feel sad about it."

Now that he had narrowly escaped what could have been a swift death from a random mortar shell (adding yet another similarity to the list of commonalities Jones shared with young Hemingway, who was wounded in 1918 when a single mortar shell exploded in the trench where he was distributing cigarettes and snacks on behalf of the Red Cross), Jones's perspective was altered.

"When at any second you may die," he flat-out insisted, "there is no adventure; all you want is to get the fighting over with. You don't spend any time consoling yourself that if you die, you will be dying for your country and Liberty and Democracy and Freedom, because after you are dead, there is no such thing as Liberty or Democracy or freedom. But in spite of all this, you keep on fighting because you know that there is nothing else for you to do."

Jones also spelled out for Jeff some other epiphanies:

"I also learned that in spite of all the training you get and precautions you take to keep yourself alive, it's largely a matter of luck that decided whether or not you get killed. It doesn't make any difference how you are, how tough you are, how nice a guy you might be, if you happen to be at a certain spot at a certain time, you get it. I've seen guys move and watch the hole they were in get blown up a minute later. And I've seen guys stay and watch the place to which they intended to move get blown up. It's all luck."

If it's surprising that the military censors allowed all that to remain in Jones's first letter home after being wounded, it is extraordinary that his next few sentences were transmitted freely. From the microcosm of his individual observations and first-person exploits, Jones segued to the macrocosm of his war-born generation: "The guys who are fighting now will have less of a chance of being alive when the war is over than the guys who haven't started fighting yet."

Just as suddenly, he highlighted his personal sense of how precarious his life was:

"I've sort of got a hunch that I'm not going to make it [emphasis added]. Partially that comes from seeing how much luck has to do with it and because from now on until the war ends I'll probably be in and out of action all the time. Then, part of it comes from being hit. Until you get hit, there's a sort of egotism in your subconscious mind that, even while your conscious mind is tearing itself apart with fear and anxiety, gives you confidence in the fact that this might happen to others guys but not to you; you can't conceive yourself getting hit. After you've been hit, you lose that confidence. The more fights you go thru without being hit, the

stronger it gets. But once you're hit, you realize as an individual you'll have to be God damned lucky to get out alive."

Only six months earlier, Jones had been enrolled in his English courses at the University of Hawaii, experiencing that rarest of opportunities in an academic setting—namely, to be emotionally expressive and welcome to make any number of connections about one's own thoughts, feelings, and experiences in the context of embracing the best writing accomplished by others in human history.

Now, as he recovered from his wounds on the other side of the world in a combat zone that at any moment could claim his life in some unpredictable way, Jones recalled with poignant pride that Professor Laura Schwartz once shared her view that a gifted young man was in her milieu. Jones related this to Jeff anecdotally: "This girl, Peggy, I told you about told me once that the day after my last pass, Dr. Schwartz, during her lecture to Peggy's class, said something about how much talent would be lost without anyone having guessed it existed because of this war. Peggy told me that she [thought] Schwartz had me in mind when she said that. If I get it, no one will ever know to what heights I might have gone as a writer. Maybe if you wrote about the promise that was there, all wouldn't be lost."

Almost one month later, on February 19, 1943, the impact Professor Laura Schwartz had made upon Jones was detailed again when he wrote to Jeff about how he might evolve as a young author, if only the opportunity to live and to write were allowed: "I had a letter from Laura [Schwartz] a while back. She said both she & [Dr. Carl] Stroven think college would help me a lot at this stage of the game . . . Stroven is to quit teaching in June & give all his time to running the Library. I hate that, but I think he'd take time to work with me if I ever came back there. All of them believe in my ability and want to see me make good. What would you say to my going back there? I even imagine I could stay with [Professor] Stroven if I wanted to."

On every level (psychological, spiritual, emotional, intellectual, and physical) Jones experienced a transformation in the wake of his wounding.

*   *   *

When soldiers speak of a "million-dollar wound" it means one thing and one thing only: It's a wound or injury serious enough to justify one's removal from the combat zone. It is an honorable way to be extricated from battles or the threat of battles. It is (one hopes) a one-way ticket away from the front or off the line or out of the sand or far and away from the fields of fire, with no questions about one's hardiness, durability or essential toughness. It is, at bottom, an exit visa from wartime peril.

In Jones's case, after he stayed for one week in a field hospital on Guadalcanal to recuperate from the head injury caused by shrapnel, he was returned to duty. In the middle of March he made his way to the divisional hospital, after once again dislocating his injured ankle. Rendered incapable of walking, trotting, running or marching with consistency or reliability, the damaged ankle that initially resulted from playing football back at Schofield Barracks became now a variation on the notion of a "million-dollar wound." Jones was examined again by a combat surgeon, who concluded that Jones had no business being in the infantry. "He looked at me and grinned," Jones recounted, alluding to the surgeon's nonverbal communication; the fact that the surgeon "grinned" was tantamount to a one-way ticket home. "I grinned back. If he could only have known how I was hanging on his every word and expression. But perhaps he did."

Jones was then sent to Naval Hospital #3 in the New Hebrides (nearly one thousand miles away from Guadalcanal) for surgery on his mangled ankle. A procedure known as "an open reduction and fixation" was performed, wherein silver-colored wires are meticulously put into place in order to keep the bones in a functional, stationary capacity. "The operation took nearly three hours, and during the last twenty minutes," according to one scholar who researched this episode of Jones's life, "the anesthetic wore off." Apparently there was a stringent limit on the amount of anesthesia at their disposal. Remembering that he tried to bury his face in the comforting midriff of a nurse standing beside him, Jones vividly recalled "the belly of the nurse who stood on my left and kept running her fingers thru my hair and wiping the sweat off me." The operation necessitated a long-term recuperation period and Jones was sent to the 39th General Hospital in Auckland, New Zealand, where he was officially admitted and logged in on April 27, 1943.

In New Zealand, his doctors concurred that he needed more surgery. Jones was put aboard an Army hospital ship and returned to America in May. He spent most of 1943's remaining months in stateside Army hospitals: first at Letterman General Hospital in San Francisco and then a longer hiatus at Kennedy General Hospital in Memphis, Tennessee. This extended period of convalescence allowed Jones ample time to observe the frantic pace of life in what was now an economically booming wartime home-front society, and, at the same time, to be in the company of others who were injured in the recent campaigns involving America's armed forces.

Combat vets who were grievously wounded everywhere from the South Pacific to Attu in the Aleutian Islands to North Africa and Sicily were in Jones's presence for much of 1943; the amputees and burn victims abounded. This wrenching epoch provided the harrowing background framework for Jones's last novel: *Whistle*.

Jones was horrified by the sight of young amputees and grief-stricken by the plight of those who had been blinded. In comparison, his injured ankle seemed to be a minor problem: "I myself was somewhere in the middle of all this. I wasn't there because of a wound—but I had been wounded . . . and I tended to associate mentally with the overseas men, and could understand what they were feeling, because I was feeling it myself." Indeed, his infantry sergeant had said: "If it [stays] as bad as what I saw, you got no business in the infantry!" That observation was wholly validated.

*   *   *

It would not be until later in his career as a professional author that Jones could articulate what it was like to engage in a bout of hand-to-hand combat. And when he did so (in his 1962 novel *The Thin Red Line*), it was fictionalized. Jones allowed himself a modicum of distance by opting not to write in the first-person singular.

What happened could not have been more basic. Or more primitive. Hardly more dehumanizing for both men involved. And now, with long days and interminable nights unfolding throughout the weeks and months of Jones's slow convalescence, his hyperactive imagination and turbo-charged emotional intensity were doubtless recapitulating, re-choreographing, and forever replaying in his mind the shocking and ultimately life-threatening brutality of one murderous incident.

That's what it came down to. In order to survive, Jones had to commit murder by hand. Although his act of self-defense could be justified by any military tribunal or for that matter held up as justifiable homicide in the act of self-defense against a hostile assailant under the strictest laws of civilian society, *still* . . . what happened in the context of a debased, ludicrously violent, random confrontation was a nightmare that haunted him all his life.

One day on Guadalcanal, Jones selected a spot in order to shit. He had his pants down around his ankles as he squatted in the bush. He was surrounded by jungle foliage, and finished his business. Out of nowhere came a Japanese soldier who appeared semi-crazed and intent upon killing Jones as quickly as possible. Perhaps thinking that there was food or water to be taken from the defecating American GI, the Japanese soldier, dressed in the ragged remnants of his uniform, assaulted Jones with bayonet brandished. Although probably half-starved and racked with disease (the island festered with dysentery and contagious fevers) he attacked ferociously.

Swinging wildly, and lunging again and again as Jones struggled with his pants, grappled with his belt, and did his level best to avoid being stabbed, the marauding Japanese soldier continued to attack. Conceivably, the Japanese infantryman had been lost and without food or water for a significant period of time. In later years, Jones would recount his emaciated appearance, but weakness was not evident. Quite the other way. The Japanese soldier was frenzied.

One thing led to another. Despite his torn ligaments (Jones's ankle had to be heavily taped each day for him to be able to walk at all) he managed to execute a hyper-kinetic football move, after he secured his pants and belt. It was all over in a matter of minutes—maybe five minutes. But it had to be five minutes that felt like a decade on Death Row. Jones's options were brutal: to kill or be killed. So, he fought back. And he prevailed. After managing to wrestle the Japanese soldier into submission, Jones finished him off.

Years later, in his novel *The Thin Red Line*, he would re-create this pivotal experience with punishing clarity. Giving the name Bead to an infantry private modeled on himself, Jones deployed in his fiction the accursed details of this miserable milestone: ". . . alternately sobbing and wailing, Bead rolled aside, seized the enemy rifle and on his knees raised it above his head and drove the long bayonet almost full length into the Japanese chest. The Japanese man's body convulsed in a single spasm.

His eyes opened, staring horribly at nothing, and his hands flipped up from the elbows and seized the blade through his chest. Staring with horror at the fingers which were cutting themselves on the blade trying to draw it out . . . [Bead] began to vomit."

After reassuring himself that his adversary was dead, Jones rifled through the pockets of the Japanese combatant. There he found a small wallet. Inside the wallet he saw identification with dates showing that they were about the same age. But in the case of the Japanese soldier, there was also a family photo: a small picture of a man and his diminutive wife holding their infant child. That broke Jones's heart.

Other incidents were not nearly as violent, yet just as heartbreaking. "I once served on a Grave Registration detail on Guadalcanal, after the fighting was all over," Jones recalled in *WWII*. Their mission was "to go up in the hills and dig up the dead lost in some attack. The dead were from another regiment, so men from my outfit were picked to dig them up. That was how awful the detail was. And they did not want to make it worse by having men dig up the dead of their own. Unfortunately, a man in my outfit on the detail had a brother in the other outfit, and we dug up the man's brother that day."

*   *   *

By the time Jones returned to the United States on May 19, 1943, and throughout the following summer and into the fall of '43, his state of inner despair intensified. The thought of being sent back into action was anathema to him.

Knowing what he knew about the escalating war and that not just hundreds of thousands but millions of GIs were being trained for the imminent invasions of 1944 (both in Europe and the Pacific), it was clear to Jones that if his ankle healed, he was sure to be reassigned to a combat division. Soldiers with his experience were highly valued; especially since so many green new draftees were being rushed through basic training's harried maneuvers.

At the Shenango Replacement Depot in Greenville, Pennsylvania, newly trained GIs not yet bloodied in combat were closely observed by a soldier-in-transit named Sebastian Sampas, who wrote in March, 1943, to his beloved friend Jack Kerouac. Sampas reported as follows:

"Jack . . . A brief note from the Replacement Center, where I am stationed for the next two weeks. —Here I am having all my records straightened out, previous to my departure for a Port of Embarkation.

"It really is a hell-hole here, with about one third of the soldiers in the guardhouse including twenty-two lieutenants, two chaplains, and one major—Practically one third of the soldiers have gone AWOL and one can hardly blame them.

"There has been an average of two suicides every three days and yesterday morning another body was found swinging in the latrine, a nineteen-year-old kid.

"The soldiers have already gone on two strikes because of the horrible food and treatment. My barrack is an Infantry Camp, made up of Anti-Tank Gunners and 'Wash-outs from the Paratroops.' . . . Sorely disgusted, Sebastian Sampas"

Since the mid-1990s and the rise of the "Greatest Generation" industry, tons of mass-marketed WWII hokum has avoided the clammy fact that untold numbers of Jones's peers were exceedingly anxious, deeply depressed, and all too human in their frailties, panic, and vulnerabilities. Sebastian Sampas was killed in action at Anzio on March 2, 1944, amid the grim Italian Campaign. He was a combat medic.

Jones's response to the acute mental stress of expecting to be sent back into combat and possibly killed ("I knew that my luck had run out" he later averred, recalling that his intuition, battle experience, and sense of foreboding made him absolutely sure he would not survive the war, unless he got out) was to binge-drink more, raising hell in the Memphis bars when he had a pass from the Army doctors.

He also squandered a small fortune in back pay for rooms at the Claridge Hotel, and the two-room suites at the Peabody Hotel in Memphis. "In addition to flocks of ground troops and administrative troops in the area," he recollected in his text for *WWII*, "there was a Naval Air Training Station in Memphis, as well as an Army Air Force field."

Jones never forgot those days:

"It was a regular stop and center for the Air Transport Command also. Apparently before the war the Peabody had been the chic place in Memphis, and it sported a Starlight Roof with dancing music and dinner. Money was not much of a problem. Nor were women. You could always go up to the Starlight Roof and find yourself a nice girl and dance with her a while and bring her down [to the suite]. Everybody screwed. Sometimes it did not even matter if there were other people in the room or not, at the swirling kaleidoscopic parties. Couples would ensconce themselves in the bathrooms of the suites and lock the doors."

Jones and other GIs threw round-the-clock parties, the booze flowing as radios blared the riffs of Tommy Dorsey's "Swing High," Lionel Hampton's "Flying Home" and the Memphis blues all night long. Rampant and freewheeling sex was indulged in by any and all party-goers, including Jones and the footloose local female war workers. This spree went on for months, thanks to the windfall Jones received, which he considered "one lovely lump sum." It was, in fact, "eleven months' back pay at a corporal's rate," compounded quite significantly when Jones cashed out "an allotment I'd been sending home to a bank for years to go to college on when I got out." Totaled up, Jones had more than four thousand dollars. In a devil-may-care bacchanalian outburst, he squandered every last dime. "My four thousand dollars was gone," he later rued, "and all I had to show for it were two tailored uniforms. That, and a lot of memories. Memories I didn't want, particularly. It was during a period when nobody wanted to remember things."

Oddly, Jones opted for Limited Duty service, although he was offered a discharge when his ankle was deemed a serious disability. Perhaps survivor's guilt impelled him to choose the Limited Duty alternative.

Yet, when his new orders were cut, Jones was reassigned as an infantryman to a division then training at Camp Campbell for what was assumed to be the invasion of France, at some point in 1944. Feeling betrayed by the Army for its utterly cavalier turnaround (offering him a disability-based discharge on one hand, and then ordering him to train with the 26th Infantry Division on the other hand, having rescinded the offer of Limited Duty service) and furious after his request for a 30-day furlough was denied (Jones had hoped to visit his brother Jeff, who now lived in Miami, working for the Red Cross), he repeatedly committed a military infraction; ensuring nothing but trouble. Time after time, Jones went AWOL.

After being released from Kennedy General Hospital in Memphis in August 1943, Jones was stationed at Camp Campbell, Kentucky. From there, in the autumn of 1943, he once again went Absent Without Official Leave. On this AWOL sojourn, he boarded a bus taking him from the outskirts of Camp Campbell, Kentucky, back to his hometown in east-central Illinois. Jones's bus rolled into Robinson on Friday, November 5, 1943, and during a weekend of family conflict and furious drinking, he was introduced to a childless, married woman who was seventeen years his senior.

Quickly they became confidantes, lovers, and impassioned visionaries sharing the belief that James Jones was destined to be the Thomas Wolfe of his generation.

James Jones met Lowney Handy on the weekend of his twenty-second birthday.

5
THE WOMAN ~ LOWNEY HANDY

She told him that perhaps her destiny was "to furnish a haven" for him, and certainly her presence inspired him.
~ Frank MacShane, *Into Eternity*

In the hours, days, and nights prior to meeting Lowney Handy for the first time, James Jones managed to find plenty of booze, some family conflict, and even a brush with the law over that first weekend in November 1943. He was at a tipping point.

Angry. Vulnerable. Frantic. He did not know that someone awaited.

For the first time in four years, he was in Robinson, Illinois. What did that mean? That's forty-eight months. One thousand and four hundred and sixty days. In many ways he was no longer the cocky young man he'd been when boarding the train to leave for the Army, way back in autumn 1939. Four years earlier. Another life.

Now, on the first Friday of November 1943, one day prior to his twenty-second birthday, Jones sat on a bus slowly making its way to the depot in Robinson. The unease of returning to his hometown is evoked on the first page of Jones's second novel *Some Came Running*, where his return is a leitmotif:

Of course, he knew the town when the bus slowed into it. . . . A man's home town, the one where he was born and raised, was always special. It was as if secretly all those years your senses themselves had banded together on their own and memorized everything about it so thoroughly that they remembered them even when you didn't. Even with the things you did remember, your senses kept remembering them first a split second sooner without permission

and startling you. And it didn't matter if you loved the thing or hated it. . . .
Your senses didn't feel. They just remembered. He looked out again . . . Under
the November sky, it had made him think of El Greco's View of Toledo. And he
had had that same devilish weird unearthly feeling of foreboding.

* * *

It was Jones's Aunt Sadie (the wife of his Uncle Charley, one of his father's brothers) who steered the angry, troubled, and reluctant young man to 202 West Mulberry Street in Robinson on the weekend of November 7, 1943.

Aunt Sadie, risking the wrath of Jones's Uncle Charley (who wanted next to nothing to do with his belligerent and resentful nephew), hoped that a local woman named Mrs. Lowney Turner Handy might somehow offer guidance, advice, and encouragement about writing. Jones was admitting to anyone who would listen that his ambitions about writing were not a matter of pretense; he was deadly serious.

And Aunt Sadie knew Mrs. Lowney Turner Handy was impassioned about books and the lives of authors, especially the obstacles faced by individuals yearning to write. In varied ways (including her name: Lowney rhyming with Tony), she stood apart; especially as the wife of Harry Handy, a prominent local executive. They were a power couple, childless, with secrets they'd long kept buried. Lowney confided to Jones that prior to marriage, impregnated by Harry, she'd had an illegal abortion; then, after marrying Harry, her philandering husband infected her with gonorhhea. Finally, she had a hysterectomy.

In Robinson's close-knit community, the church ladies gossiped about perennial efforts made by Lowney Turner Handy to help the downtrodden. Lowney was considered a kooky oddball. Her concern for social outcasts mystified some and irritated others. Visiting prisoners in the county jail? Lowney did that. Never damning, but, instead, assisting unmarried pregnant runaways? Lowney did so. She took in unwed pregnant girls or offered aid and comfort to convicts, because she had compassion for the dispossessed and aspiring artists alike.

Lowney's personal touch as an empath derived from being the eldest of nine children born to Fanny and Jim Turner down in Kentucky's Bluegrass region, during the first two decades of the twentieth-century. As the first-born child and eldest daughter, Lowney gradually assisted her mother in every aspect of rearing all the children. When the large Turner family made its way from Kentucky to Marshall, Illinois, the seat of Clark County, Jim Turner (a former railroad yard detective) was duly elected Sheriff. The family's living quarters were adjacent to the jail. It was in those early years of her life that Lowney routinely helped her mother prepare meals for prisoners in the county jail. Animated by boundless energy, a lively mind, and curious about others' true-life stories, Lowney proved to be an avid listener. She harbored deep feelings of being an "outsider" herself, especially after the Turner family resettled from the wilds of Kentucky to small-town Illinois. Ridiculed in high school for her "hillbilly" accent and her height, Lowney fought back with words and fists. She was always strong and extroverted.

At bottom, Lowney made a personal mission out of embracing pariahs: the misfits, ostracized, and discarded. Aunt Sadie knew that this unusual woman would not say no to a troubled soul. Lowney's husband's social status protected her.

In her most flamboyant imaginings, Aunt Sadie never could have projected just how fatefully she functioned, as she lured Jones toward this ultimate encounter. From the moment he crossed the threshold at the home of Mrs. Harry Handy on the first day after the debacle of his twenty-second birthday, James Jones was in the realm of a life-transforming mythic figure whose influence would be profound, and whose effects on Jones were both unique and peerless.

The night before, Jones had made a spectacle of his distress at the Robinson Country Club, where Uncle Charley was more than a member in good standing; he also served on the Board of Directors. After a dinner party intended to celebrate Jones's twenty-second birthday ended, harsh words were hollered and conflict erupted. Jones had been drinking heavily ever since hitting town on Friday, and at the Country Club he began yelling when dinner concluded. He ranted about the knotty, conflicted family issues bedeviling the Jones clan. And then, his disgust and howling disdain were aimed at the hypocrisy and conformity of Robinson's upscale movers and shakers, including his Uncle Charley.

While Jones was overseas, his Aunt Sadie and Uncle Charley had managed in deft maneuvers to exploit the family estate to their advantage. They now occupied the mansion that had once been the home of George W. Jones, the paternal grandfather whose reputation and legacy loomed large even in 1943, fourteen years after his death.

Jones suspected that inheritance monies, hidden stocks, cash, and other fiscal benefits were denied to his father and two other uncles, while Uncle Charley rigged the estate to favor himself and Aunt Sadie.

There was still no other home in Robinson that could compete with the old Jones mansion for sheer size and royal ambiance, and part of the reason for Jones's rage at Uncle Charley was that Jones assumed, given Uncle Charley's slick manipulations as a lawyer (and the fact that he had been the sole family member handling legal matters in the aftermath of Ramon's suicide), that everything had been officially tweaked and somehow finessed so that Uncle Charley and Aunt Sadie could ascend swiftly in their small-town quest for social mobility and upper-crust status. They were ravenous materialists, as far as Jones was concerned; and Uncle Charley, in particular, evinced nothing but skepticism and disapproval regarding Jones's passion for writing. At the end of his birthday party on the night before he met Lowney Handy, not only did Jones bellow and rage as he made an impromptu speech attacking the values and mores of those at the Country Club, but he smashed highball glasses and glass ashtrays. He also threatened to write a novel exposing all of Robinson's secrets: the adulteries he knew about; its drunkards and cheats; the town's seamy underside.

Later that night, after drinking even more as he reacquainted himself with the downtown Square and some Robinson saloons, Jones was picked up by a squad car and brought by two police officers back to the old mansion, presumably to stay the night. Uncle Charley was having none of it. He refused to allow his nephew to enter the premises, and having been turned away from "home," a bitter rift between Jones and his Uncle Charley solidified. There would never be any reconciliation.

However, because she had already gone to the trouble of indicating to Mrs. Harry Handy that she desperately wanted her husband's nephew to meet her and perhaps find common ground and possibly inspiration regarding his constant talk about writing, Aunt Sadie insisted that Jones meet Lowney. And so he did.

*   *   *

Throughout Robinson, Illinois, and Crawford County at large, Lowney Turner Handy was known as a maverick. Her personality was considered offbeat; and at times scandalous. And yet, she could not be either publicly criticized (not too much, anyway) or privately consigned to oblivion, because in Robinson's small-town, calibrated social rank, Lowney Handy sat high atop the totem pole.

She had married Harry Handy (a University of Illinois graduate in engineering) on July 31st, 1926, three years after she graduated from high school. They lived in Robinson, where Harry was eventually appointed superintendent of the Ohio Oil Refinery. Harry Handy was well connected on every level of Robinson's social pecking order. He was, indeed, a man whose modesty and goodwill were admired and appreciated. And, as the chief executive officer at Robinson's largest source of local employment, his wife automatically received deferential respect.

But then, she acted like she didn't give a damn. In truth, she didn't. Lowney was an authentic rebel who was not just married to a powerful man. She was also a proudly self-educated woman who read voraciously, had an encyclopedic curiosity about a vast array of topics (including the religions of India and the Far East), and constantly encouraged others to go their own way. By corresponding with aspiring writers who sought her advice and opinions, as well as in her living room at home on Mulberry Street, Lowney constantly emphasized the need to trust in one's own silent intuition. More than a half-century after the day she met James Jones, a profile of Lowney Handy, written by historian and literary archivist Thomas J. Wood, appeared in the Summer 1997 *Illinois Historical Record*. Wood highlighted the essence of Lowney's offbeat persona, by quoting from one of her idiosyncratic messages of hope to an aspiring artist. In a note to one of her students, Lowney Handy wrote: "Strangely enough – if we go our own way – say nothing, just keep at work – all the people who denounce and are angry because we are not following in the groove, will finally become the first to praise. IT IS NEVER IMPORTANT WHAT – 'They' – SAY!'" And then Wood further states:

Lowney Turner Handy (1904-1964) lived most of her life as if she did not care what "they" said. And yet, her family, friends, and enemies had much to say about her generosity, stubbornness, enthusiasm, anger, eccentricity, and above all, her individuality. But she lived in a time and place where what "they" said about the expected behavior of women seemed very important indeed. She chose, however, not to follow "in the groove" laid down by small-town Illinois society.

Family backgrounds gave Jones and Lowney plenty to talk about when they met on the Sunday after Jones's dissolute twenty-second birthday. Distinct similarities abounded, despite the fact that Lowney, born on April 16, 1904, was seventeen years older than Jones.

She was the eldest daughter of Jim Turner, who years earlier had been Sheriff up in Marshall, Illinois, twenty-eight miles north of Robinson. Jim Turner's larger-than-life reputation as the former Clark County Sheriff was a matter of local legend, as were his days serving as the elected Road Commissioner of his precinct. He'd been a powerhouse figure in the local contingent of the Democratic Party, and his zestful egalitarian ethics were inherited by his daughter Lowney.

Similarly, Jones's paternal grandfather had once been an icon of the community with his esteemed law practice, his mansion with its Southern-style pillars, and his towering Lincolnesque mien. George W. Jones was still remembered for wearing his fine tailored black suits as he promenaded to and from the office, during his heyday. Lowney's Kentucky ancestors and Jones's pioneer forebears were deeply embedded in the tumultuous, violent Americana of the 1800s; their long-gone family members had fought on both the Union and Confederate sides during the Civil War.

Another similarity: Jones's mother made Christian Science tenets the central focus of her life; Lowney's mother never ceased in her Baptist proselytizing and hellfire rhetoric. Like Jones, who despised his mother's fear-based incantations, Lowney disdained her mother's zealous brand of Southern Baptist faith.

Lowney's family had roots in the blood feuds of Kentucky. As a schoolgirl and later as a young woman she was continually mocked—no matter how far her family progressed in Clark County and then Crawford County's power structure—and told repeatedly she was "a hick." She had been teased for being "a stupid hillbilly" throughout all of her years in school, much as Jones had been ridiculed for being a "four-eyed" bookworm whose short stature impeded every effort he made to shine athletically or otherwise. Height figured prominently in Lowney's life, as well.

In her case, it was her taller-than-average physique that made her appear ungainly. About that she didn't give a damn, either. In a culture where women—literally and figuratively—were assumed to rank below all men in stature, status, career paths, income, and social mobility,

Lowney was a strikingly tall, confident woman glorying in her vigor. She did not walk or saunter; she *strode*. Brisk daily walking was a favored form of exercise for her. She also practiced Yoga, believed in homeopathic folk remedies, and favored a vegetarian diet. Lowney enjoyed manual labor and also exulted in the sacred texts of Hinduism and Buddhism, steeping herself in mystical literature. In her daily life, she went braless as often as possible. With her breasts swinging freely beneath a light gray sweatshirt that she enjoyed wearing atop her rolled-up denim jeans and moccasins, she scandalized the local ladies who were aghast at Lowney's provocative aura. She didn't care if her nipples visibly hardened, just as she didn't care if others considered her offensive for her lack of a girdle, bra, stockings, white gloves, and the other ornaments of standard lady's attire. When necessary, though, Lowney could perform as the executive's proper wife. And when she wanted to, she could "play the part" required of her by Harry's career and attend banquets, country club dinners and social dances. But she preferred her renegade persona.

Author John Bowers was a close observer of Lowney and Jones, and in his 1971 memoir, *The Colony*, he described the earthy impact of Lowney's presence: "She was striding out of the *Ramada* as I was walking up. Her tanned skin was coffee-colored, there were strands of gray through her hair, and her eyes were huge. Her arms were short for her torso, thick around the upper arms, and—lo and behold—she wore no brassiere. Her large breasts jumped—the only word for it—inside a sweatshirt, and I saw, with a catch in my throat, the outline of nipples. I kept my eyes raised, not wanting her to think I was interested in such things."

She and Jones overflowed with libido. Their sapiosexual attraction to each other was chemical, psychological, spiritual, emotional, and certainly physical. The first thing Jones noticed after she welcomed him into her living room at 202 West Mulberry Street, was that she had multiple stacks and shelves of diverse books. He knew from his Aunt Sadie that Lowney also aspired to be a writer. Years earlier, in 1936 (when Jones was a high school sophomore), Lowney had enrolled herself in a correspondence course for writers, titling one of her essays "Write Me as One Who Loves His Fellow-Men." Lowney's self-awareness in relation to her deep yearning to nurture others later manifested in varied ways —especially with striving writers. In the meantime, she excelled as an autodidact and made herself an avid reader.

Recently, in fact, Aunt Sadie and others around Robinson had picked up on the story of Lowney's sojourn to New York City. She had made her way to Manhattan—that in itself was a brazen endeavor, given that most of Robinson's citizens rarely made their way to Chicago—in order to show her work in progress to a professional book editor at one of America's leading publishing houses. She had been diligently working on a novel for quite some time. Glancing at her pages, the New York editor quickly dismissed her manuscript. "What he really meant, though," she later surmised, "was that I was a frustrated, childless, middle-aged woman trying to find something to do, and that I had better go home and find something else." Lowney left his office with a furious desire to return someday. Triumphantly. A journalist would later ascertain that "[Lowney] had gone home carrying in her heart a bitter determination to show them all. But anybody who had anything to do with writing made her very angry this soon after her experience." That explains the exasperated reaction that Lowney had when Aunt Sadie said about Jones: "He thinks he wants to write." To which Lowney retorted: "Oh, my God, no! Not a writer!"

In this respect, she and the angry young man she welcomed had something else in common. Each of Jones's short-story submissions had been rejected thus far by *Esquire* and other Manhattan-based magazines. But there was no doubting his love for books and his passion for literature. Within a few minutes of greeting each other on that Sunday, Lowney recalled, Jones sat on her living room floor removing her library of books from the shelves, as though he wanted to devour them for the nourishment and sustenance they promised. She later said: "You should have seen him then. He swaggered; he wore dark glasses; he even asked me to read his poetry aloud. He had obviously come over for a free drink. Then he saw my books. Jim got out of his chair and began to take out the books. He flipped through them and plopped them back as if he were gulping down what they had in them."

That image has a streak of Thomas Wolfe about it, with certain passages from Wolfe's novels coming to mind about his word-drenched, book-starved, poetically flailing young heroes in spacious libraries reacting with visceral enthusiasm to reams of print in their midst. Wolfe was an author beloved by Lowney, too. Of course, an erotic Wolfe-like passion was in the air and it was satiated the very next day when, according to Jones, he and Lowney spent the entire day in bed.

There was a fiery, highly charged, erotically combustible attraction between Jones and Lowney Handy. Her unconventional life, unorthodox marriage, and enthralling rebelliousness made her a perfect match for him. Most of all, she harbored a wildly intoxicating medley of personal characteristics that caused Jones to fall in love in a way that obliterated all of his preexisting notions about sex and romance, women and men. Having endured the sexual deprivations of Schofield Barracks and the combat zones in the Pacific, it was no surprise that while he convalesced in Memphis and had an excess of back pay to blow to smithereens, Jones engaged in frantic episodes of alcohol-fueled casual sex at hotel-based all-night parties where partners shifted, switched rooms, and made the rounds as Tango dancers do at a traditional *milonga*. "I had a two-room suite at the Peabody six weeks straight and loaned the key to anybody who wanted it when I couldn't get into town," he later explained, when outlining his "wild time" in Memphis during the summer of 1943.

But *this* was different. This was not transient. Nor was it all soaked in alcohol.

Lowney did not care for drinking, so while Jones probably had some amount of booze in his system as they became lovers almost instantaneously, it is highly likely that he was not nearly as drunk as he had been during his past sexual exploits. As such, his lovemaking with Lowney was almost certainly a new experience in that he was inevitably more sensitive to all sensations, more alert in his willingness and ability to be responsive to her needs and desires; and most of all not ready to flee.

In almost all of the fiction that Jones later wrote both exploring and evoking the sexual gamesmanship of the wartime epoch, there is a horrendous kind of manic, frantic, get-it-while-you-can, wham-bam, hurry up and dump her kind of sex. It is for most people involved not just a booze-sodden, angry mess . . . it is also unfulfilling, depersonalized, and deeply unhappy. Everything was the opposite with Lowney.

And doubtless the fact that she was seventeen years older than Jones intensified this. Not only was the beaten-down AWOL combat vet making love to a prominent married woman who flouted social conventions with a free-spirited *joie-de-vivre* shrug of her shoulders that rivaled his unconventional attitudes, but, she was old enough to be his mother. Being attracted to her bespoke an act of rebellion. Being intimate with her was an affront to every moral precept held dear (then and now) about the meaning of marriage and the strictures of monogamy. Being adulterous with her was an admixture of libertine indulgence and unethical malevolence, in the eyes of the upright citizens of Robinson. And being consumed by her, caressed by her, kissed, comforted, and indulged by her was, probably, for James Jones at age twenty-two, the most sacramental reprieve he was able to know from his chronic, raging, interior emotional disarray. Far different in every way from the whiskey-soaked episodes of hurried, anger-inflected, oftentimes anonymous sex he had known during his Memphis hiatus, the newfound erotic immersion he shared with Lowney was enmeshed with their mutual visions of creativity as writers and their dual commitment to achieving lives that weren't hamstrung by social propriety.

Although in recent years such a trans-generational attraction has been culturally acknowledged (usually with hackneyed stereotypes about Cougars or MILFs), the fact remains that back then, and even now, a sexually charged rapport between a younger man and a woman nearly two decades his senior is often looked at askance.

Both Jones and Lowney refused to give a damn for the ways that others were likely to speak or think or react to their impassioned commitment to each other. The oddity of all this in the heart of small-town America in the wartime Midwest of 1943 cannot be stressed too much. Yet it was commonly known, even before Jones returned to Robinson, that Lowney and Harry Handy had a childless, exceedingly untraditional marriage. The expression "open marriage" was not then in vogue, but it is apropos. Harry Handy had his girlfriends; now Lowney had her younger lover.

In the weeks, months and years to come, Jones would learn a great deal about the radically unusual liberties that Lowney and Harry granted unto each other. Indeed, their lives would provide fodder for Jones's mature fiction. An ambitious first novel was already taking shape in Jones's imagination and it was largely inspired by the crass new booming wartime America he saw all around him, as well as the weekend crises of his twenty-second birthday. Titled *They Shall Inherit the Laughter*, it became Jones's ultimate literary preoccupation over the next two-and-a-half years.

Meantime, Lowney and Harry Handy conferred, and then Jones and the Handys vowed: Once extricated from the Army, Jones would move in with them; they would support him in his quest to be a great writer. They were in harmony.

All three believed that destiny beckoned. Their collective blind faith in 1943 is hinted at by literary scholar George Hendrick, who offered this summing up in 2008 to the *Illinois Times:* "Most writers' colonies were along the East Coast [e. g., the MacDowell Colony or Yaddo]. They provided no training and were only open to those writers who were already established or had glowing recommendations. Lowney was looking for people who were just out of the Army, or in two cases, just out of prison, who had a lot of experience, but most of them had no training in the arts. That's quite different from the usual writers' colony. There's nobody like her, as far as I know."

Yet, the main question facing both Jones and Lowney after their encounter on that Sunday segued to their love-at-first-sight sexual ecstasies on Monday (about which Harry was aware and indifferent, with his attention, as usual, focused on his own private life, his career, and also his prodigious drinking and philandering) was this: How to get Jones out of trouble with the Army? Like it or not, he was AWOL. He could not stay too long. After two weeks, he returned to Camp Campbell, where a sympathetic sergeant magnanimously "fixed" Jones's paperwork, officially marking it as "Delayed Two Weeks En Route." That allowed Jones to sidestep a court-martial.

At this time, Jones made the final break with what remained of his family in Robinson. Bitter and humiliated because his Uncle Charley did nothing to prevent him from being tossed in jail for vagrancy one night (after he was found passed out in the wee small hours of the morning at the Mission Tea Room downtown), Jones wrote a blistering letter to his uncle, reflecting on his recent visit to Robinson and their toxic level of caustic tension. It was a letter addressing past, present and future:

"[Your] attempt to humiliate me by having me thrown in jail was foiled by me: I made it a deliberate point to tell everyone I saw about my being thrown in jail and also pointed out to them, in case their obtuse thinking didn't catch it, what a damned good joke it was on me. I also told them all about your telling the night-cop to put me in. I think that foiled it—everyone is of the opinion I enjoyed it I think. I know that I have allegedly done several things that you do not think were in keeping with the Jones name and the burden of keeping it unsmirched. I, too, am proud of the name Jones—but I am proud of the name in the same way that I am proud of Dad's committing suicide. None of my beliefs are in accordance with yours—I can see that much more clearly now than I did before. I am not under your jurisdiction, being legally an adult. Neither have you in the least part tried to understand my beliefs—altho

I sweated blood in a self-conscious agony when attempting several times to explain them to you. You shut your mind to them. I shall not bother to try to tell you about them anymore."

Invariably, his newfound allegiance to Lowney Handy deepened. By this time, Jones doubtless saw her as Thomas Wolfe once described Aline Bernstein, the married older woman who became his lover and patron: "She was so lovely, so ruddy, and so delicate, she was so fresh and healthy-looking . . . eager and full of belief in life, radiant with beauty, goodness, and magic."

*   *   *

The magnetic, charismatic and nurturing aspects of Lowney Handy's persona had always been noted by those who met her. Jones was far from being the first individual to react viscerally to her. Their swift plunge into love and sex, however, was definitely a rare development for both of them. Most of the time, in those years, Jones had found himself straining for any sort of sexual opportunities with whomever it was that he hoped might provide erotic fulfillment. Yet ever since he had been in the Army, his yearning for a genuine romantic companion and a generous sexual ally had been thwarted. Instead, he had suffered through an admittedly disconsolate series of assignations over the years, wherein the sex he was able to obtain was soaked in alcohol, often in the company of others who were also drunk or just plying their trade (Jones retained a fondness for the transactional simplicity of prostitutes well into the 1950s).

Now, though, he had crossed a threshold. Lowney was a new friend who was well placed to play the role of mentor, while also offering immediate release from the sexual frustration that had plagued Jones throughout adolescence and into young adulthood. Moreover, there was in Lowney's realm of ideas about art, spirituality, psychology and literature in particular a set of common denominators that galvanized Jones's deepest convictions about his good fortune in meeting her.

Whenever others first met Lowney Turner Handy, they too were struck by the power of her personality. Toward the end of the 1940s, one of Jones's childhood schoolmates (Sylvanus "Tinks" Howe, with whom he reconnected as pals after the end of World War II) got married in Robinson. When his new bride was first introduced to Lowney and

Jones, who at that time still labored in obscurity on what would emerge as *From Here to Eternity*, it was Lowney who made the greater impression on Helen Howe:

"She was one of the strongest women I think I've ever met," Howe recalled in an interview. "She was demanding, extremely honest and fair. And I am sure that . . . all of the people she worked with, she controlled and ruled."

By the time Helen Howe met Lowney in 1949, not only Jones but a handful of other aspiring authors were under her wing. The difference was that Jones was not under her tutelage, strictly speaking—whereas with other writers she agreed to mentor, it was understood that they were her "pupils." In Jones's case, it was understood that he worked on a higher level of autonomy than the other students in Lowney's circle. Still, the universal element was the force of Lowney.

Helen Howe (whose future career led to her teaching for decades at Lincoln Trail College in Robinson, Illinois, where she and others also founded The James Jones Literary Society, which thrives to this day) was deeply impressed by the eloquence and intelligence Lowney exuded:

"She had marvelous ideas," Howe said. "She had a beautiful command of the language. She had a tremendous talent. She provided the motivation for all of the people who were" in her tutorial environment, whether they were the local high school students who gravitated toward her or the future members of the writers' colony that she, her husband and Jones inaugurated later on. The one constant ingredient was the centrality of Lowney's fixed ideas about writing in particular and life in general. She touted the values of discipline, strict routines, vegetarian dietary limits and other protocols considered not just unorthodox but downright maverick.

Her younger brother Earl Turner minced no words when speaking about Lowney: "She was bullheaded," Earl told scholar J. Michael Lennon. Whereas Earl's wife, Belva Turner, put it this way: "She was domineering." When asked to elaborate, Earl concluded: "She was stubborn. She and I didn't get along. We'd argue." And yet, Belva also recalled that Lowney "was generous to a fault," and when it came to helping someone else, Lowney would "give anyone anything."

One woman who spent her career teaching English at different levels in the Robinson public school system was Alberta Eagleton. James Jones was never enrolled in one of her classes, but Eagleton did teach Jones's younger sister, Mary Ann, when she was in eighth grade. By that time,

Jones was in the Army and away from Robinson. But it was precisely during those years, as the Second World War metastasized between 1939 and 1943, that Eagleton became increasingly aware of Lowney's reputation for opening her home to bookish high school students, whose ardent interest in writing and other arts baffled their parents and annoyed most of their peers.

It was not a mystery to Alberta Eagleton, who was once asked about why such students were drawn to Lowney. "I think," Eagleton mused, ""it was because Lowney had provided a place for them to come . . . where they could express themselves. I think it was [also] that she simply had a love of life and found that she could express that to the young people. It was a pitched war between the mothers, grandmothers and fathers of these children. They weren't exactly children, they were high school students, probably juniors and seniors—but were attracted to Lowney's home. So the pitched battles were between the parents and Lowney and the kids were caught in the middle."

Gossip was rife. Rumors swirled about. And in Robinson, where the ladies' network of affiliations and associations was a hornets' nest, the fact that the childless wife of the superintendent of the Ohio Oil Refinery (the town's largest employer) had set herself up as a kind of mentor to creatively inclined young people generated not just controversy but downright suspicion. "I think they thought Lowney had a devil's cult out at her home," Alberta Eagleton once said: "[That she] was dragging these youngsters down there in the evening and having them participate. I don't think they understood what Lowney was trying to do. You must remember: the town at that time didn't have much entertainment for those students. There was no place for them to have that kind of an outlet where they could express themselves and be themselves. She offered that kind of a place for them. [Then] they would shut themselves up in their rooms or up in the house somewhere and retreat from the family; they would read and they would try to write. It was alienating these youngsters from their families."

In Jones's case, however, there was more than family strife at hand.

During his second AWOL excursion to Robinson (a three-day hiatus that coincided with Thanksgiving in 1943), Jones accompanied Lowney on a road trip to Morris, Illinois, to visit her brother Harold and his wife Margaret. As the oldest of twelve children (eight girls and four boys), Lowney had always sustained a profound sense of loyalty and kinship with her siblings, even though her own life differed greatly from theirs. Lowney's temperamental traits were rooted in the 19th-century clan sensibilities of the Bluegrass region of Kentucky, where she had been born and partly raised. At bottom, no matter how her interests diverged from the priorities of her more traditional siblings (whose conventional marriages and child-rearing agendas were worlds removed from the open marriage and artistic adventuring Lowney established for herself), she was always attentive to the notion of maintaining her family ties.

But she was even more attentive to the increasingly erratic behavior of Jones. Margaret Turned recalled in one interview how Jones's odd deportment manifested during that pre-Thanksgiving '43 AWOL period:

"Harold and I had just been married a short time and ... it was in the fall of 1943. We had an apartment in Morris and Lowney brought Jim up to see us. I don't know whether they were on their way to Chicago or what, but they stayed there long enough for me to get dinner for them. And the thing that really I couldn't understand [was that] Jim wouldn't eat at the table. He wanted his food in on the living room floor. He was sitting by the record player listening to Alec Templeton, one of his records. So I carted the dish in with all the food on it and his drink and everything and plunked it down on the floor in front of him. And he ate it in there. I thought he was really strange. That was the very first time I'd ever seen him."

Jones's remote attitude may well have been a ploy to avoid anything resembling standard small talk around the dinner table. He deliberately retreated from the socializing going on nearby, and kept to himself.

Lost in the music of popular radio bandleader Alec Templeton, Jones's self-absorbed posture and his comparative silence—"Lowney did most of the talking. He was very quiet that day, very quiet" Margaret recalled— was likely a coping mechanism. He could hardly be expected to speak for long in any typical dinnertime setting without the topic turning to the subject of the war. Still in uniform and with his convalescence from both his shrapnel wounds and his injured ankle apparently complete, the subject would have inevitably shifted to Jones's future in the Army. And if there were one issue he wished to avoid more than his AWOL status, it was the issue of being returned to combat sometime in 1944.

It was during the first six months of 1944 that Jones's psychological stress reached a breaking point. Although not punished severely after returning to Camp Campbell, Kentucky, following his second AWOL sojourn (Jones later recounted that he lost his corporal stripes and was "busted to private," and then reassigned and thus "became latrine orderly"), he nonetheless began a downward spiral that coincided with the one-year anniversary of his Guadalcanal wounding and all of the stress, trauma, fear, dread and disorientation that both preceded and then followed that pivotal experience one year earlier. In the year now past, the likelihood of an anonymous death and not just an unfinished life but a life that left no legacy or anything to be remembered by caused Jones new depths of despair. "It is hard enough to accept dying," he mused. "But to accept dying unsung and unknown except in some mass accolade, with no one to know the particulars how and when except in some mass communiqué, to be buried in some foreign land like a sack of rotten evil-smelling potatoes in a tin box for later disinterment and shipment home requires a kind of bravery and acceptance so unspeakable that nobody has ever given a particular name to it."

After more than thirty years of reflection, Jones concluded in the mid-1970s: "I don't think I ever learned . . . the last steps in the EVOLUTION OF A SOLDIER . . . my EVOLUTION OF A SOLDIER stopped short of full development. I remember lying on my belly more than once, and looking at the other sweating faces all around me and wondering which of us lying there who died that week would ever be remembered in the particulars of his death by any of the others who survived. And of course nobody else would know, or much care. I simply did not want to die and not be remembered for it. Or not be remembered at all."

In the winter of '44 Jones was thrown in with more than a hundred other so-called "physical misfits" and ordered to serve with the 842nd Quartermaster Gas Supply Company. It was grunt work. And yet for a brief period, he was pleased to be in the company of a Jewish-American Lieutenant who shared with the busted-down private a passion for books and writing. By the spring of '44, Jones was briefly promoted to sergeant and put on duty in the company's Orderly Room. Just as swiftly, though, that Jewish-American colleague was relieved of command and in the turmoil of officers' rotation, a gruff disciplinarian replaced him. At this time, writing in fits and starts and trying his best to make progress with a first novel that chronicled the distress and the drama he experienced during his first drunken AWOL spree back in early November of '43 (Robinson was renamed Endymion in homage to Keats; and the archetypal "Lowney character" was dubbed "Cornelia Marion"), Jones had every reason to regret his prior decision not to accept a discharge when it had been offered. His latter-day loyalty to "the old company" and doubtless his perceptions of bravery, shame, cowardice, and other intangibles had impelled him to stay in uniform. But now his fatalism left him stricken by thoughts of again being sent overseas. In May 1944 the war in Europe was fast approaching one of its peak periods, and American soldiers (not by the thousands or the tens of thousands or hundreds of thousands, but two million GIs in Europe) would soon be embroiled everywhere from the ongoing Italian Campaign to the gargantuan landings in Northwestern France that would soon make the name Normandy dominate headlines.

"I got drunk one night on 3.2 beer in the PX, and I did not see any point in any of it," Jones later reflected. "I felt outraged for our Jewish Lieutenant who was on the shitlist at the 2nd Army Headquarters; I felt degraded at having to answer the beefy Captain's damn phone; *I knew we were shortly going to Europe and I felt that I had done all that they could expect of one man . . . and I felt in my bones that I had used all my luck up, that if I went to Europe I wouldn't be coming back* [emphasis added]. I caught the bus at midnight, aware that I was leaving for good, though I didn't know where or how or what would come of it, and didn't much care, and left the Post, and looked back from the bus and watched the lights fade away. At the risk of seeming sentimental, I will say I loved the Post I was leaving, all of it. I also hated it." This third AWOL episode in May of '44 would be Jones's last. It is stunning to ponder the amazing luck that followed. Inexplicably, in the same season that found untold numbers of other experienced soldiers more entrenched than ever in military duties, and with the need for replacements and experienced hands soon reaching an all-time high in every theater of the worldwide conflict, Jones was not only spared a court-martial for his third AWOL infraction, he was fatefully maneuvered right out of harm's way.

By the time of the initial D-Day landings on the five bloody beaches of Normandy on Tuesday, June 6, 1944, a letter from Jones was en route to brother Jeff. Written on Saturday, June 3, 1944 (just two days prior to the Allied entry into Rome, which was quickly eclipsed in the news by the landings of Eisenhower's armies at Omaha, Utah, Gold, Juno and Sword beaches on Tuesday the 6th), it was a letter of defeat:

"I suppose you've already had a letter about my being AWOL," he wrote to Jeff: "So it won't be a surprise to you to know I'm in jail. I'm in the psychiatric ward of the station hospital. If you write, write the letter to my old address of the 842nd [Quartermaster Gas Supply Company]. When I got back and had the customary interview with my C.O., I was sent here for mental observation and treatment. What happened was very simple: I had stood the army as long as I could."

On the day he wrote that letter, Jones had been in the U. S. Army for one thousand and six hundred and fifty-five days.

Obviously Jones highlighted his newfound rapport with Lowney Handy in earlier letters to Jeff, because she required no introduction in his letter dated June 3, as Jones explained that "Lowney had a letter from my C.O., which made me believe you probably got one, too. She didn't know I was gone, but when she got the letter she started calling around & found me. She said that she half-suspected that [I] was where I was. She came over to Indianapolis & got me & talked me into coming back. I had intended to stay until I finished the book or else got caught."

He was working feverishly on a first novel entitled *They Shall Inherit the Laughter.* Simultaneously, Lowney was at work on a different mode of fiction. On June 2, 1944, the day before Jones wrote his explanatory letter to Jeff and summed up by saying that "[Lowney] came over to Indianapolis & got me & talked me into coming back," a crucial letter was typed by Lowney and sent to Captain Eugene A. Mailloux of the 842nd Quartermaster Gas Supply Company at Camp Campbell, Kentucky. It proved to be a letter that would seriously influence Captain Mailloux and spur him on in his effort to help Jones receive a discharge.

It is clear that in her first letter to Captain Mailloux, it was Lowney's intention to lay the groundwork for an all-out effort to secure Jones a legitimate discharge as soon as possible. She did so by pushing from both sides at once.

On one hand, she began her letter of June 2, 1944, with a circumlocution that was not an outright lie, yet it was not the whole truth either: "In answer to your inquiry concerning the whereabouts of Sgt. James R. Jones, I regret that I am unable to be of any help to you." Read quickly, her statement seems to say that she does not know where he is. Or was.

Yet, the chronology of overlapping correspondences proves that she knew exactly where he had been (Indianapolis); for in Jones's letter to Jeff, it is Lowney who is credited with persuading him to return from his AWOL hideaway and turn himself in back at Camp Campbell. "If it wasn't for her I'd still be gone," he admitted.

The question is: When did Jones turn himself in back at Camp Campbell?

When Captain Mailloux responded to Lowney's letter of June 2 with his memo dated June 7, 1944, he confidently stated that "Jones returned to this organization on the 30th of May." And so, because Lowney had gone to Indianapolis and persuaded Jones to return to Kentucky and he then appeared back at Camp Campbell on May 30th, surely the claim in her letter of June 2 (that "I am unable to be of any help to you" in regard to "your inquiry concerning the whereabouts of my friend, Sgt. James R. Jones") is a bit of a ruse. She sent in that letter and feigned ignorance, when in fact she had personally hunted down Jones in Indianapolis and convinced him to report back to Camp Campbell, come what may.

On the other hand, now that she was in direct communication with Captain Mailloux, and now that she doubtless knew that despite her claim to the contrary, Jones *had* returned from his latest AWOL caper, she went into rhetorical overdrive. With a calculated intention (to get Jones out of the Army) and with political finesse (insisting that "I also want it on the record that I will not assume any responsibility for his erratic decisions"), Lowney typed the remainder of her single-spaced page-and-a-half letter, arguing that Jones was a rare, exceptionally talented man.

But she also made it plain that he was unstable, unpredictable, and in no way a further asset to the military. "Not that I especially mean this as derogatory," she wrote. "However, since you say you have checked with the men and studied his record I am certain you understand what I mean. I can furnish all sorts of proof from anyone living here in Robinson, his home town, as to his instability as an ordinary citizen."

Swiftly, though, Lowney insisted that Jones "[is] harmless if left alone to work at the one thing he cares about."

The "one thing," of course, was writing. And the bulk of Lowney's long first letter to Captain Mailloux is a testimonial to Jones's potential—yet there is also one more tour-de-force example of Lowney's calculated verbal dexterity. "He is a writer of very rare promise," she insisted. "This is not only my opinion but I have shown samples of his work to a number of people and they have been unusually impressed. Among these was Tom Uzzell, former fiction editor of *Collier's Weekly*. All agree that [Jones] is brilliant, undoubtedly [a] genius. If he is a poor soldier, this will account for it, for genius is almost invariably astute in one line and utter failures in all others . . . my friends agree that he is in a class with Ernest Hemingway, [Thomas] Wolfe, [and] John Dos Passos.

"Jones is an artist. He is very sensitive, and certainly far from conservative in his thinking. Like all artists, he is not aware of any law, so cannot predict what he may do; and [I] am positive that he has never understood the term ethics as you and I define it."

Then: Lowney interjected a startling sentence, but just as swiftly pulled back and mused that it may very well have been a bit of hyperbole on Jones's part: "I have heard him say," Lowney wrote, "that when he was overseas he meant to kill his commanding officer and that the only reason he did not do so was that the opportunity did not present itself. This of course could have been a form of showing off, but I felt at the time that he had spoken truth."

Fabrication or not, that claim held Captain Mailloux's attention in a great big way. When replying on June 7 to Lowney's letter, he flat-out admitted: "Your letter will be one of the exhibits to prove that he is mentally unbalanced." Yet, that assessment was not nearly as negative as it sounds. Captain Mailloux's letter of June 7 goes on to say: "Now, don't misunderstand me. I don't think he is mentally unbalanced . . . I have come to the conclusion that he is a conceited, egotistical, selfish individual who thinks he is a genius because a few people have told him so. On the other hand, his colossal conceit has led him to a state of mind where he might, to dramatize a situation, do something drastic, and I wouldn't want to be held responsible for any of that." It borders on the fantastic that Jones was lucky enough in June of '44 to be protected, as it were, inside the military system, by a Captain who was so judicious.

Every step of the way, as Mailloux followed by-the-book procedures and protocols, he also managed to keep in mind Jones's humanity, his past service, his having been wounded, and more. As he explained to Lowney: "As soon as he reported to me, I of course, put him under arrest. As I saw he was under some mental strain and in a very depressed mood, I called the Detachment Surgeon and had him placed under observation. They in turn are now taking action toward a possible discharge . . . I do appreciate the fact that he has been wounded and I have made inquiries as to what steps he could take to get a discharge on that basis. And as far as I'm concerned what the Medical authorities decide will also be my decision."

By the time Captain Mailloux wrote those words, Jones had already had several interviews with "the Medical authorities." In describing to

Jeff what had recently been discussed, he explained: "I talked to one of the psychiatrists here and to a Red Cross Social Worker. I told them everything I could: that I am a genius (although they probably won't believe that); that if they attempt to send me overseas again I'll commit suicide; that if I don't get out of the army I'll either go mad or turn into a criminal—which is just next door to an artist anyway; that all I want to do is write, and that nobody and no thing means anything to me except writing. I don't know whether they believe me or not. I'm afraid they'll [think] I've cooked up a story."

Nobody thought Jones was malingering. And he was never branded as one who had "cooked up a story." What gave Captain Mailloux reason to pause was the omnipresent realization that in June of 1944, the war's many crescendos made any one individual's personal needs quasi-irrelevant.

"Our lives, during this crisis" Mailloux wrote to Lowney, "do not belong to us but rather to a cause. If we want to change the world, one way or the other, the important thing is first to settle the present problem [and] then make the changes. We can't do this if some of us take the attitude [of] 'I didn't start this. Why should I stick my neck out?' If Jones is returned to me for duty, I will do all I can to keep him contented. On the other hand I will expect him to do his duty as a soldier of this company, whether or not he agrees with the decision handed down. I will see to it that he gets every opportunity to exercise his talents . . . but on the other hand he must realize that I have duties to perform and that as far as I am concerned, the group comes before the individual."

That said, Captain Mailloux asserted: "I have made further study of [his] case and I'm convinced that Jones, who is undoubtedly very brilliant, could be made to realize that no matter what his personal feelings are, we all have a job to do these days and that personal ideals should be laid to one side until that job is done."

Contrarily, Jones pulled no punches: "The problem itself—this miserable, shitty reawakening of a hope long since laid to rest—stemmed from the realization that [I] was now fighting in a war which was already won. A won war, but a won war whose fighting was going to continue for a while, and in which [I] might still be killed just the same: one of the last KIAs of a waning war." Psychologically, Jones was affected by hope's return. "Hope had pushed itself back up into [my] thoughts because the war was won. Any fool could see that . . . in 1944.

Such thoughts awakened all the pain [I] had learned so laboriously over the years to amputate at the root."

So, he railed: "I told them how I hate the army, that the army has done nothing but screw me, whether consciously or unconsciously. I just can't stand it anymore; I've reached the saturation point. If I hadn't been overseas; if I hadn't done all a man could be expected to do, it might be different. If my ankle were a wound instead of an operation as it is, I would have requested a discharge. More than once I've seriously considered sticking my leg under a train. It'd be worth the loss of a foot to get out so I could have some peace and write. I just can't take it any more."

Lowney sent another full-page single-spaced typed letter to Captain Mailloux on June 10, 1944. In this letter, she maximized all of her powers of insight and empathy. Most importantly, she isolated one peculiar sentence form Mailloux's June 7th letter to her. In that initial letter, Captain Mailloux ended a paragraph in a way that a careless reader may have missed. But a careful reader—perusing between the lines, as it were—could very well have ascertained a signal of sorts.

Mailloux wrote: "I know that [Jones] will be a tough job for somebody and I'm further convinced that you are the only person who can do it. Won't you help?" Lowney took the bait. That sentence and that one question were rife with subtext. Although Mailloux sandwiched those two lines in between his lengthy paragraphs regarding duty "during this crisis" and the notion that "duty comes first," he also hinted otherwise.

Lowney's reply to Captain Mailloux was an all-embracing appreciation of the Captain's intelligence, integrity, decency and perhaps most of all his unspoken need to make a difference. She opened her heart to him.

"I feel that you are doing much more than ordinarily expected from an officer in your effort to help Pvt. Jones. I'm certain it is necessary now, and if he is to succeed later with his work." Already she was looking forward to the future that she and Jones had outlined for themselves. No mention, of course, of their intimacy impinged on this. Instead, Lowney designed her letter as a statement on behalf of lofty themes.

"One of the chief reasons that we have so few brilliant people mature and continue successfully, completing the work of which they alone are capable" she asserted in her June 10th letter to Mailloux, "is that there are too many besetting hazards. That brings us back to the old argument: 'Am I my brother's keeper?' I feel that I am, as much as it may annoy me at times."

And rather than elaborate with examples of her years of engagement with pregnant teenage girls or the prisoners at the jail where her father presided as sheriff or the Robinson high school students who aspired to write or the local GIs who gratefully accepted the free drinks and home-cooked meals that she and Harry sometimes provided, Lowney allied herself with Captain Mailloux as a kindred spirit: "From the tone of your letter," she wrote, "I can see you too assume responsibility. I agree with your statement that Pvt. Jones will be a tough job for somebody. And since you are convinced that I am the person to undertake it, [I'll] do everything I possibly can. I am most anxious to work with you to see he gets every opportunity, as long as he is not favored above the group."

It may seem ridiculously contradictory that Lowney wrote in the same sentence that Jones should "not [be] favored above the group" while at the same time she encouraged his swift release from the group. Yet, she knew what Captain Mailloux knew and a salient detail was added onto Jones's updated records: In the spring of 1944, the official certificates awarding Jones the Purple Heart and the Bronze Star had finally been presented. And his one thousand and six hundred and fifty-plus days in the Army were also a matter of fact. No one could argue that he had not been dutiful. Clearly much was being said, albeit behind closed doors.

Two weeks later, it was Lowney's turn to receive a new letter and it came from one of Captain Mailloux's fellow officers. She was stunned.

Lieutenant Fred P. De Palma wrote to inform "Mrs. Handy" that he had been "up to see Pvt. Jones at the Station Hospital yesterday."

And then he wrote: "I informed [Jones] that I was dismissing the Court Martial charges against him. This would enable the Medical Board of Officers to review his case and render decision. I think that the Board is meeting tonight. It's almost a certainty that Jones will be discharged. If that doesn't get him out of the service, then I'll try the proceeding which would discharge him as a Purple Heart man with physical disability; with wounds which render him physically unable to do the minimum requirements of work. But I'm not worrying too much about the alternative." The confidence percolating in Lieutenant De Palma's last line suggests that he, Captain Mailloux and others had concurred.

De Palma's letter to Lowney (dated June 21, 1944) then segued to an unconditional appreciation of Mailloux as a man. De Palma took

Lowney into his confidence just as she had taken Mailloux into hers:

"Capt Mailloux isn't back and won't be until the 27th of this month. He's been gone only six days and I miss the man. He's a powerhouse of energy and enthusiasm and a heaven of goodness and fairness. Don't think I've met any other Officer or man in the Army quite like him. He's probably exhausted every possibility in helping out Jones. So, whatever I'm doing is more or less of a spark given to me by the OLD MAN. I wrote to him last night and told him what the situation was. *It's just as he planned it* "[emphasis added].

Jones's extraordinary good fortune at this time (despite the war fully raging everywhere from the blood-soaked Pacific islands to the ghastly hedgerows just beyond the Normandy beaches) was akin to a cosmic benediction. He was granted the freedom to live and to be a writer.

Only five days later, in another letter sent by Lieutenant De Palma to Lowney, the rapid new lease on Jones's life was officially confirmed:

"It's happened," De Palma wrote to Lowney on June 26: "Jones is now Jimmie. We got his records completed here as soon as possible and transferred to the casual company that actually does the discharging. So, it'll be only a matter of a couple days before he'll be sporting his civvies. Hope that he meets nothing but the best. Captain Mailloux isn't back yet but I'm going to inform him about Jones's discharge in my next letter to him. No doubt he'll be happy to hear the news."

Ten days later, on July 6, 1944, James Jones was granted an Honorable Discharge due to a medical determination of "psychoneurosis" that he had not been afflicted with when he enlisted. His discharge specified that his "disability" emerged "in [the] line of duty and not due to his own misconduct." After fifty-five months in uniform, Jones was a civilian.

He was also a pilgrim of sorts. His first significant outing occurred even before he returned to Robinson, Illinois, where Lowney and Harry Handy had agreed to house him, feed him, and support his writer's quest. Jones set out first for Asheville, North Carolina, to pay a visit to novelist Thomas Wolfe's hometown and to see an array of sites and locales that Wolfe had immortalized in his novels and stories.

Jones's impassioned identification with Wolfe had been evoked yet again in his letter of explanation sent to brother Jeff back in early June of '44. Jones had shone a light on how his dogged efforts at writing a first novel, *They Shall Inherit the Laughter*, contributed to his third and final AWOL episode.

"You know about *They Shall Inherit*. For weeks I'd been trying to work on it after hours. All during the day, when I had to work at clerking [in the Orderly Room], ideas, sentences, whole paragraphs would pop into my head--& I wasn't able to write them down. At nite I'd sit for hours trying to write & I couldn't. The atmosphere in the army isn't conducive to writing ... I'd write page after page and tear it up and throw it away. So I went over the hill. It was a force completely beyond my control. I could no more help what I did than I could help urinating if my bladder was full. I <u>had</u> to get that stuff out of me."

That passage echoes Thomas Wolfe's ruminations in *The Story of a Novel*:

"I cannot really say the book was written. It was something that took hold of me and possessed me, and before I was done with it—that is, before I finally emerged with the first completed part—it seemed to me that it had done for me. It was exactly as if this great black storm cloud I have spoken of had opened up and, mid flashes of lightning, was pouring from its depth a torrential and ungovernable flood. Upon that flood everything was swept and borne along as by a great river. And I was borne along with it."

By late summer in 1944, Jones was writing furiously in Robinson.

*   *   *

At summer's end in 1944, when Jones concluded his pilgrimage to the birthplace of novelist Thomas Wolfe and then returned to the small town of his own birth in Robinson, Illinois, the aftermath of his quest to absorb the atmosphere of Wolfe's origins was illuminated by Lowney's passion for two newly published books: *The Portable Hemingway* was now available and with its Introduction and annotations by Malcolm Cowley, it was both a bestseller to the masses and to some extent a new guidebook beheld by Lowney; also in the fall of 1944 came the novel *The Razor's Edge*, which stunned author W. Somerset Maugham and his publisher (Doubleday) by rapidly becoming a sensation. *The Razor's Edge* sold hundreds of thousands of copies in hardcover and its storyline of World War I-era disillusion and spiritual yearning enthralled Lowney, who touted the book to Jones and others. The novel's front cover promised that it was "The Story of a Man Who Found a Faith."

That notion—that one's own personal quest to evolve was valid—loomed large.

The essential nature of the rapport between Jones and Lowney at this time was not merely the magnetic physical attraction that caused local tongues to wag. Whatever happened behind closed doors was always secondary to what happened in full view of others with whom Lowney and Jones visited, socialized, and sometimes debated. Lowney's sister-in-law Margaret Turner was once asked specifically: "How did she help him?" Her answer made clear that much more than sex was at issue.

"She talked to him a lot," Margaret explained. "She talked and talked and talked. They discussed books, they read [together]; she would go over the things he wrote. They had tremendous discussions. There was just talk all the time."

Above all else, Lowney brought to Jones's daily life in the early autumn of 1944 an overflow of attention, evinced by a spirited display of interested, authentic, personal and relentless support focused exclusively on their shared devotion to writing, reading, the life of the mind, and most of all the state of the soul. Lowney's diffuse reading patterns were not limited to fiction or history. She had shelves filled with books that decades later would seem right at home in the apartment of a Greenwich Village hippie rebel in 1968. Biographies of the Buddha and stories of mystical seekers in the Far East; chronicles of journeys throughout India and the Orient; books about everything from Yoga, meditation, and the life-transforming values of ascetic practices and a vegetarian diet—there was in the living room of the Handy home a library that invited and inspired a forum of ideas that transcended all the limits and boundaries of Jones's own upbringing. And yet, when exiting the Handy home to go buy a newspaper or to run errands, Jones was again smack dab in the milieu of his youth. Physically he was back in Robinson. But mentally, emotionally and psychologically he was not *of* Robinson.

"They studied a lot of different things," Margaret Turned also recalled. "History," she emphasized. Reading together was part of their passion, yet there was more. Lowney and Jones "always wanted [to look] for something new, write down everything, remember everything . . . keep a file on everything too after [they wrote] it down."

In Maugham's *Razor's Edge*, a traumatized veteran of the First World War (a young Chicagoan named Larry Darrell) refuses to stay on track after the war and become a stockbroker and marry. Maugham's protagonist rejects the plans and arrangements that were fully in place and after his expatriate years in Paris and elsewhere, the novel peaks with Darrell's extensive recollections of his spiritual transformations in the heart of India, where he spends significant time in an ashram.

Such a narrative seized Lowney's imagination and she, in turn, made sure that Jones studied the book. It was Maugham's most remarkable triumph to publish at the age of seventy a novel that recapitulated the Great War disenchantment of the so-called "Lost Generation" of the 1920s, and at the same time and in the same book to tap into the wartime mood of dislocation and uncertainty that made 1944 discomfiting for millions in America and untold millions elsewhere. *The Razor's Edge* also forecast the future preoccupations of the Beat Generation and the Counterculture of the Sixties in relation to Eastern ideas of spiritual growth and self-actualization.

To Margaret Turner, it was all in the air at the Handy home in Robinson. At 202 West Mulberry Street in Robinson, Illinois, when it came to Lowney and Jones, one thing was clear: "They always spoke of religion. She read books of mysticism and talked about reincarnation. There was an overall knowledge that she wanted and I think that's what she wanted for him too."

All the more reason that *The Razor's Edge* held such appeal. Its very title was chosen by Maugham in order to echo the novel's sole epigram: "*The sharp edge of a razor is difficult to pass over; thus the wise say the path to Salvation is hard.*" That quotation derives from one of the *Upanishads*. Toward the end of the novel there is a dialogue between the narrator (none other than "Mr. Maugham" himself) and Larry Darrell that rivals *My Dinner with Andre* in its wide-ranging rhetorical flights. In their colloquy, the *Upanishads* figure powerfully, as Larry Darrell recalls his years in India and finally his hiatus at an ashram. Maugham's presentation of such a lengthy, soul-centered, verbally expansive dialogue (it does not advance the plot or fulfill any other slick function, yet it commands the reader's attention for several chapters in a row) is capped by his own assessment of Larry's intensity: "I do not think I have ever found myself in a stranger situation than when I sat on the red-plush seats of that garish restaurant for hour after hour while Larry talked of God and eternity, of the Absolute and the weary wheel of endless becoming."

Such lofty topics were the coin of the realm for Lowney Handy, especially in the fall of 1944. Welcoming Jones back to Robinson and opening her home to him in every way marked for her the beginning of a quest that matched Jones's visionary sense of purpose. His vocation was indisputable. He would strive to become a great writer. However, his material well-being depended entirely on Lowney's willingness to back him to the hilt. And her commitment required Harry Handy's unconditional cooperation (financial and otherwise), which was forthcoming. So forthcoming, in fact, that before a small addition was built onto the house to provide Jones a private space in which to write, to read and to sleep in solitude, visitors noticed that Harry occupied a spare room downstairs; Jones was then sleeping upstairs with Lowney.

Lowney's sister-in-law Belva Turner once said: "Anything that Lowney wanted to do was all right with Harry."

In this boldly unorthodox milieu, Jones's growth was not just ensured; it was galvanized. Mentally, physically, spiritually, sexually, creatively, and nutritionally, the private life he now shared with Lowney Handy granted unto him a re-birth of sorts. "She was a good cook," Margaret Turner remembered: "She started from scratch. I can't remember her ever buying anything ready made [or] pre-cooked. She wanted to serve French onion soup and things that were more like a gourmet restaurant. And Jim was learning how to cook too and he appreciated good foods."

On the most basic level, Lowney made sure that Jones's propensity to drink himself into a stupor as often as possible was at least somewhat checked. "She was an exercise . . . freak," Margaret Turner recalled. "Firm believer in plenty of rest, plenty of water, early to rise, don't stay up all night. Lowney was not a drinker." On the other hand, Harry Handy was a serious drinker with whom Jones sometimes socialized, either in the privacy of the house or out in the wider world. The results were predictable. Despite all of Lowney's spiritual influence and mystical insights, when the booze flowed everything else was on pause. After a rowdy fracas at the Elks Lodge in Robinson, a formal memo was sent to Harry Handy from The House Committee at Robinson Lodge #1188. The memo read: "Dear Harry ~ Because of the disorderly conduct of your guests, Mssrs. John Metz and James Jones on Saturday night, October 7, 1944, we regret to inform you that the courtesy of their presence in our Elks Grille in the future must be denied." In other words, Jones was blacklisted from the Elks Lodge. And the names of The House Committee members who were blackballing him (and assuring Harry that "With all good wishes, we remain, Fraternally Yours") were listed as

"Duncan, Hewitt [and] Jones." It was, of course, Jones's estranged Uncle Charley Jones signing off.

Otherwise, by simply being in Lowney's company and in her home, Jones's wilder impulses were tamped down. And his lifelong yen for physical fitness was encouraged at every turn. Always adept at boxing, he now kept active by practicing at swimming at the local Y and working out with weights. Most of all, however, he yielded to a daily discipline that both he and Lowney would mandate for others in the future, when they co-founded a writers' colony that revolved around Lowney's protocols. As Margaret Turner saw it: "Early to bed and early to rise, nose in the typewriter all day, no distractions. We only went out there by invitation only, because we knew what the routine was."

Lowney's younger brother Earl took note of two ways in which Lowney was years ahead of her time as she cultivated her new life with Jones. "She would buy a new pair of blue jeans and she'd fade them. She'd put Clorox in and wash them. Had big white blotches all over them. She was doing that years before it was popular [in the 1960s and 1970s]." And then there was her passion for Yoga. "She practiced Yoga a lot." Surely there was no studio or any such space to practice outside of her home. But that suited Lowney just fine. As for how she learned what to practice and how to hone her skills, Earl mused that such esoteric knowledge and came to her "probably [from] those books that she was always [studying]. But she was a Yoga person. Believed in the hereafter . . . some people do."

And yet, lofty precepts aside, there were always her down-to-earth, offbeat ideas. Writer John Bowers was startled more than once in her milieu. "You should take an enema," he recalled Lowney saying, when anyone claimed to feel unwell. "I've seen it work wonders. Wonders! If you'd get all that shit out of your system, then maybe you could write a fucking novel" she insisted. Neither age nor the passage of time would ever cause Lowney to mellow, either. In the summer of 1953, when Norman Mailer visited Jones in downstate Illinois, he was transfixed by the force of Lowney's persona: "Lowney Handy burns—I kept thinking of fanatics like John Brown when I looked into her eyes," Mailer confided that summer, in a letter to William Styron.

Doubtless many other visitors ascertained what Mailer immediately noted: "Lowney Handy and Jones . . . both of them are such extraordinarily passionate people."

Lowney's personal library invited Jones to be exposed not just to ancient sacred writings like the Hindu *Upanishads* and the *Bhagadvad-Gita* and the tales of the Buddha's spiritual evolution, but also to the core writings of the 19th-century Theosophists and their kindred spirits Emerson, Thoreau, and Louisa May Alcott.

The New England Transcendentalists of the 1800s were intoxicated by the East. And in 1944, biographer and historian Van Wyck Brooks was on the cover of *TIME* Magazine. Brooks's Pulitzer Prize-winning history of Transcendentalism in America had sold well since its publication in 1936. Titled *The Flowering of New England*, it had earned Brooks the National Book Award. It was Ralph Waldo Emerson who ignited in Thoreau a fiery curiosity and a vast admiration for the sacred writings of the Hindus, in particular. "In the morning," Thoreau testified, "I bathe my intellect in the stupendous and cosmogonal philosophy of the *Bhagavad-Gita*, since whose composition years of the gods have elapsed, and in comparison with which our modern world and its literature seem puny and trivial . . . the pure Walden water is mingled with the sacred water of the Ganges." In the 1840s, Thoreau became enthralled with the subject of India and its ancient spiritual texts. Between 1849 and 1855, he regularly borrowed a wide variety of Indian scriptures from Harvard University's library. Now, one hundred years later in downstate Illinois, the sagging bookshelves of Lowney Handy benefited Jones. Her instinctual passion for Eastern spiritual precepts was validated by the vivid endorsements offered up a century earlier by the likes of Emerson and Thoreau.

Henry David Thoreau was also a devout believer in reincarnation. He once averred: "I lived in Judea eighteen hundred years ago, but I never knew there was such a one as Christ among my contemporaries." In almost any Western milieu (academic or otherwise), such a claim would induce scorn and derision. But to Lowney and Jones, steeped as they were in their fascination with Eastern notions of karma and reincarnation, Thoreau's statement seemed plausible and wise. It helps here to offer a summary of such elevated ideas, which the West has barely been able to assimilate, despite the wholehearted appreciation of certain American literary sages (Emerson, Whitman, and others) who have all been posthumously lionized.

In *The Seekers: The Story of Man's Continuing Quest to Understand His World*, scholar and former Librarian of Congress Daniel J. Boorstin summed up as follows:

" . . . two quite specific dogmas, shared by Hindus and Buddhists in various forms, diverted them from the problem of the origins of evil and the suffering of the innocent. First, most distinctive and ingenious—and convenient—was the idea of *karma* (from Sanskrit *karman*, 'deed,' fate, or work). This was a byproduct of belief in the transmigration and reincarnation of souls. Karma was a name for the force of all a person's acts—good or evil—in all past incarnations shaping his destiny in the next incarnation. So karma was an ingenious way of giving each person some responsibility for prosperity or suffering in the present life and, at the same time, of affirming a fatalism that left the person little power to change the fortunes of the present life. It was conceivable that a devout ascetic, renouncing all corrupting desires, might struggle free of his karmic debts."

In a letter written to a friend, Louisa May Alcott concluded: "I think immortality is the passing of the soul through many lives or experiences; and such as are truly lived, used, and learned, help on to the next, each growing richer, happier and higher, carrying with it only the real memories of what has gone before . . . I seem to remember former states and feel that in them I have learned some of the lessons."

Ralph Waldo Emerson was equally immersed in such exalted thoughts: "It is the secret of the world that all things subsist and do not die, but only retire a little from sight and afterwards return again" Emerson wrote in "Nominalist and Realist." And in his *Journals*, Emerson further mused: "Life itself is an interim and a transition; this . . . is my one and twenty thousandth form, and already I feel old Life sprouting underneath in the twenty thousand first, and I know well that he builds no new world but by tearing down the old materials."

Jones became especially fond of Emerson's essay "Compensation," and doubtless he and Lowney took note of the fact that in the essay "Immortality," Emerson quoted from the same *Katha-Upanishad* that had given Maugham's *Razor's Edge* its motif: "The soul is not born; it does not die; it was not produced from any one. Nor was any produced from it. Unborn, eternal, it is not slain, though the body is slain; subtler than what is subtle, greater than what is great . . . Thinking the soul as unbodily among bodies, firm among fleeting things, the wise man casts off all grief."

Such ideas would qualify as blasphemous to Jones's mother and her Christian Science cohort; and equally blasphemous to Lowney's fundamentalist Baptist mother. But as Lowney and Jones continued to read widely and eclectically, their studies confirmed that myriad great and divergent minds often concurred. They were neither faddists nor dilettantes. Jones and Lowney deeply pondered the ultimate issues of human life, and in their realm others invariably did so too. Three decades later, in 1975, when interviewed by Laura Adams, author Norman Mailer harked back to his 1953 visit to see Jones and Lowney. Asked about his newfound use of the words "karma" and "reincarnation" in varied writings, Mailer credited James Jones by saying: "He gave me [in 1953] the standard explanation, which is that we are not only reincarnated, but the way in which we are is the reflection, the judgment, the truth, of how we lived our previous life . . . Jones went on about it and I said, 'You *believe in that?*' Because I was an atheist and a socialist in those days. He said, 'Oh, sure. That's the only thing that makes sense. . . .' I thought about it over and over and in the last three or four years I began to think, 'Yes, that does make sense.' Jones was right."

Author George W. Russell (known as *AE*) had gone on the record, stating that "the *Bhagavad-Gita* and the *Upanishads* contain such Godlike fullness of wisdom on all things that I feel the authors must have looked with calm remembrance back through a thousand passionate lives full of feverish strife . . . [before] they could have written with such certainty of things which the soul feels to be sure."

One of the acolytes of H. P. Blavatsky's 19th-century Theosophical movement was Annie Besant, whose book *The Ancient Wisdom* shone a light on the very type of teacher-student rapport being cultivated in the Handy home: " . . . for here the powers of the most advanced souls find their exercise, so far as they can be expressed in the world of form. Here the kings of art and literature are found . . . students of the deeper knowledge, the eager, reverent pupils who sought the Teachers . . . who longed to find a Teacher."

Ever since his days at the University of Hawaii, Jones had longed for a guide. A mentor. An authority upon whom he could depend for sage advice about his writing. Fate precluded any English professor from assuming that role. But as the autumn of 1944 unfolded, Lowney Handy rose to the occasion. And with The Viking Press having recently published *The Portable Hemingway*, with its meticulously selected panorama of short stories, excerpts from novels and *The Sun Also Rises* in its entirety, a radical notion touted by Lowney would be adhered to by Jones.

Annie Besant's *The Ancient Wisdom* highlighted that "many a student on earth, all unknowing of these subtler workings, is preparing for himself a place . . . as he bends with a real devotion over the pages of some teacher or genius, over the teachings of some advanced soul. He is forming a link between himself and the teacher he loves and reverences."

By New Year's Day in 1945, a unique variation on that theme had become gospel to Lowney and Jones. While he continued working on his first novel, Jones was ordered by Lowney to begin the regimen that came to be known as "copying."

Believing that one could learn by osmosis the rhythms of dialogue, the flow of transitions, and the architectural intricacies of narrative structure by retyping not just passages and pages from a great writer's work, but entire stories and even full chapters of novels (if not the whole novel), Jones set to work copying *The Portable Hemingway*. Hours each morning were devoted to the task of retyping page by page, section by section, the array of classic Hemingway works that the expert editor Malcolm Cowley (who was also a poet, translator and critic) chose to anthologize. This protocol was later mandated for everyone Lowney mentored. To a hopeful student, Lowney once summarized: "THE WHOLE KEY TO SUCCESS IN THIS WRITING SYSTEM is ever the copying. Everything in life we do is copying—from the mannerisms we pick up to the way we learn to drive a car—eat our food—anything."

In his memoir *The Colony*, author John Bowers (who also published novels and works of military history) recapitulated Lowney's orders: "Copy Hemingway, *The Sun Also Rises*. It's got some of the best dialogue ever written. And copy midway in *Tender is the Night*. Boy, Fitzgerald got inside people, women, the way no other writer has. Leave [Thomas] Wolfe alone. Try some early Caldwell, and parts of *Light in August* by Faulkner. John Dos Passos is one of the greatest living writers we've got. Copy 'Art and Isadora' from *U.S.A.* He can write rings around Hemingway. But copy, copy, copy. Don't think while you do it. Let it seep into your brain, and it'll stay there."

Invariably, this dogged approach yielded rhetorical and narrative lessons that Jones absorbed as he mentally inhabited Hemingway's literary terrain with such devotion to detail.

Later in January of 1945, Jones would physically inhabit Hemingway's literary terrain when he calmly talked his way into the New York office of Maxwell Perkins, the most esteemed book editor in America. With the typescript of his first novel in hand, and knowing full well that Perkins had guided the careers of Thomas Wolfe, F. Scott Fitzgerald, and Hemingway, it fell to Jones to find a way to meet the elusive and famously private mentor. How Jones did so was impromptu, and yet mythical.

It ultimately determined his fate.

6
GOING TO MEET THE MAN ~
MAXWELL PERKINS

Writing ... can only be done by those who
have eyes and ears. ~ Max Perkins

For more than a quarter of a century, Maxwell Evarts Perkins affected the destiny of American authors in his role as editor, mentor, advisor, guide, ally and all-purpose advocate. In the winter of 1945, he was the top editor at one of the most distinguished publishing houses in New York. And yet, one of his colleagues, John Hall Wheelock, later recounted: "head editor" was "a title, however, which he, in his modest and unassuming way, never acknowledged."

By early 1945, Perkins (at age 60) was a celebrated figure in his own right, much to his chagrin. His new fame was due largely to a widely read two-part Profile about him that *The New Yorker* magazine published one year earlier, on April 1st and April 8th, in 1944. The author of that in-depth profile was Malcolm Cowley, the critic, poet, and translator whose career was enmeshed with the post-World War I writers of the Twenties: the so-called Lost Generation. Serious attention from Malcolm Cowley ensured vast publicity. And in a revelatory letter, Max Perkins expressed his personal reaction to such national exposure. He wrote:

"I can tell you that Profiles in *The New Yorker* are things to dread. I dreaded this one for a couple of years, and even consulted a lawyer as to what means might be taken to prevent its publication." And yet, in the same letter, the dry New England wit for which Max was also appreciated managed to emerge, as he concluded: "But when it did come out, I said

'I wouldn't mind being that fellow,' and secretly I thought he was a great sight better person than myself."

The ultimate hallmark of Perkins himself (aside from his impeccable manners and a stately sense of decorum: never would he think of appearing at the Scribner office in any attire other than a dark suit and a white shirt; his conservatively-patterned silk tie properly set with a Windsor knot; his suspenders in place) was self-effacement. He refused almost every invitation he received to speak or appear in public and be presented in some special light.

The notion of celebrity was alien to Max Perkins, and the degree to which Malcolm Cowley's two-part *New Yorker* profile increased the weekly avalanche of unsolicited manuscripts and query letters at Scribners overwhelmed his staff.

Cowley was a peer of the writers he assessed in his autobiographical coming-of-age chronicle *Exile's Return*. Like Hemingway, e. e. cummings, John Dos Passos, and others, Cowley volunteered as a college-aged youth with one of the ambulance organizations that recruited Americans to serve in the fields of wartime Europe during World War I. Also, like many other writers of the Twenties, there was in Cowley's heart a profound love for Paris as an American expatriate's utter paradise. Most of all, he deeply appreciated the authentic efforts made by a cadre of post-World War I authors to break new ground in poetry and prose fiction.

When *Exile's Return* first appeared at the nadir of the Great Depression in 1934, it did not receive the attention it deserved. More than a decade later, however, by the time that Malcolm Cowley accepted *The New Yorker's* assignment to write a lengthy prose portrait of Maxwell Perkins, the best work of the World War I's literary progeny was becoming more and more entrenched in the world of academe.

Thus the lore about all that Max Perkins had done to guide the careers of several iconic writers was at long last becoming as legendary as some of the novels that evoked, in retrospect, the essence of the 1920s.

Oftentimes dubbed the Roaring Twenties or the Jazz Age, the decade of the Twenties had been far more complicated and contradictory than such flippant references implied. But one indisputable fact was that some of the most durable novels to illuminate and illustrate the new directions being taken by American writers in the Twenties—*The Great Gatsby* by F. Scott Fitzgerald and Hemingway's *The Sun Also Rises* and Thomas Wolfe's *Look Homeward, Angel* to name a few—were shepherded by Maxwell E. Perkins.

After writing for *The New York Times* following his graduation from Harvard in 1907, Perkins spent several years in the advertising department at Scribners before he was promoted to his nascent editorial duties on the fifth floor of the stately old- world offices at 597 Fifth Avenue. By 1920, however, when Perkins' single-minded devotion to a twice-rewritten first novel by a then-unknown F. Scott Fitzgerald finally managed to get *This Side of Paradise* into print, more than Fitzgerald's vital and influential career in American literature was launched. The genteel, staid, Edwardian texture of the venerable House of Scribner was also transformed. As Cowley pointed out in his *New Yorker* profile, looking back a quarter century to 1919-1920: "In those days [*This Side of Paradise*] seemed to be the terrifying voice of a new age and it made some of the older employees of Scribners cringe."

Cowley described the office into which James Jones would walk in the middle of January 1945, where a feeling of time long past prevailed. Cowley reported:

"In 1920, the furniture looked—and some of it still does [in 1944]—as if it had been purchased from the estate of a very old country doctor. Most of the employees were even more elderly than their desks, and in publishing circles people said that nobody left Scribners until he was carried out. Scribners did not publish the realists who emerged during the so-called American Renaissance—Dreiser, Anderson, Sandburg, and so on. Instead, the firm took a sudden leap from the age of innocence into the middle of the lost generation.

"That leap was the result of suggestions made by Maxwell Evarts Perkins, then one of the younger editors, but he offered them so quietly that hardly anyone noticed what was happening until the revolution was under way."

In addition to the increased fame Perkins acquired through Cowley's *New Yorker* profile, he was also renowned for his long-term associations with Marjorie Rawlings (whose bestselling novel *The Yearling* remained a perennial favorite with the book-buying public), and poet Allen Tate.

Ultimately, though, in 1945, with Fitzgerald and Thomas Wolfe dead, Max Perkins was most famously allied with Ernest Hemingway, whose one-year wartime assignment as a correspondent with *Collier's Magazine* had recently ended and from whom a great new work about the Second World War was widely anticipated.

In league with Perkins and under the highly regarded rubric of the Scribner imprint, Hemingway had sustained a phenomenal career between 1925 and 1945, with his body of work consisting of a slew of titles that loomed large in the American imagination. All forty-nine of his short stories (most of which originally appeared in separate volumes with the lapidary titles *In Our Time, Men Without Women,* and *Winner Take Nothing*) were collected in one volume in 1938. And, unlike Fitzgerald and Faulkner, whose novels were mostly out of print in the 1940s, all four novels by Hemingway remained in print despite wartime paper rationing. They also sold perennially, thanks to the author's reputation being burnished by Hollywood productions (*For Whom the Bell Tolls* in 1943 and *To Have and Have Not* in 1945).

Ernest Hemingway's reputation was further enhanced by the degree to which contemporary critics, reviewers and professors ranked *A Farewell to Arms* and *The Sun Also Rises* as modern classics. It was no accident that The Viking Press made *The Portable Hemingway* one of the first in its "Portable" series in 1944. And it was no accident that Perkins had ascertained Hemingway's talent early on.

The pattern that had evolved with Perkins and Hemingway, F. Scott Fitzgerald, and Wolfe was a pattern Perkins repeated time after time in the Twenties, Thirties and Forties. Soon enough it would manifest in the extraordinary way that he would inspire and invest in Jones.

The key issue came down to one word: *talent.* Max had an uncanny ability to sense when someone's writing—however flawed—was rife with talent. When reflecting on the career of Perkins in a special introduction that was written in 1950 for a posthumously published collection of letters titled *Editor to Author,* another one of Scribners estimable staff members—poet John Hall Wheelock—had this to say:

"With this deep care for talent, there went, in Max's case, an instinctive perceptivity that was uncanny . . . he seldom failed in recognition of work of a high order: he knew it instantly when he came across it in the manuscripts of writers now famous, but at the time unknown or little known, who had through him their first publication. For Max, that was enough. The work might not be publishable, but there were glimmerings of talent. Into his already swollen briefcase it would go; a weekend was devoted to it, in the hope, not always unrewarded, that something could be salvaged."

John Hall Wheelock also wrote (apropos of Perkins): "Among an editor's various roles, one of the most important is that *of the listener*" [emphasis added].

And it was precisely in the role "of the listener" that Perkins first connected on a moment's notice with young James Jones. No appointment was scheduled. Jones had not made a preliminary phone call or even sent a standard query letter.

Usually, when unsolicited manuscripts were delivered to the office, they arrived over the transom from unknown writers whose enclosed letters were often barely disguised desperate pleas.

Not this time, however.

Instead, one day in the midst of January 1945, as the news of Hitler's collapsing Nazi Germany competed in the press and on the radio and through the newsreels with the up-to-the-minute accounts of President Roosevelt's fourth and final inauguration plans, a frustrated Jones (whose attendance at New York University on a Vocational Rehabilitation Award yielded good grades but little fulfillment) stood at the front desk on the fifth floor of the Scribner building in the heart of Midtown Manhattan. Making this type of "cold call" in person was not something Perkins' long-term secretary, Irma Wyckoff, considered appropriate.

Although they had worked in concert for decades, Perkins still called her "Miss Wyckoff." She, like her boss, had manners and protocols that harked to the past.

Yes, she understood that Jones wished to see Mr. Perkins. And yes, indeed, she did understand why the aspiring author wanted personally to greet the great editor and submit a manuscript on site. But, as Irma Wyckoff explained, that wasn't feasible. According to her, Mr. Perkins was out of the office. And that was that. She did vow to hand over to Mr. Perkins the typescript that Jones had stuffed inside a typewriter-paper box. She promised that Mr. Perkins would receive the manuscript forthwith.

But Jones refused to budge. He would not take her at her word. Perhaps that left Irma Wyckoff flummoxed. No matter what, he would not do as he was told and then courteously *exit*. James Jones kept standing there. Yet, he was not rude at all.

Suddenly, she excused herself and entered Perkins' small office. After a minute, Irma Wyckoff returned to her front desk and informed Jones that Mr. Perkins had returned to his office via the back entrance. Jones was invited to meet the editor.

In the near future, Jones would soon learn that no such back entrance existed.

In the meantime, at age twenty-three, the restless ex-GI from downstate Illinois (who was insecure about continuing his university studies at NYU) introduced himself to the man whose devoted mentoring of novelist Thomas Wolfe was a shimmering mythic tale.

Less than one hour earlier, Jones stood outside of the imposing, magisterial building that housed on six floors the array of operations for Charles Scribner & Sons. It's even likely that before he crossed the Rubicon and entered the building and rode the elevator to the fifth floor, he stood alone in broad daylight as the streets of New York in all of their glorious cacophony receded into the background, and perhaps pondered one of the chapters in Thomas Wolfe's last novel, *You Can't Go Home Again*. In chapter two, Wolfe's doppelganger (this time named George Webber) bucks himself up as he prepares to enter the fictional equivalent of Charles Scribner & Sons. In Wolfe's novel, it is James Rodney & Co., and the reader is told:

"If the traffic policeman on the corner noticed a strange young man in front of the office of James Rodney & Co. that morning, he would never have guessed at the core of firm resolution with which this young man had tried to steel himself for the interview that lay before him . . ."

Indeed, by this time Jones must have cultivated his own "core of firm resolution." His spring semester at New York University—which involved a full program of study with five courses, most of which met fours days per week—was starting and though he had appreciated his teachers and proved yet again that academic success could be his, if he so desired, Jones felt out of sorts and believed that he was too old to be just beginning a four-year bachelor's degree program. All that truly mattered was the novel he had been working on for more than a year. Nothing else.

Doubts persisted, though. Jones had yet to place one of his short stories with a magazine. He had no track record. The best he could say was that some of his professors had shone a light on him.

When Jones left Illinois for New York after NYU accepted him as a student enrolled with a Vocational Rehabilitation Award, he arrived in Manhattan with one contact to whom he was referred by Lowney: a literary agent named Max Aley, who along with his wife ran an established literary agency. Aley and his wife had seen most of the first novel that Jones now carried in his string-tied box. By this time, however, Jones was tiring of the repetitious disagreements he and Aley were having about the book. Both Max Aley and his wife did believe that *They Shall Inherit the Laughter* possessed merit. But neither thought it was ready for the marketplace.

About that Max Aley was absolute: "A final word on the book--get the neuroticism out of it," he told Jones. "The [new] piece in the *Saturday Review* indicates just how unwelcome neurotic soldier novels are going to be. Compassion and a deep sense of pity are one thing—neuroticism and self-pity are another. [There] is an editorial from the *Herald-Tribune* which shows how seriously the [new] article [in the *Saturday Review*] is being taken. There are some 'neurots' coming out of the army just as there is a certain proportion of them in life. But I'm happy to say that I [find] very few among . . . the boys I see getting back into civilian life," Aley wrote to Jones.

The arrogance in those lines (and between the lines) is mind-boggling. Aley, though, illuminated a mass-media phenomenon already underway. The linked communications conglomerates of newspapers and magazines, radio, and movies, and even a literary periodical like *The Saturday Review,* were devoted to the jaunty cultivation of G. I. Joe as an archetype of boundless optimism, upright ethics, and a thoroughly unrealistic capacity to endure war's horrors; and then readjust quite nicely after shedding one's uniform. "Neuroticism" would be anti-Americanism.

Compounding his negative assessment of Jones's protagonist as a boorish neurotic, Aley disliked the chapter where Cornelia Marion (a stand-in for Lowney Handy) proclaimed the need for artists to transform society. "This chapter is a crucial one for revision," Aley insisted. "You can literally see her mount to the pulpit—she delivers lectures. It won't do."

So, rather than do what was expected of novice writers and defer to the experienced judgment of his literary agent, Jones took the lead, concluding that the one authority whose verdict he would consider unimpeachable would come from Maxwell Evarts Perkins. In these lines from Thomas Wolfe's *You Can't Go Home Again,* which by now were surely burned into Jones's memory, the crossing of this threshold was spelled out in vivid words, offering a blueprint to Jones:

Finally, as he came abreast of the entrance . . . he quickened his stride and seized the door knob—but at once, as though it had given him an electric shock, he snatched his hand away and backed off, and stood on the curb and looked up at the house of James Rodney & Co. For several minutes more he stood there, shifting uneasily on his feet and watching all the upper windows as for a sign. Then, suddenly, his jaw muscles tightened, he stuck out his under lip in desperate resolve, and he bolted across the sidewalk, hurled himself against the door, and disappeared inside.

*   *   *

The deep-bowled ashtray on Perkins' desk likely put Jones at ease, because Max's own chain-smoking habit was a match for Jones's compulsive puffing. It's no stretch to imagine that a minute or two after shaking hands, both Perkins and Jones lit up and allowed the bonding that smokers have always instantly shared to establish for them an immediate rapport.

Even more likely is that the abundance of books and manuscripts piled higher and deeper throughout such close quarters created for Jones a sense of kinship with Max, which was then enhanced by Perkins' great gift for listening.

They conversed for more than one hour about Jones's wartime experiences. Perkins made no effort to hurry things along. There was in the personal behavior of Perkins a sense of deep appreciation for someone else's authentic need to communicate and if Max sensed that such a person was not in any way putting on airs, or merely hustling to "sell himself," then that person's reward was Perkins' full attention. After listening to Jones for the better part of an hour, Max agreed to have Jones's first novel evaluated and set the manuscript box to the side. They kept on talking as the afternoon waned. Jones did most of the speaking.

That was not a problem. It was part of the Perkins communication style to listen more than he spoke. What indicated his degree of interest or appreciation was not the percentage of words he uttered. Instead, it was the look in his eyes. A younger Scribners editor, Burroughs Mitchell, who would play a major role in Jones's career in the future, recalled the power of Max Perkins' active listening: "Max Perkins had the most remarkable eyes. There was nothing judgmental in their steady look; it was calm, receptive, and curiously warming. His eyes made all the more impression because of his silences. The silences of Max Perkins had become famous in the publishing world."

When all the other Scribners staff had left for the day, Jones and Perkins were still deep in conversation. Comparisons and contrasts were likely made with the works that now formed a canon of World War I literature. Jones had a detailed sense of what he thought was right and wrong with everything from *What Price Glory* (a play that for years was the most familiar dramatic work to evoke WW I themes) to the fiction of Hemingway, Erich Remarque, and John Dos Passos. The young man's profound appreciation for past writers made an indelible impression on Perkins.

And yet, Jones was not stuck in the past or interested in emulating others' forms. He had his own powerful sense of the need for new works to tell contemporary stories.

Already, the first important books by eyewitness participants in World War II had landed on the best-seller lists and even earned some critical approbation. It was not yet the spring of '45 and though the war against Hitler was winding down there was every expectation that the war against Japan would drag on into 1946.

Nonetheless, John Hersey's *A Bell for Adano* had been a major success in 1944, and as a first novel, a film, and then as a Broadway play, it continued to thrive. In 1945, Robert Lowry's novel *Casualty* was finished, and by 1946 there would be other debut novels (Alfred Hayes's *All Thy Conquests* and Gore Vidal's *Williwaw*) that quickly inaugurated new careers in letters.

But there was in Jones's vision something different. Eventually, as night fell, the aspiring young author and the editorial guru he sought most of all found another way to bond. By this time in his life, Max Perkins was drinking quite a bit more than ever before. Five Martinis a day were not unusual. He and Jones left the Scribner offices and made their way to the bar at the Ritz Hotel, conversing all the while.

* * *

In any part of the world, at any given time, two men who share a mutual love for tobacco and alcohol are likely to become fast friends. Or instant acquaintances.

In the case of Perkins and Jones, however, much more than chain-smoking and Martinis were in the mix. Aside from their ease with each other over drinks and cigarettes, the two of them had not just common interests—writers and books, in particular—but they shared an unlikely amount of past experiences and personality traits that made Perkins (who would turn 61 later that year) and Jones (whose 24th birthday would follow in the fall) naturally complement each other.

Superficially speaking, this was not obvious. Back at the office, no doubt, Irma Wyckoff—the stalwart "Miss Wyckoff" who had been Max's secretary for decades—would never have thought that the impromptu "cold call" made by Jones that day (with his manuscript stashed in a box tied with string and his pencil-line moustache, his twangy Midwestern accent, and a suit bought off the rack of a department store back in Robinson, Illinois) would lead to such instant rapport.

Each man was personally fascinated by the other. And both the older, respected, much-lauded prestigious editor and the aspiring, busted-down, striving ex-GI author had a gift not just for listening intently—but also for asking probing questions.

Perkins inquired about all sorts of Army-related issues. But he did not do this merely to humor Jones. As a Harvard student earlier in the century, Perkins had experienced a deep sense of being an "outsider," because he attended Harvard on very limited funds and never felt as though he belonged in any true sense amid all the Gold Coast young men whose family fortunes allowed them to breeze through life with their devil-may-care insouciance. Perkins apprehended during his years at Harvard that one's mind could be superior and one's grades superlative, but when membership in the right clubs was impossible or when the frayed cuffs on one's trousers and the shabbiness of one's few suits were seen, all judgment was negative.

Similarly, as Jones was all too willing to acknowledge, the Army itself was a caste system; a parallel universe within which everything from ethnic heritage to rank and ratings branded one as worthy or unworthy—just as the issues of money, property and family pedigree branded one in the Ivy League one way or the other.

In terms of family, a critical paternal element also united Perkins and Jones. Both of them had been exceedingly fond of their fathers; and both men lost their fathers at a young age. When Max Perkins was fourteen, his father died of pneumonia at the age of forty-four. As best as he could (immersed as he was in the New England Yankee values of stoic, upright, responsible behavior) Max tried his best to assume the role of head of the family. He tended with care to his widowed mother and his younger siblings. He never felt, however, that he was quite able to rise to the task at hand.

In Jones's case, now that his older brother had relocated from Ohio to Florida and with his younger sister, Mary Ann, at loose ends as she struggled to find her place in the world (Mary Ann would live periodically with brother Jeff; then take off and move everywhere from Florida to California; her life was a peripatetic scramble), there was no sense of a unified family. Jones yearned palpably for what was lost, but also knew that looking backward was fruitless and that he had to carve out a future.

Both men yearned a great deal for things that were either lost or had never been had at all. Perkins was the father of five daughters and his long marriage to his wife, Louise, was never shattered by adulteries or fiscal catastrophes. Yet, it was in many ways an unhappy marriage and the perennial, deeply confidential correspondence that Perkins sustained for many years with Elizabeth Lemmon would doubtless be categorized today as a prime example of emotional infidelity. But Jones would have been the last one to harshly judge such an extra-marital attachment. In his own life, Jones was more attached than ever to Lowney Handy; and both Lowney and Jones were dependent as always on the financial support of Lowney's executive husband, Harry. Shortly after Jones began his spring semester at NYU, Lowney had visited New York and the two of them stayed together in the small apartment that Jones had secured near Central Park West.

They continued to cultivate their love and passion, while at the same time renewing their commitment to the notion that Jones could be, should be, and would be the heir to Wolfe and Hemingway. Lowney Handy's praise for Jones's first novel was almost unconditional, and thus the tough-minded critique given to the book by agent Max Aley had stung Jones. It was that criticism that impelled Jones to unilaterally seek out Perkins and ask him for an ultimate verdict.

And by this time, Perkins had spent more than a few months corresponding at great length with hopeful, ambitious, aspiring writers who were stationed all over the world and forever wondering if they'd survive the war and then find the time to write the books that were detonating in their imaginations. These younger men, all of whom knew about Max's track record with iconic authors, inquired about topics ranging from the value of university classes to the worthiness of repeated revisions.

With gracious patience and his innate commitment to excellence always uppermost in mind, Perkins had dictated replies to unknown, forward-looking writers that in every way equaled Rilke's instructive, unselfish, artful *Letters to a Young Poet*.

Most of all, throughout his adult life Perkins had yearned for a son. Although he was an attentive and loyal father to his five daughters, there was little doubt that Max's monumental sense of concern and his downright devotion to his most successful younger male authors (at varied times it was either Fitzgerald, Hemingway or Wolfe) served as a substitute for the son (or sons) he was never fated to raise.

Now he sat at the bar at the Ritz with a young man who in so many ways needed a father figure as much as Max needed a surrogate son. The two of them were a perfect match. And by the time drinks were reordered, some of their mutually rough edges were probably being smoothed out. Booze is always a lubricant.

If Perkins was relentlessly intrigued by Jones's wide-ranging array of Army stories, there's no reason to doubt that Jones was equally intrigued by Max's anecdotes about once having been a police reporter for *The New York Times*. That phase of Perkins's career was rarely written up, but before he made the House of Scribner the centerpiece of his life, Perkins had known plenty of shady, rough, grim episodes.

In 1916, Max's Army service was on the Mexican border with the United States Cavalry. And once when he was still on staff at *The New York Times* and dashing off copy as a police reporter, Max volunteered to be strapped into an electric chair at Sing Sing, in order to report with visceral accuracy what a convict with a death sentence faced at his end. There was more than a Harvard degree on his resumé.

*   *   *

As an undergraduate at Harvard (Class of 1907), it had been Perkins' good fortune to be able to land a spot in the freshman composition class of a maverick Instructor named Charles Townsend Copeland. At that time, before having a terminal degree was the *sine qua non* of academe, a man like Copeland (lacking a Ph. D.) was still able to make a career of teaching at the highest echelon of education in America.

Perkins never forgot what made Charles Townsend Copeland unique: *passion*. Pure and simple. Copeland had a tangible, omnipresent, overflowing devotion to words and the authors who wrote them. His classes were never lectures in the dry and dusty sense. He was not dependent upon stale notes, textbook summaries, workbook exercises or any other dread mode of rote learning. Instead, his fiery and impassioned love of language, ideas, narrative, form and most of all the power of a well-told story (or a well-crafted poem or a well-structured play) was contagious.

And though Max graduated from Harvard with a degree in Economics (a subject about which Perkins used to wryly observe that no serious person ever called him "a businessman"), it was as a writer that he first saw himself somehow making his way in the world. Yet, after a few years of police reporting and its irregular hours, plus the low pay and most of all the harried, manic, relentless deadlines that Perkins knew were deleterious to any effort at serious writing that would somehow last, the segue to Scribners ensured normal hours, a salary, and, at last being in the milieu of literary writers who did not have their writing shredded by editors' rewrites.

On this issue, too, Jones and Perkins were in tandem. Aside from being homesick, feeling too old to be at the start of an undergraduate program and always short of money, the biggest frustration for Jones at NYU was the mandate of the Vocational Rehabilitation Awards. The operative term was "vocational," and when Jones told an academic advisor that he wished to take an array of creative writing courses, he was advised that such studies were not considered practical; he had to sign up for journalism classes and other liberal arts requirements instead. Thus he ended up with a five-course program of study consisting of a journalism class taught within the English department; Math and French; plus a philosophy class and one elective.

The fact that Jones had completed his first novel entirely on his own and at such a young age no doubt impressed Perkins.

Just hearing Jones speak, at ease, about the scope and the intention of his completed first novel (without yet reading it, he ascertained that Jones's furious discontents with America's booming, cynical, wartime surfeit offered the possibility of a new voice in literature) was enough to convince Max Perkins that classroom protocols wouldn't meet Jones's needs. In the spring of 1945, Perkins offered sage advice to another military veteran whose desire to write was colliding with his confusion about the value of college:

"As to perhaps a couple of years in college, I should think that that might be of great advantage, in a general sense, but don't try to learn about writing there. Learn something else. Learn about writing from reading. That is the right way to do it. But then it can only be done by those who have eyes and ears, by seeing and listening. Very few of the great writers had that formal education, and many of them never mastered spelling or grammar. They got their vocabulary by reading and hearing. But the way they teach literature and writing in college is harmful."

While Perkins never forgot the spellbinding classes of Charles Townsend Copeland, he also never failed to recall that Copeland had been not just a maverick, but truly the odd man out; an exceptional teacher who was also the exception to all the rules.

Jones was no less a maverick and for that reason he was also not suited to the notion of being pigeonholed with a major in journalism, on the assumption that newspaper writing was his métier. Nothing could have been further from the truth.

By definition, "métier" is understood to be "a field of work or other activity in which one has special ability or training." This was the issue vexing Jones the most.

The process of completing *They Shall Inherit the Laughter* had convinced him that he was a novelist. Not a journalist. Not a short-story writer. Certainly not a poet in any traditional sense. And yet, this conclusion set the bar so high it was dizzying.

And practical matters were as challenging as the mysteries involved in developing oneself as a novelist, which in itself called for a long-range vision and a discipline that simply had to be an organic part of the writer's personal nature; it could not be taught or induced through classroom calisthenics. Far less mysterious, though, were all the workaday issues of life; money being the primary problem.

There existed in the history of American letters a pattern of evolution connecting the legacies of late 19th-century authors as divergent as Ida B. Wells and Mark Twain to early 20th-century writers as innovative and idiosyncratic as Dorothy Day, Theodore Dreiser, Sherwood Anderson, W. E. B. Du Bois, and Ernest Hemingway. One word summed up that pattern: Journalism. It had been the gateway—in a variety of forms— for all those writers (and many others). Writing for pay and supporting oneself as a journalist who quickly wrote articles on any number of subjects (politics, war, sports, travel, adventure in all its forms, and social crises ranging from prostitution to lynching) was one of the few ways that an aspiring author could make a living while practicing one's trade and hoping that eventually a career as a book author would develop.

If one did not produce a novel or a book-length work of nonfiction early on, there was the possibility that a collection of one's articles might catch on with a publisher who would take a chance on such a medley of pieces. But this pattern was not in the cards for Jones.

Nor was it a pattern designed to fit Joseph "*Catch-22*" Heller, his peer and future colleague in America's fraternity of postwar white male novelists. Jones and Heller attended NYU at the same time, yet never met while there. They also shared a brush with the school of thought mandating that anyone with a knack for writing should be a journalist. In Heller's case, his detour was swift: "I had applied . . . with a major in journalism, thinking, without thinking clearly, that there'd be a lot of reading and writing involved and that newspaper work," Heller mused, "by its very nature would be invariably arresting, if not always electrifying," he wrote in his autobiography.

Fortunately for Heller, he "noted the required courses, such as copy editing, rewriting, proofreading, and layout." That's when Heller did an about face: "I switched like a fugitive to a major in English and with a deep breath relaxed and blessed my luck. I had a deep feeling of relief that I'd escaped, by the skin of my teeth, an irreparable and very great disaster."

The fundamental necessity for journalism is speed. The ability to write quickly, briefly, clearly. The capacity to see, and to report right away. But Jones was not wired for this in any way, shape or form. Max Perkins had discovered, toward the end of his own journey with *The New York Times* decades earlier, that such speed was alien to his own sense of quality writing. "I do think," Perkins said, "writing for a paper, when you must produce, say, half a column in half an hour, with a copy-boy standing by to tear the half sheets out of your machine, does tend to sloppy writing."

When Perkins decided to leave journalism and enter the advertising department at Scribners, he had a Harvard degree and a personality suited for office hours; he yearned for the regular structure of a low-key office milieu. Calm. Diligent.

Contrarily, Jones knew in his bones that he was a fish out of water in any nine-to-five office realm and a college degree was not in the offing and nothing was going to alter the fact that when he wrote, it all came with difficulty. Explaining once to a trusted ally just how unpredictable his output was, Jones admitted: "I work very slowly, and painfully. Now and then I'll write like mad for a week or two and knock myself out and then it's a page or two a day until another spasm seizes me. In the overall, it's very very very slow going."

None of this was the result of laziness or sloth on Jones's part. Quite the other way. He was, to a certain degree, hamstrung by the largeness of his ambitious visions. In a reflective mood as he one day wrote about his stalled efforts, Jones concluded: "I guess my greatest struggle is the struggle to achieve form. And it struck me that [Thomas] Wolfe did somewhat the same thing with his novels. He *created* form, of his own, and withdrew to live in it. I ache to do something like that; I ache to discover an un-severed thread that will run continuously through everything I write."

But even ruminations as seemingly relaxed as that one were, in truth, anxious thoughts expressed with the silent awareness that Jones harbored about the degree to which he was dependent on Lowney Handy; and by extension dependent wholly on the financial support of her husband Harry. Without them, he had nothing but his ambition, discipline, talent, and vision. None of which could buy his food. Or pay his rent. Or allow him to write full-time and cultivate a great work. Not just yet.

When they parted company after sharing their drinks at the celebrated bar of the Ritz Hotel (the symbolism was surely not lost on Jones, who had probably thrice-read F. Scott Fitzgerald's famous story "A Diamond as Big as the Ritz"), it was with the understanding that Jones's first novel would be scrutinized with an eye toward publication. Jones had spoken enough for Perkins to know that *They Shall Inherit the Laughter* was a contemporary narrative that took a sledgehammer to society.

There was also no doubt that it was a thinly disguised autobiographical novel.

Perkins may have also fully understood that he was so taken with the power of Jones's personality that an objective, cold-eyed reading was not possible. Contrary to what the young author expected (and fortunately, for the sake of his nerves, Jones was not informed until later about this), Perkins decided not to be the first to have a look at *They Shall Inherit the Laughter*.

Instead, he handed it over to two of his trusted colleagues. Neither of them had a wholly positive reaction. Talent was present; there was no doubt about that. The force of Jones's storytelling power was palpable. They agreed on that. But all things considered, it was their consensus that *They Shall Inherit the Laughter* was not a novel ready for publication. It lacked a streamlined narrative form. Its characters, major and minor, were too often found making speeches about society's failings or other lofty pontifications. Most of all, it was without any firm resolution.

Matters may have ended there if not for that long late-afternoon and early-evening dialogue and Jones and Perkins shared at the Scribners office and then at the Ritz. There was something about James Jones that Max was not able to forget. Although his two colleagues offered reader-reports that were lukewarm, Perkins set aside his mountainous pile of other manuscripts and took a close look at the typed draft of *They Shall Inherit the Laughter.*

"We do not feel," Perkins reported, "that 'They Shall Inherit the Laughter' quite comes off as a novel, nor does it turn out to be anything for which we could make an offer." In that regard, Perkins' reaction was what Jones's agent, Max Aley, feared all along. All the more reason that Aley was suggesting an overhaul of the whole book.

On the other hand, Max Perkins saw something beyond this first book-length typescript; something more than what was on the page or even between the lines.

"It is," Perkins announced with conviction, "a serious attempt to do a big piece of work." Anyone with eyes to see might have said that in response to the 700-plus pages of typescript. But there was something else: "And the author has the temperament and the emotional projection of a writer," Perkins insisted.

Those qualities wouldn't have been ascertained without meeting Jones in person.

While declining to work on the novel in its current form, Perkins did not dismiss Jones outright. The novel had been treated with tremendous respect and sincere courtesies by all. But would Max read a revised version of the novel in the future?

What mattered now was that Jones had to make decisions about whether or not to continue at New York University; whether or not to retain Max Aley as his agent; and whether or not to return to Robinson in the future. He was at a crossroads.

To retain his monthly disability pension (and Jones needed every dollar, because his stipend paid fewer than fifty dollars per month), he had to submit on a regular basis to evaluations at the Veterans Administration Hospital. At summer's end in 1945, Jones's record was updated as follows: "The patient dislikes society, he has always been a nervous high strung individual who has no interest in anything other than being a writer, is resentful of regimentation, loses his temper, and as he says, if he has a plan in mind he will carry it out regardless of consequences involved."

Meantime, the United States and the world at large reached a tipping point unlike any other in history. Between May of 1945 (when Nazi Germany's unconditional surrender led to Victory in Europe Day) and August 1945, when America dropped atomic bombs (first on Hiroshima and then Nagasaki), the Second World War ended.

As tens of millions of Americans joined with hundreds of millions of others throughout the world and danced in the streets, Jones isolated himself and wrote.

By Thanksgiving week in 1945, having vowed to rework his novel from start to finish, having exited New York University with superb grades but no plan to go back, and after staying everywhere from a cabin in the Smokey Mountains (where Jones heard locals talking about something "atomic" ending the war with Japan) to Florida and then back to Lowney's house in Robinson, Illinois, he was ready to reach out again.

On November 20, 1945, while working part-time on a fishing boat off Marathon, Florida, a letter from Jones was sent to Perkins. The editor was approached anew:

"I am writing to you in reference to *They Shall Inherit the Laughter.* I have just completed a new, finished draft of the book, which has entailed my rewriting most individual chapters at least several times and occasionally more often than that. I am now preparing to go over it again, copying it up in [manuscript] form and making what smoothing and finishing changes I will find necessary. I expect to have the completed [manuscript] done within a month or five weeks from [now].

"I am writing you first to see if your firm would like to see it before I attempt to contact anyone else. I am no longer with Mr. Aley . . . by a mutual agreement we have dropped the association, and I am now handling the thing entirely by myself."

Earlier that year, after *They Shall Inherit the Laughter* made the rounds at Scribners, it was agent Max Aley to whom correspondence was directed. Thus it was possible for Jones to evaluate differing reactions to his original typescript, and to note that one of Maxwell Perkins' principal colleagues who read the book was the distinguished poet-editor John Hall Wheelock. Jones put his cards on the table:

"Mr. Aley was kind enough to give me the letters of both yourself and Mr. Wheelock and to report some of your comments to me verbally. One of the chief complaints with the [manuscript] you saw was that it 'lacked resolution' . . . While I did not understand that criticism at the time, I think I do now, and I am grateful the book was not published as it was. I am offering it to you now first, partially because I still have a soft spot for the character [Thomas] Wolfe drew from you, but mainly because I feel I owe you a debt of gratitude for not publishing the book as it was when I submitted it. I will wait to hear from you before I start trying [to] contact anyone else."

One week later, Jones received a letter from Perkins. Yes, Perkins averred. It'd be fine to resubmit *They Shall Inherit the Laughter* to Scribners. Best of all was this reply ended on a personal note: "I have often wondered how things are going with you." And then Perkins widened the circle by his use of the plural: "We've been wondering what happened to you."

What happened to Jones in the next three months determined, in many ways, the trajectory of his life.

7
FAITH LIKE MUSTARD SEEDS

Sisyphus (in Greek Mythology) the son . . . condemned to the eternal task of rolling a large stone to the top of a hill, from which it always rolled down again. ~ Webster's

That letter from Maxwell Perkins (regarding *They Shall Inherit the Laughter*) was dated November 27, 1945. It galvanized Jones. Now his self-imposed deadline was January 1st, 1946. He and Lowney stayed in Florida, avoiding the winter miseries in Illinois. Lowney believed in the value of solitude, and sometimes she retreated on her own to a small cheap hotel or a cottage for rent.

To his dismay, Jones could not complete the rewriting, revising, and the retyping of his book by New Year's Day. Crestfallen, he wrote again to Perkins, early in January, vowing to do his best to speed things along.

Writing back with calm and paternal assurances, Perkins reminded Jones that writing was not an exact science; nothing could be calibrated, calculated or strictly timed as though it were a formula. Concluded Perkins: Send the fully revised draft, when the book was completely retyped. Jones dug in his heels and finished the task.

On January 17, 1946, he mailed his thoroughly revamped version of *They Shall Inherit the Laughter* via U. S. Parcel Post. A confirmation receipt was sent to Jones when it was delivered.

The whole effort took a heavy emotional and psychological toll on him. The omnipresent autobiographical content structuring *They Shall Inherit the Laughter* ensured that as he reworked the material and analyzed episodes, dialogue, plot points, character issues, and conflicts, Jones was impelled to think again, to see anew, to feel once more and to shine a light for the umpteenth time on personal experiences that had scarred him deeply in recent years.

After the retyped new draft of *They Shall Inherit the Laughter* (more than 700 typed pages) was sent to New York, the waiting and the wondering soon agitated Jones. He tried other endeavors. He wrote varied pieces of short fiction. Although he never saw himself as a short-story writer in general, Jones often had stories in mind that he devoted himself to when not consumed by work on a novel. He also drafted notes on ideas and incidents he thought might be useful for future books.

In a spontaneous burst of hopefulness, he began outlining a second novel. Weeks passed. Finally, on February 10, 1946, Jones wrote these words to Maxwell Perkins:

"Since the notification of the receipt of my [manuscript], dated Jan. 22, I've had no other word from you. I realize the time necessary to study a [manuscript], etc.; a number of people have to read it, then discuss it, then make suggested changes or perhaps a heightening of a certain scene. All that takes time and a lot of it . . . But I guess that besides being a moralist by nature, I am also naturally impatient.

"But I have a number of plans I'm champing to get into action, and all of them hinge on this book: whether it is accepted or rejected, whether you will consider that it needs more work (personally, I'm sure it doesn't, but it's just possible my judgment may be biased), and of course the money angle, how large an advance and how soon. I'm stony broke right now."

He was not exaggerating. Jones's $46 monthly Army pension translated to a budget of a little over $1.50 per day. Which meant Jones had pocket money for cigarettes, Beef Jerky, and cheap beer. He also had a pittance of a dividend from the remnants of his family's once-robust stock in oil, but that paid only a few dollars per month. Limited help from Harry Handy financed their food and gas; and so, Jones and Lowney pinched every penny. He further explained to Max Perkins:

"I suppose you're used to being drafted as a father confessor. I have been making unintelligible notes on more than one future novel. I'm all ready to start in on one now, but . . . I can't reasonably free my mind to concentrate it on this new idea when the possibility exists that I may have to do more work on this one."

After typing out a long paragraph to Perkins highlighting what Jones foresaw as "a pure combat novel," he turned on a dime and shared his most life-transforming, perceptive idea: "In addition, *I have always wanted to do a novel on the peacetime army, something I don't remember having seen* [emphasis added]. Do you think such a novel . . . would be badly received now? I'm quite capable of writing it now, but it may be that the reading public is getting fed up with army and war . . . I wanted to ask your advice on that point." Jones explained how a soldier named Stewart, whom he'd observed at Schofield Barracks, suggested an archetypal protagonist.

Perkins offered more than "advice on that point." Jones had outlined his travel plans, so Max knew he planned to "go to an address in Illinois . . . I'll send you that address where I can be reached."

When Jones returned to Robinson, Illinois, later in February, a telegram from Maxwell Perkins, dated February 15, 1946, stunned him:

WOULD YOU CONSIDER PAYMENT FIVE HUNDRED DOLLARS NOW FOR OPTION ON STEWART NOVEL AND SETTING ASIDE "INHERIT LAUGHTER" FOR REASONS I'LL WRITE? SOME FURTHER PAYMENT TO BE MADE AFTER WE READ SAY FIRST FIFTY THOUSAND WORDS. WISH TO COOPERATE BUT HAVE MORE FAITH IN SECOND NOVEL AND HAVE FURTHER REVISIONS TO PROPOSE FOR "LAUGHTER."

Unexpected. Unusual in the extreme. Perhaps unprecedented. An unknown writer with no track record in journalism and without any stories in print amid the many popular magazines of the day (Jones's only publication had been a short story in the undergraduate literary periodical at New York University in May 1945) was hereby offered five hundred dollars . . . *not* for the manuscript he had submitted, but for an unwritten work that he'd barely outlined. And the offer came from the top editor at Scribners. A publishing legend. Only one answer was possible.

On February 17, 1946, James Jones sent a telegram to Maxwell Perkins:

PROPOSITION ACCEPTED. PLACING MYSELF IN YOUR HANDS AND AWAITING LETTER HERE. WIRE FIVE HUNDRED DOLLARS ANYTIME TO 202 WEST MULBERRY ROBINSON ILLINOIS.

Jones and Lowney were back at the Handy house in Robinson. In the next few days, while waiting for the five-hundred dollar advance to be wired, this act of faith on the part of Perkins was discussed by them as the ultimate validation of Jones's talent; and also the ultimate vindication of Lowney's instincts.

For more than two years now, Lowney had been insisting with her dogmatic, single-minded intensity that Jones was another Jack London. The next Thomas Wolfe. A new John Dos Passos. Against all odds, and with the effrontery to dismiss outright the thoughtful input of an established agent like Max Aley or anyone else she perceived as an obstacle, the unwavering faith that Lowney placed in Jones was unconditionally offered up. She often said to anyone who would listen that an artist had to have, no matter what, the innate "faith of a mustard seed," and like a mustard seed grow and evolve and develop.

The Biblical allusion to "the faith of a mustard seed" was usually amplified by her relentless references to the mythic tale of the Phoenix. Rising from one's ashes, time after time, overcoming the dead past with spiritual renewal in Time Present, was all that mattered. In Lowney's view, Jones was now manifesting the flight of a Phoenix.

When Jones collected his thoughts, he communicated his loyalty and his faith to Perkins directly: "I trust your judgment from past knowledge of your work and your tremendous experience with such things that I don't have. And I'm willing to ride along. As I said, I'm putting myself in your hands, not Scribners exactly, but you personally, because I have more faith in your ability to see further and clearer than anybody I've met or heard of in the writing game."

To Jones, this turning point was surreal. He knew all too well that in *You Can't Go Home Again*, Thomas Wolfe had ended an early chapter of that novel by summing up his protagonist George Webber's first meeting with book editor "Foxhall Edwards," who was of course Maxwell Perkins (as transformed by Wolfe's robust imagination): "It was a check for five hundred dollars. His book had been accepted, and this was an advance against his royalties."

* * *

The key difference in Wolfe's fictional account of his own experience with Perkins and the *acceptance* of *Look Homeward, Angel* was just that: Thomas Wolfe's five-hundred dollar payment was received in 1929 because his first novel had been "accepted" for publication. Contrarily, in Jones's case—making the payment of five hundred dollars even more unexpected, if not downright astounding—the offer on the table was for an "option": the money wired to Jones gave Scribners exclusive rights to the work-in-progress, with the option of continuing or discontinuing their commitment to the developing book at intervals of their own discretion.

Now more than ever, the forum of ideas touted by Lowney Handy on any given day became the bulwark supporting Jones psychologically and spiritually. He knew that without the material support of Harry and Lowney Handy, he would be an ex-GI with no parents, no home to go to, almost no money, and limited scant prospects. But even with the infrastructure provided by Harry Handy (mostly to appease Lowney and to support her own quest to make her mark by lifting up others), there was the matter of Jones's need to start all over again. The blank page loomed.

If a blank screen is a writer's nightmare in the 21st-century, then blank pages were in Jones's era the leading cause of anxiety. He had his pages of notes, however, and along with the Lowney-inspired regimen of copying vast portions of published works by approved writers like John Steinbeck, Hemingway, John Dos Passos, and others, the processing of ideas and the constant recycling of images, notions, themes and variations that one could produce in notes were a valuable inventory to possess.

Above all else, though, was the need to possess faith. Not wavering faith. Not the kind of periodic faith that ebbs and flows in relation to one's good luck or fortune. Instead, as the need to begin an entirely new narrative commenced, Jones looked deeper into the wisdom of the words that Lowney most often repeated. Although she was very well read in the sacred literature of the Far East, it was the constant repetition of a Biblical phrase about possessing "the faith of a mustard seed" that Lowney favored. She was an ardent admirer of the words attributed to Jesus in the New Testament of the Holy Bible, and she swore by Chapter 17, Verse 20 of the Gospel according to Matthew: *"And Jesus said unto them, Because of your unbelief: for verily I say unto you, If ye have faith as a grain of mustard seed, ye shall say unto this mountain, Remove hence to yonder place; and nothing shall be impossible unto you."*

And there were other such allusions. In Chapter 13, Verse 31 of Matthew, there is this quotation attributed to Jesus of Nazareth: *"He told them another parable: 'The kingdom of heaven is like a mustard seed, which a man took and planted in his field'."*

This was a heady time for Jones. His situation was peculiar. Everything depended not on the revising of work already accomplished, but instead on what might soon be achieved if only her were able to get beyond outlines and notes and into fresh new writing itself. Meantime, he shared a surprising development in this new season of possibility with a West Coast long-distance relative.

Jones had recently written to his Aunt Molly Haish (his mother's sister), who lived out in California. He had visited her before shipping out to Hawaii, shortly after his Army enlistment. Now he wrote warmly to her of his boyhood memories of "the little gadgets" and "the Xmas presents you used to send to us kids in Robinson."

Memories aside, he told her: "I've also been doing a lot of looking into religion. Bought myself a grand $14 Bible which has everything including even a history of the books of the Bible and how and by whom they were written. As you probably remember from my old letters, I was pretty fanatically anti-religious. It took me a long tome to overcome the antipathy to religion that the churches of Robinson, Ill., had instilled in me. But now I've learned that if a man can disregard and forget the churches, that there's a tremendous amount of knowledge in the Bible."

That passage highlights one way in which Jones expanded his mind. Like many who lived before him, and many who have lived since, he was never capable of being aligned with doctrinaire, dogmatic, institutional religious protocols. Yet, he was a spiritual seeker. Being spiritual was not synonymous with institutional traditions.

In that same letter to Aunt Molly, there was another reminder of the yearning nature of Jones's mind and soul, as he elaborated on his newfound readings:

"I've also been reading a man named Paul Brunton, who spent a great many years in India, studying their religion. He's studied the ancient Egyptian and Greek 'Initiate' religions. He's written a number of fine books on religion, and its good points of truth."

Lowney's influence was in the air. Her library was at Jones's disposal and it was back at 202 West Mulberry Street in Robinson, Illinois (the epitome of a church-centered small American town with its population of approximately six thousand) that he found himself not just studying the Bible as literature, as history and also as a source of wisdom, but it's where he also had access to Paul Brunton's *A Search in Secret India* and *A Hermit in the Himalayas*, along with other works by kindred spirits such as Annie Besant, who was a devotee of Theosophist Madame Blavatsky.

Jones was a chain-smoking, two-fisted former soldier who was prone to fits of anger and drunken outbursts, but he also immersed himself in sacred texts. He personified the pairs of opposites that symbolized the

Yin and Yang of the Tao of Life: light and dark, passive and aggressive, optimistic and pessimistic, and so on.

He shared his fears, insecurities and contradictory inner world not just with Lowney Handy, but also with Maxwell Perkins.

On March 27, 1946, just a little more than a month after Jones accepted Scribners's offer of a five-hundred dollar option on his untitled, unwritten, "peacetime army" novel, a letter was sent from Max Perkins to Jones. It's a letter that overflows with patient tutorial advice, deep understanding, and fatherly kindness.

"I was greatly pleased by the last sentence in your letter," Perkins assured Jones, "telling of how 'a host of hazy memories come back clear and sharp' from looking at your manuscripts."

Jones had been compulsively studying his notes and outlines, as he ramped up to write chapter one of his new novel. And his primary discovery was that all his large themes, all the abstract narrative motifs and all his burning visionary zeal congealed not around a plot twist, but instead around one character: "Prewitt." Concluded Jones: "Prewitt is the real protagonist of the book. It is with him that the main theme and main stream of action deals."

Always noted for his ability to ask direct questions and probe ideas with vigor, Jones now focused upon the sole ultimate question: "What do I want to say in this novel?" he asked in his notes. He answered himself:

"The first thing, *the main thing*, is I want to tell the story of the guys in the peacetime army. They are sons of bitches, but the fault is not theirs. The fault belongs to the society, the system under which they live—not only the economic system, but the moral system of righteousness.

"This creates a natural problem: how to show them as the sons of bitches they are, and at the same time create sympathy for them with the reader.

"To do this I have chosen the story of Prewitt. His story must be a tragedy, as the army is a tragedy."

The themes that Jones listed as paramount in his summation of the peacetime army, pre-Pearl Harbor, were: "Caste, Privilege, Favoritism, Politics, Arbitrary Authority."

On top of which Jones added: "the political corruption, rank favoritism, friendship before efficiency or justice, that is so prevalent—

then or now. At one time I hated these things—*mainly because I was not a recipient of them. If* I had been in position to accept the benefits from them, would I not have gladly taken them, like everybody else? No need to ask . . . of course I, or any other human, would."

Jones grappled with the omnipresent contradictions and the subtle and not-so-subtle aspects of the world-within-a-world that his vision evoked. Although he had several specific characters already in mind, it was their situation and their setting over which he brooded at length before composing his first chapters.

Again and again, he asked pressing questions in his journals, notes and letters: "What is the nature of the story I want to tell? What is its tragedy?"

One revelation he could not escape was that in the case of his new book, all of the autobiographical ligaments of *They Shall Inherit the Laughter* were atrophied.

"I'm having troubles I never had before," Jones realized. As he mulled over his several tentative beginnings and groused about false starts and dead ends, he recognized that all of the advantages of his earlier effort no longer served him.

As he explained to Max Perkins: " 'Laughter' was largely autobiographical and I had a ready-made plot and characters who followed it; all I had to do was heighten it and use my imagination."

Things had changed, Jones confessed to Maxwell Perkins: "But [now] I have nothing to go on except certain people I knew in the army and what made them tick," Jones elaborated. "There is no plot at all except what I create. I'm not even a character in the book myself, except in so far as I am every character. What I have to draw from is 5 ½ years experience in the army."

All of which reminded Jones that he was working with material that set him apart from the vast majority of the more than twelve million men who donned uniforms after 1941. Most of the veterans now being discharged in record numbers had enlisted after December 7, 1941, or had been draftees whose civilian lives were truncated by Pearl Harbor and the three and a half years of America's war effort in 1942, '43, '44 and the larger part of 1945. But Jones's story far preceded all of that.

"My material is the peacetime army," he insisted. "The war has nothing to do with this material, except as it overshadows, unmentioned, the whole book."

And yet, he knew all along that his novel would climax with a full-blown re-creation in fiction of the Japanese attack on Pearl Harbor. He explained to Max Perkins: "The climax is tied in with the event of Pearl Harbor," which of course begged the question of how all of his characters' lives would be altered, affected, upended, transformed or summarily ended by that event.

Throughout 1946, Jones repeatedly discovered that no matter how many outlines or notes he prepped for his new endeavor and regardless of how boldly he proceeded to pile up the first one hundred typed pages (or more), he had to halt. He was impelled time and again to start over after concluding that he had steered the narrative off course. His frustrations were palpable. He fretted constantly.

The distress signals were heard by Perkins. Loud and clear. To encourage Jones and at the same time to help him cultivate a mental discipline that might diminish his doubts and anxieties, Perkins suggested a favorite tactic that he freely admitted none of his other authors had followed through on: "Now this is something I have told many writers," Perkins began, "and I do not believe any of them have done it."

Right there he put the anguished young author in control. The protocol that Max touted was for Jones to decide on. He could take it or leave it. If he shrugged off the advice, then he was in the majority. Such an astute appeal may have caused Jones to believe that he, in fact, would be the first of Perkins' authors to benefit from the editor's sage counsel about the efficacy of keeping an orderly set of note cards.

Perkins had a definite scheme in mind: "Most [writers] keep notebooks, and they certainly should," he reminded Jones. "But they should keep them this way, I think: They should get a loose-leaf note-book and put into it preferably stiff cards, and they should make notes all the time about everything that interests them or catches attention. Then, each thing should have a separate page, and at the top of the page should be put some key word like, say, 'Fear.' Then, just let the cards accumulate for quite a period, and then group them together under the key words. I think if a writer did that for ten years, all those memories would come back to him, as you say, and he would have an immense fund to draw upon."

The very nature of this long-distance tutorial reinforced Perkins' bedrock faith in the notion that Jones was, indeed, every inch a writer. And he further reinforced his belief in Jones by reminding him in no uncertain terms: "One can write about nothing unless it is, in some sense, out of one's life—that is out of oneself."

It may have been that line that inspired Jones to share with Perkins the initial blueprint—the first template, as it were—for what would emerge over the next three decades as the capstone achievement of Jones's career: his World War II trilogy. At this time, however, Jones believed that everything he eventually wrote in three long novels was somehow going to be contained in one vast novel. In the meantime, no working title was yet given to the magnum opus Jones summarized.

Yet it all mirrored—chronologically and geographically—the trajectory of Jones's life. His insecurities aside, he was conceiving a tale "out of one's life—that is out of oneself." Nonetheless, he remained frustrated and periodically despondent.

Each time he felt hamstrung, though, he also realized that one or another of the suggestions made by Max served as a diversion and sometimes even as a lesson in what did not work, but was worth trying. Perkins' hidden agenda was actually hidden in plain sight: To keep Jones mentally stimulated as the intangible subconscious work necessary for the new book had its chance to percolate.

Meantime, Jones's funks would segue to better moods: "I enjoyed your last letter very much. So much so that I went out first chance I got and bought myself a small looseleaf notebook and filled it with stiff cards. I've already started making notes in it. The idea you wrote me about is the best system for keeping notes I've seen," he reported.

And yet, he immediately informed Perkins that he was already at loggerheads with the whole concept. "Of course, how far I shall get with it is something else again. I am depressed because it isn't perfect. Already I've made notes that I'm incapable of classifying generally. They're not Fear, tho some have fear in them. And they aren't courage. They aren't Sadness, although they have elements of sadness, and they aren't Pathos, Joy or Bitterness. Yet almost all of them have two or three of these elements in them. You see what I mean by a German mind? I'd need a Dewey Decimal System, only I don't know how to read one very well. Tomorrow I begin plugging away again."

Jones may not have had a Dewey Decimal System, but he had a sharp eye for his own tendency to overwrite. The primary trouble was that even though he sensed that he was providing too much detail, risking digressions, straying from anything resembling a linear plot-line or in general not getting on with his story, he believed that everything he wrote was essential if he were to achieve his ultimate vision.

"I think my writing has the same trouble," he candidly admitted: "Not a plethora of words but a plethora of detail, all of which needs to be there to get just the right shade of meaning." Such a notion had Jones sounding like a painter, with his concerted efforts to varnish the "detail" and "just the right shade" in his prose.

It was not too far removed from an insight offered once by Perkins, when he was reassuring Jones about his gift. "I remember reading somewhere," Max told Jones, "what I thought was a very true statement, to the effect that anybody could find out if he was a writer. If he were a writer, when he tried to write, out of some particular day, he found in the effort that he could recall exactly how the light fell . . . and all the quality of it . . . would be part of the frame of reference, for instance, if they were writing fiction. They would use that day in the fiction, and they could get the exact feel of the day. Most people cannot do it . . . but that ability is at the bottom of writing, I am sure."

Could there be a more direct analogy between the arts of writing and painting than the image of an author trying to "recall exactly how the light fell"?

Such tidbits from Perkins, shared in letters that were spaced apart by weeks or months (long-distance phone calls were not the norm), served as catnip to Jones.

After one of his anxious periods had passed, he again shared with Max how much in harmony he felt they were—but with a difference or two or three. Which was fine.

"I have concluded, somewhat hopefully, from your letter" Jones confessed, "that I am in essence a writer, although it works a little differently with me: Instead of remembering the exact day, sharp and clear, I seem to remember with equal sharpness and clarity, not that day itself, but the way that day should have been for the particular scene I'm writing. In effect, the day, the temperature,, all the thousands of little things fit themselves to the scene, the way they should be for that particular scene. I guess, tho, that that is only another way of saying exactly what you said."

Even as he thrashed at his typewriter, banging out a letter to Perkins, it was possible for Jones to make an editorial decision, as his mind worked its way into high gear: "Since I began writing this letter," he signed off on April 9, 1946, "I have made a note to cut out the first three chapters entirely (about 15 or 18 pages); they are good writing and give a reader a fine picture of what I'm leading up to, but I guess they are more or less superfluous." Nobody knew better than Perkins that such an act of editorial excision was precisely what F. Scott Fitzgerald suggested to Ernest Hemingway twenty years earlier, thus ensuring that *The Sun Also Rises* began with less background and more momentum. The song remained the same.

* * *

"What I want to know is do I write too much?" Once again that question was dogging Jones when he again unloaded his frustrations and fears on Max Perkins at the end of May in 1946. "And if so," he also wanted to know, "[then] how does one go about not writing too much?"

Jones's struggle with the shapeless, overwritten early drafts of his new book were problems that were familiar.

"The obvious abnormality of the length of [*They Shall Inherit the Laughter*]," he confided to Perkins, "[based upon] Mr. Mitchell's report, is bothering me, and it has been daily becoming more depressing. It's got to the point where it bothers my working." Jones was still irked by the official reader's report of Burroughs Mitchell, a young Scribners editor who served as a junior officer in the Navy during the war.

Burroughs Mitchell and Jones were worlds apart in some ways (Jones was seven years younger, and Mitchell had a degree from Bowdoin College); yet simpatico in others. What mattered is that Mitchell was a new Scribners editor who symbolized the World War II generation, and the imminent new wave of postwar authors.

In a memoir written more than three decades later, Mitchell clearly remembered his engagement with Jones's earliest work: "The first I heard of James Jones was early in 1946," he recounted, "when Max Perkins handed me a manuscript called *They Shall Inherit the Laughter*. This was Jim's first novel, revised after correspondence with Perkins. A clumsy, ill-proportioned book, describing a soldier AWOL in his hometown during wartime and raising persistent hell, the novel nevertheless had a power that impressed us—Perkins, Wheelock and me. But its faults looked too big to make another try at revision seem promising." Nonetheless, certain scenes were still vivid in Mitchell's mind three decades later, when he said to one-time *Harper's* editor Willie Morris that an episode in which the intensely excitable Lowney-figure, steering the AWOL soldier around a bookstore and rhapsodizing about literature, "was a sort of catalogue of great books; long-winded and naïve, but . . . touching."

Self-consciousness was the problem that tormented Jones most of all, as he fought to get control over his new material. His confidence had been shaken by the repeated rejection of *The Shall Inherit the Laughter*, even as his talent was affirmed by the willingness of Perkins and his colleagues to offer payment on an option for "the Stewart novel." Jones was caught betwixt and between. As he struggled to gain traction with his current narrative, he remained distressed at the fate of *Laughter*.

Simultaneously, as he worked in fits and starts and realized that the new novel had yet to congeal and find its own rhythm, Jones's self-confidence took a beating:

"I am oppressed with what seems to be the disjointedness and pointlessness of practically all I've written to date. So much so that I have difficulty going ahead," he explained. Exasperated by his own penchant for long-winded paragraphs and hefty passages of densely textured detail, he highlighted his own contradictions: "I was stuck the other day on a passage which seemed too long for the overall of the book, and yet it was not too long for the passage."

Being emotionally upset was not the only symptom of Jones's distress. As he noted his heightened state of confusion over the fact that he was knowingly writing too much, he also insisted that "I know everything I have written so far is interesting, readable, and an important facet of the lives I'm trying to show." All of which led to serious physical manifestations of his creative tension.

"The ambivalence of it keeps me from sleeping, eating and enjoying myself when I'm not working" he explained to Perkins. And doubtless Max Perkins shared some of this information with the two colleagues to whom he had entrusted *They Shall Inherit the Laughter*. All the more reason that Jones's self-consciousness had to weigh him down. Not only did he feel beholden to Maxwell Perkins but he wrote with the omnipresent awareness that a poet and editor of great repute (John Hall Wheelock was then routinely compared to Pulitzer Prize-winning poets a' la Mark Van Doren and W. H. Auden) was also giving his work close readings. Atop which there was now the input of "Mr. Mitchell" to wonder about. Jones kept on writing.

But he did so with constant conflict. "As it is," he groused, "I find myself muzzled by the necessity of restraint when I want to say something I feel needs to be said. So then I think this doesn't need to be said, because it's taking up too much space. Which puts me in a position where I don't know what does need to be explained and said and what doesn't."

The crux of Jones's problem was that organically he was a maximalist. He wished to tell everything about everyone, and that meant writing with saturation details to explain everything – about anything. His impulses were the polar opposite of other recently discharged veterans who by the end of 1946 had already published first novels. They were novels of modest intent, though. Gore Vidal deliberately set out to craft "a small, cool, hard novel" when he wrote *Williwaw*, which succeeded on its own terms as a wartime tale in a realm (the Aleutian Islands) that most readers knew little about. Similarly, Robert Lowry's *Casualty* was tight, lean, condensed. And it also had, from page one forward, echoes Hemingway's terse early style.

James Jones, however, did not wish to echo Hemingway and he couldn't minimize. All his life he harbored a Homeric need to conjure up a comprehensive, fictive *Iliad* and *Odyssey* to illuminate and illustrate the enormity of his era's war. But it wasn't yet developing as his vision dictated, and he was wise enough to know this. "It's depressing as hell," he exclaimed: "And I'm beginning to wonder if I can write at all."

And yet, already he was recycling chapters and realigning large chunks of the first 200 pages, and invariably he was beginning to render order out of semi-chaos.

By now Jones surely knew that his initial expectations were somewhere between untenable and absurd. In the letter written six months earlier, when he first floated the idea of "a novel about the peacetime army," Jones had proclaimed that "the army novel I mentioned can be written and completed in six months, I think, what with the advantage of all I've learned in writing the first one." That was wishful thinking.

In early June of 1946, however, at least Jones was able to assure Max Perkins and his colleagues that a major effort had, indeed, commenced. "If you like," he said, "I can copy up Book I and send it to you. You said that after the first 50,000 words were approved, there was a possibility of further payment. I could sure use another advance. Having read of your trouble with [Thomas] Wolfe, I guess you ought to know something about this. I am hoping that you can tell me something that will help me."

*   *   *

Women who conceived and announced their pregnancies at the time that Max Perkins read Jones's plaintive words (in June 1946) knew that nine long months lay ahead before they delivered their babies in March 1947. Similarly, in Jones's case, the same nine long months now passed as he experienced the writer's equivalent of carrying a child. The difference being that after another nine months of writing and rewriting; endless revisions and structural reorganizing; going off on tangents and managing somehow to rein himself in and get back on track, only to discover that with his increasingly large cast of characters he had to backpedal and begin anew in order to lend his story cohesion and a sturdy narrative architecture, he was in a panic.

"I had written three hundred pages of *Eternity*," Jones later remarked, "before I realized that [Sgt.] Warden was going to have an affair with Karen Holmes. So I had to go back and bring that about. But even then I didn't know how it would end. I knew only that because of their situation it wouldn't—couldn't—work out."

He told Perkins on March 16, 1947: "The truth is things aren't going so well." And it was not just the particulars of his manuscript that were distressing him. The agenda itself seemed unwieldy. It was almost in a shambles. Or at least it looked that way to Jones, when his fears really took hold.

"I think I'm getting so I'm almost afraid of it," he admitted. "Which is something that never happened to me before. I have a fear of failing that I never used to have. I think it's because I've never actually published anything. I guess it's silly, but I keep feeling I should have published something by now."

Eventually, Jones stopped looking at newspapers and magazines as he focused exclusively on what he struggled with at his desk: "I don't need to tell you," he reminded Perkins, "writing is my life; if I couldn't write I don't know where the hell I'd be. But writing without publishing is like eating without swallowing."

Lowney Handy continued offering unconditional support, but all was not well on the domestic front at this time. Invariably, tensions would heighten between Jones, Lowney, and Harry Handy, regardless of how all three purported to accept their brazenly unorthodox arrangement.

Although they periodically retreated from each other (with Jones staying at the house with Harry, while Lowney went away by herself; or with Jones visiting his out-of-state brother Jeff, letting Harry and Lowney have the house in Robinson to themselves), there was also evidence of a new commitment. By the summer of 1947, a crew of workers hired by Harry from the oil refinery he supervised would complete all the work required to add a private room for Jones at the back of 202 West Mulberry Street. In addition to having a room of his own with a fireplace and home office space, the addition also included a private bathroom.

Still, nothing felt as settled as it should and nothing would feel centered or balanced until the all-important first long section of the work-in-progress finally snapped into place. One long year after setting to work, Jones was still wrestling with Book I.

But at least his new work now had a title: *From Here to Eternity*. Of that Jones was sure. He thought that the words derived from a Yale drinking song. Perkins quickly advised him that the Yalies had borrowed the phrase from one of Rudyard Kipling's "Barrack-Room Ballads." That seemed apt all around.

In Jones's mind, his panic was also apt. Looking back, he agonized over how many times he had put Book I through the wringer in the year now past: "I rewrote what I first sent you two different times," he summed up for Perkins, "cutting a lot and adding many more scenes, a great many of them written before you saw the first part. There is much you have not seen, so I don't know where to start to tell you about or to ask your help. The help I need is in the plotting, in the discovering of *external events* which will display the undercurrents I'm working with, and I guess I have to do that alone."

Again and again for a year now, Perkins replied to Jones with sage advice and quiet counsel. Even though Jones had convinced himself that he might lose control of his narrative vision and the book at large, he began at the same time to narrow his focus. Then he projected to Perkins not just that the novel would have five major "books," but that the leitmotif of each book was well in hand: "At present I've divided it thus . . . Book One--"the transfer" Book Two—"the company" Book Three—"the women" Book Four—"the stockade" Book Five—"the reenlistment blues." And there was more change afoot. Originally, Jones had envisioned a narrative that would commence in 1930 and go forward to war's end. Now he reconfigured that.

"At present," he finally announced, "the time sequence runs from April '41 to December '41, and the climax ties in with the event and emotional turmoil of Pearl Harbor. I have had to abandon the major wartime Hawaii part for a later book. I can't do it justice here. The same holds true with the combat part."

Jones telescoped his story to reveal as much as possible about his characters as their lives unfolded in 1941. In that way, he tapped into one of the most universally applicable, shared elements of the whole World War II demographic: No matter who you were or where you were or whatever you thought about current events, nothing was the same after December 7, 1941. It was not a number on a calendar like any other random date. Nor was it merely a milestone. It was a Rosetta stone.

Out in Manhattan, as Perkins and Burroughs Mitchell and John Hall Wheelock perused Jones's letters and conferred about his periodic reports, there was no talk of abandoning the project. A second payment of five hundred dollars had been sent, even as Jones continued to beat Book I into submission. This financial endorsement was crucial to sustaining Jones's fragile confidence, yet it added to his anxiety.

"I worry about your having advanced me so much money," he said. (At this time you could purchase a brand new car for fewer than a thousand dollars.) "I worry about the responsibility I have toward you personally. And it is taking so damned much longer than I thought, and over half of it not even done in first draft yet."

Nonetheless, the cast of characters had by now almost fully emerged. What had begun as narrative rooted in conflict and competition between two professional soldiers named Private Robert E. Lee Prewitt and Sergeant Milton Anthony Warden had grown exponentially to now include an adulterous love affair between Sgt. Milt Warden and Karen Holmes, who is the wife of Captain Dana "Dynamite" Holmes, the unscrupulous Commanding Officer of G Company at Schofield Barracks.

Then there is the high-strung and forever rambunctious Angelo Maggio, with whom Prewitt will carouse and converse, brood and booze up, sing the blues and in the end serve time in the Stockade (the Army's version of jail). Other major characters were invariably emerging, demanding attention and inspiring Jones to see anew that he was presenting to the reader nothing less than a fully populated parallel universe: Chief Choate and Corporal Bloom are characters as fully developed as Corporal Maylon Stark; and varied civilians of Hawaii are also omnipresent. Soon enough there would be a secondary love story in the works, as Prewitt and a whore named Alma (she uses the name "Lorene" when on the job) find themselves as doomed by the Fates as Karen Holmes and Sgt. Warden.

"I do not know the book well enough to be able to envision it as a whole," Perkins reassured Jones, "and so I cannot fully understand the significance of the ways in which you are dealing with the parts. But whenever I can understand them, I agree with what you say. For instance, the motivation in the case of Prew . . . seems to me a distinct improvement and, in fact, almost everything you say seems to me to go in the right direction."

Perkins' calm words were like a raft to a man who feared drowning. The same can be said for the life-sustaining impact of a sudden windfall that unexpectedly brought Jones more than six hundred dollars. The state of Illinois was now issuing bonuses to veterans who had served overseas and "since I was overseas almost the whole time," Jones explained, "I'll get around $660."

As always, Lowney had a plan. She wrote to Jones almost daily when he stayed at his brother Jeff's house for a visit in May of 1947, and suggested "that you keep half of your $600 for a trip to New York – but that you wait until you have re-written the first full draft." Her letters were streams of consciousness within which she never failed to convey everything from local gossip to updates on Harry's travel plans; in addition to mystical bromides—"the last 15 minutes before falling asleep are powerful"—and her visions of a future with Jones: "Vera said she ordered a book from the library, and when she saw it she thought of me – It's [about] how to build your own adobe house. We can go anytime we get tired of working here and build a house on our own—the car is wonderful." Recently, Lowney had persuaded Harry to buy her a new Pontiac. The freedom it granted to her was liberating and joyful.

"I find that having the car has made a tremendous change in my mental attitude and feel that it will in yours," Lowney told Jones in a letter mailed to him while he stayed with his brother. The increased independence the Pontiac gave her made her think that the most recent tensions at home would subside a great deal, now that she had the ability to drive off on a moment's notice. Yet, spending money was not only tight—it was nearly non-existent. About this Lowney was also forthcoming.

"After [June] first, maybe I can knock down a little on grocery for car money." As always, Lowney's monthly budget was dominated by the cost of buying whatever it took to cook everything from scratch and to feed herself and others in a way that was entirely contrary to America's burgeoning postwar Del Monte "can" culture. By this time, as the summer of '47 began, there were also two other local boys (Don Sackrider and Willard Lindsay) who were not long out of high school and now seeking Lowney's advice and guidance about their hunger to write. Whenever anyone visited her home, food and beverages were offered. And it all added up.

Nothing, however, superseded her commitment to Jones and the cultivation of his new novel. Having had his weeks away at Jeff's in May of '47, Lowney now wrote of her renewed hopes: "[I] wouldn't be at all surprised that you will be able to go to work when you get back ... and finish your book right here [in Robinson]." She also alluded to the recent period of awkwardness that had affected her marriage and Jones. "My feeling of thwart and Harry's subtle domination or whatever you call it was influencing you through me. I have also done something about that, too. If I keep calm and contented and without worries, I notice that *you* are better also. So while you have been taking a rest, I've been getting things ironed out [with Harry]."

Before Jones's hiatus at Jeff's house late that spring, his domestic tremors had been so discomforting that he confided to Max Perkins about wanting to leave Illinois for once and for all. Without sharing personal details of his *menage a trois* arrangement with Lowney and Harry, he admitted: "I must get out of this town. I know now that I can no longer stay here and write as I wish to. Probably it's because it is my hometown and it is so small. I have hated the prospect because of several reasons, not the least of which is that I used my thousand bucks to outfit a perfect place for working, *with some outside help* [emphasis added]. A very wonderful place, and I have hated to face the necessity of leaving it."

With good reason. All tensions and emotional undercurrents aside, Jones knew that most of the time—especially when Harry traveled, which he did often—he had a set-up that was ideal for concentrating exclusively on a major work. But during those times when Harry and Lowney experienced friction with their open marriage, and the odd aspect of Jones living in the newly built addition to the house at 202 West Mulberry Street, not only was Jones reminded of his precarious state—but there was really nobody to vent to about his situation.

He did manage to say this much to Perkins: "It is terribly depressing, it makes you lose your faith in yourself, to be viewed as a sort of ne'er-do-well who is living, as one of my acquaintances phrased it recently, 'a country gentleman's life of a little reading and a little writing.' *And here it goes much deeper than that. . . .*" [emphasis added]

It's quite possible that the ridicule about "a little reading and a little writing" came from Harry Handy, probably after a few drinks. To Lowney, though, all that truly mattered was that Jones return to Illinois, and again occupy his room.

"You can see that the promise of other things will lift the pall of gloom and melancholy that has been hanging over us. I think that all you'll need to do is go to work [on the new book]. Sit down and put it through [the typewriter] in three months like you did 'Laughter.' Just make this place do. We can't go running away from ourselves forever. We can't escape our lives here."

In a different but equally direct way, Max Perkins also offered Jones a powerful dose of encouragement. Jones had written frequently of his troubles with technique and his bewilderment about the intricacies of plot, structure, and character development.

Even after all this time, it was an issue that tormented Jones: "I sometimes despair of ever learning technique," he lamented, "so I can just sit down and write. I have trouble with transition in the middle of chapters. There is, I am told by ever so many books on it, a technique to the novel. Yet nobody ever says just what it is, or how to acquire it."

The mysterious issue of plot development particularly bedeviled Jones. He sharply noted: "The only plotting I know is to have a man do what he would do in his life, but that apparently is not enough. Plotting is supposed to be an improvement on life. I wonder if there is any direct and systematic way to learn the technique of the novel. I'm constantly worried about the plotting taking the life and the truth out of it."

Perkins intervened on this matter. He did not lecture. And he did not pontificate. But he steered Jones away from a stack of "How-To" books that were mentioned in Jones's letters.

First and foremost, however, Perkins reinforced Jones's own intuitive choices: "I think your plot—about which you ought not to concern yourself so much—is right, [and] that the events must rise out of the actual characters and their environments."

Then: One by one, alluding to Jones's repeated references to Thomas Uzzell's *The Technique of the Novel* and other "How-To" guides that promised to reveal the secrets of the literary arts, Perkins discouraged Jones from perusing such works while he was attempting to create his own new novel: "When you come to such books," Max advised, "and [I] could probably get you [from Scribners bookstore] much better ones than you have been reading," they ought not to be read "until you finish your novel, for I do not think you ought to read about writing while you are writing."

Perkins also predicted that the novel would, inevitably, be finished and published. Yet he was cautious and remained superbly tutorial: "I do not know whether this book will sell," he admitted, "and I think there will be a very hard struggle in cutting it and shaping it up, *but I think it exceedingly interesting and valid* [emphasis added]. The Army is *something* and I don't think anyone ever approached presenting it in its reality as you have done. I think though that one reason it needs a great deal of cutting is that you explain too much. You give too much exposition. When you come to revise, you must try to make the action and talk (which is a form of action) tell us all, or almost all."

Although the book was slowly taking shape, Jones had presented enough material to convince Perkins that a novel of unprecedented realism was in the making. That "reality" of the Army that Perkins ascertained in the work-in-progress was grimly accentuated in one of Jones's letters when he forecast a scene "in the Stockade . . . [where] O'Malley is beaten with pickhandles, his ears torn from his head (I *saw* this same thing, incidentally, when I was in the Prison Ward of the Station Hospital at Camp Campbell, Ky.), and confined in the Black Hole, a pit dug under the stockade with no bunk, no floor, a #10 can for a latrine, bread and water."

In the last paragraph of a letter sent to Jones on May 28, 1947, the words of Max Perkins communicated to Jones an image and a truth that induced a new burst of fresh writing and a surge of confidence: "I do get a little afraid," Max admitted to Jones, "that in thinking of the theory, and so much of the plot—though I suppose you cannot avoid it—you may become sort of muscle-bound. That is, *you must be flexible* [emphasis added]. A deft man may toss his hat across the office and hang it on a hook if he just naturally does it, but he will always miss if he does it consciously. That is a ridiculous and extreme analogy, but there is something in it."

There certainly was "something in it." That final paragraph opened Jones's mind. It had the effect on him of a Zen koan bringing forth sudden illumination. It inspired him. As did a gift book sent to Jones by Perkins, who explained in his thoughtful letter why he sent *The Art Spirit* by Robert Henri (a collection of essays originally delivered as lectures). Perkins wrote:

"Yesterday, without naming you, I was trying to explain to a prominent and able writer what you were trying to get across in your book, and the great difficulties of it . . . for she is very intuitive. Then I told her you had been reading [about writing] and she was shocked by that and agreed with me that while writing you should not be reading about writing. But then she spoke of a book. I have sent you [*The Art Spirit*]. I had read it years ago and thought it most revealing. [It is] not about writing, but by inference enormously illuminates the problem. It is concerned with painting, and is derived from the lectures of Robert Henri."

One month later, it was clear that the book had affected Jones profoundly.

"I am working now and feeling high. God, there is no abyss like that of a writer who wants to write but can't and sits around all day wanting to write and not able to and every word he types is horrible," he exulted to Perkins.

"I think the key was in your other letter where you mentioned the *intuitive* woman writer and in Henri's comments about Yogis and that the thing was to attain the 'trance state' first and then the art was a natural result. I think I've been, as you said with the man tossing his hat, trying to calculate and figure too much. I've stopped that now and am trying not to worry and just let it come out, because apparently it is all there, in your mind, in the subconscious, and the trick is to throw your conscious mind out of gear and just let it flow thru."

These subtle epiphanies and notions harmonized with the Eastern spiritual ethos that Lowney affirmed and touted for years. Jones was in a state of excited renewal and gratitude. His recent readings in *The Art Spirit* had him making connections to others who had written or spoken about ethereal matters. He reported to Perkins: "[*The Art Spirit*] has turned me recently to an interest in the Yogis and their various paths of attaining the Overself, as Paul Brunton and Emerson put it, which exists someplace in every man's mind, the God in every man. I've been reading a good bit about them and of them lately. (Is Paul Brunton the man Maugham drew his protagonist for *The Razor's Edge* from? I've a hunch he is, although Maugham seasoned it up a lot, and apparently didn't know much about Yoga.)"

Celebrating his revived creative powers, he thanked Max Perkins with a flourish: "Anyway, the trick is to release the trigger of your conscious mind, it seems to me, and then things write themselves that you have forgotten you even knew. To do that, I have to, as you suggest, put technique, plot and calculation aside and just let it come out willy-nilly . . . I'm very, very thankful that there is man in the publishing business who can see what you are driving at when you tell him . . . I'm damned glad you are there at Scribners and that I came to you."

Jones now felt it was time to make another pilgrimage to New York, and to see Perkins in person again. But he wanted to wait until more new work was done.

"I still plan on coming to New York when my bonus comes through," he confirmed. "But, if I can keep working the way I am at present, I don't intend to come to New York permanently, like I did before. I have a fine place to work, and comforts here that I could never have in New York by myself. And if I can work here, it's smarter to stay. So, I sort of plan on making a temporary trip there . . . I certainly want to come to New York, at least for a while to see you. I feel that there is so much I can learn from you that will help me," Jones wrote on June 23rd.

Max Perkins did not read those words. After too many years of overwork (he rarely took time off; and he stuffed his briefcase with manuscripts every weekend), too many decades of compulsive smoking, the chronic heavy drinking that hurt his health, plus his minimal eating habits, he collapsed with "an advanced infection of pleurisy and pneumonia," according to his official biographer A. Scott Berg.

Unbeknownst to Jones, who quit reading newspapers and magazines as he surged forward on the writing of *From Here to Eternity*, it was on Tuesday, June 17, 1947, that Maxwell Evarts Perkins suddenly died.

James Jones at 15. He attended Robinson High School in his hometown (Robinson, Illinois). In one yearbook, JJ was described as "a scrapper" and "a napper."

G.I. Jones in 1943. He was AWOL, on a hell-raising weekend, when he met Mrs. Lowney Handy. JJ had survived the attack on Pearl Harbor and combat in the Pacific, where he earned the Purple Heart and a Bronze Star.

Jones writing circa 1947 in the additional room built for him by Lowney and Harry Handy.

Lowney Handy and James Jones wintering in Fort Myers, Florida, in 1949.

LEFT:
Poet John Hall Wheelock (esteemed Scribners editor) championed *From Here to Eternity*.

BELOW:
Scribners Editor Maxwell Perkins met the unknown Jones in 1945, guiding him until June 1947.

Lowney and Jones made wintertime road trips to Arizona,
New Mexico, Florida, and California.

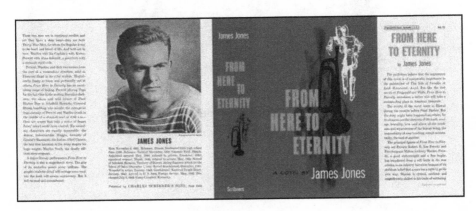

Scribners first-edition jacket copy compared
Jones to Thomas Wolfe and F. Scott Fitzgerald.

Lowney Handy and James Jones in 1951, glowing
with the blockbuster success of his debut novel.

National Book Award winners, 1952: (L to R)
Marianne Moore, James Jones, Rachel Carson.

Manhattan 1952: (L to R) Actor Mickey Knox,
artist Adele Morales, James Jones, Norman Mailer.

Lowney Handy & James Jones on the Handy Writers' Colony property in the mid-1950s.

James Jones, Handy Colony member Don Sackrider, and JJ's sister Mary Ann Jones, circa 1951.

Actor Montgomery Clift visited Jones to consult
extensively about *From Here to Eternity*.

Montgomery Clift and Jones bonded deeply and their
friendship lasted until Clift's death in 1966.

Lowney Handy and Montgomery Clift got along well when he visited the Handy Writers' Colony.

Hawaii-bound: (L to R) Frank Sinatra, Montgomery Clift, Deborah Kerr, Burt Lancaster, JJ, and Oscar-winning director Fred Zinnemann.

The cast of *From Here to Eternity* (L to R) Frank Sinatra (as "Maggio"), author James Jones, and Montgomery Clift (as "Prewitt").

Monty Clift studies JJ's novel in paperback, for which New American Library paid $100,000.

After visiting the Handy Writers' Colony, author
Norman Mailer dubbed Jones "a pirate captain."

Jones and Lowney had a long love affair (1943-1957) unlike any
other in American literary lore.

At his custom-built house on Colony grounds, Jones visits with Lowney and Harry Handy (right).

A New York wedding for Colony bestselling novelist Tom T. Chamales. Jones (left) was best man.

Some Came Running appeared in January 1958. By then, JJ had married and left Illinois forever.

Lowney Handy on Colony grounds near the end of her life. She died on June 4, 1964, at age 60.

8
RISING FROM THEIR ASHES

phoenix *(in classical mythology) — a unique bird that lived for five or six centuries . . . after this time burning itself on a funeral pyre and rising from the ashes with renewed youth to live through another cycle.*
~ Webster's

In no way was Jones being led on. Burroughs Mitchell recalled this period with clarity: "As sections of the novel began to come in to me, I had the exhilarating experience that is an editor's highest reward: the increasing certainty that he is watching the growth of something uncommonly fine and perhaps enduring."

A crucial issue to Mitchell was the topic of Army jail time. Jones had decided that Book IV of *From Here to Eternity* would be subtitled "The Stockade" and as he had made plain in one of his letters to Perkins, his writing about the brutal treatment of Army prisoners by Army guards was a topic going to break new ground in American fiction. Jones would have it no other way. Ever. He was committed to dramatizing everything from the soldiers' sexual deprivations and their enforced acceptance of a hierarchical system of authority that dehumanized the enlisted men (while the officers, by comparison, lived regally) and he was just as committed to exposing the Stockade's ferocity.

Mitchell welcomed this discomforting material. Furthermore, he wanted to help Jones acquire the *TIME* Magazine articles that had first appeared in 1946, when news of gross abuses at an Army prison in Lichfield, England, shocked the public.

"Mitchell is especially strong and adamant about the part on the Stockade," Jones excitedly informed Lowney, "and is very interested in my getting it down true. I mean he really wants to see it written."

Perhaps Mitchell's own sensibilities as an officer and a gentleman were so outraged by the Lichfield revelations that he decided to spur on Jones's fierce, grim realism. Mitchell had his own disquieting memories from his time in the Navy. "He told me several things he had seen and heard," Jones admitted, "such as the brig marines' guards running the prisoners through the gauntlet with belts, etc. He really wants to see ["The Stockade"] written . . . although he is reserved sort of and did not come out with a harangue or anything like that."

It was back on September 9, 1946, that *TIME* Magazine had published a major story on the inhumane treatment of U. S. soldiers by their compatriots at the Army prison near Lichfield, England. When Jones wrote Book IV of *From Here to Eternity*, he had his characters emphatically informed that prisoners were no longer to be considered soldiers in any way, thus they were unworthy of any decent treatment. At all. If they were prisoners, they were not entitled to the courtesies or the rights or the basic human dignity that even a buck private had. And certainly they were not to be accorded the human rights of any citizen.

TIME made its case in plain English, calling the revelations about the Lichfield stockade "the most shocking Army scandal of World War II." One officer, in particular, had been brought to trial and it was in regard to his notorious legacy that the Lichfield trials proceeded. His name was Colonel James A. Kilian, and the primary charge against him was that he had condoned the violence inflicted on the soldiers who had been sent to Lichfield's stockade.

When the story first broke in 1946, Jones had not yet begun his boycott of newspapers and magazines. He was aware of the story and had alluded to it in one of his letters to Max Perkins: "I've started spending a certain amount of time every day . . . in clipping news items from various papers and following up the stories from day to day, for example . . . the Lichfield army trials, which I'm particularly interested in."

When *TIME* reported fully on the story in September of 1946, readers were shocked. The trials had gone on for months, and some testimony was grotesque.

Reported *TIME*: "Men had been beaten there with fists and rifle butts till they were unconscious, then revived and ordered to clean up their own blood. Prisoners who complained of hunger were gorged with three meals at a time, then dosed with castor oil. Hours of calisthenics, of standing 'noses and toes' to a guardhouse wall were routine punishments. . . . There was even a ghastly, sardonic slogan among Lichfield guards: 'Shoot a prisoner and be made a sergeant.'"

Such revelations grimly reinforced Jones's assessment of the fate of enlisted men in the Army. In notes he drafted for *From Here to Eternity*, he ascertained this: "The meaning of the army for me is one of personal degradation, a degradation that is inescapable once a man is hooked, a degradation rising directly out of the system of caste and privilege and arbitrary authority."

Furthermore, he concluded with no qualms at all: *"I assert it is impossible to escape this degradation unless a man allows his own moral nature to be corrupted.* This is a fact by the very nature of the army now, and will remain so until it is changed."

The details that came out at the Lichfield trials shone a blinding light on "the system of caste and privilege and arbitrary authority" that Jones sought to illuminate in his new novel. And the resolution of the charges against Colonel Kilian reinforced his worst assumptions about what glued the officers together in opposition to the enlisted men (or the draftees): "Caste, Privilege, Favoritism, Politics, Arbitrary Authority." Indeed, as *TIME* verified, many of the six thousand GIs sent to Lichfield as prisoners had been sentenced for infractions as minor as being AWOL for hours (not days or weeks or months, but hours).

Although Colonel Kilian was found guilty of "permitting" the vicious abuses inflicted upon the prisoners at the Lichfield stockade, he was acquitted of the charge that he "knowingly" approved or sanctioned the behavior of the guards. In the end, Kilian paid a fine of five hundred dollars.

In a letter sent to Lowney when Jones was in New York, he confirmed that thanks to Burroughs Mitchell, abundant research information would be gleaned: "Tomorrow I'm going over to *TIME* and see Mitchell's friend. They said it would be alright for me to bring a portable [typewriter] and copy some of the stuff about Lichfield."

Other issues were also resolved. Scribners renewed its option on *From Here to Eternity* and Jones received an additional one thousand dollars. By the time he returned to Robinson, Illinois, he was transparently aware of his good fortune.

"You people have been wonderful to me," he proclaimed to Burroughs Mitchell on December 7, 1947. The irony of writing such words on the sixth anniversary of the attack on Pearl Harbor could not have been lost on Jones, who then noted: "If there's ever been a writer who's been advanced $2,000 for a just-begun novel and who had never published anything, I never heard of it."

Jones's progress on *From Here to Eternity* actually nullified the idea that his was "a just-begun novel." All of Book I was clearly in the bag, and whatever editing or paring down it required would occur in due course. Book II was well underway and Jones's newfound research regarding Book IV ("The Stockade") was known by all.

If anything, the fact that Jones still dubbed his book "a just-begun novel" indicates the scope of his vision, and the vastness of his ambition. As was the case with Max Perkins, there was to Jones's mind no novel greater than Leo Tolstoy's *War and Peace*. Perkins read and reread that massive novel throughout all of his adult life. He touted the book to everyone. And Jones, surely, was under Tolstoy's spell. As hubristic or as delusional as it may have sounded to anyone else, Jones intended to compose a work that readers would concur belonged on the same shelf as *War and Peace*. He was also impressed with Stendhal's *The Charterhouse of Parma* and made no secret of his goal to do for his generation what Tolstoy and Stendhal had done for theirs. In short, that was to write the ultimate novel of his era's crucible.

Meantime, he acknowledged to Mitchell that the sequence of events in his life since 1945 had a mystical glimmer. "Nobody will ever know how glad I am [that] I broke off with [literary agent Max] Aley and then swallowed my pride (I had to do that, you know) to write Perkins another letter and ask him to look at 'Laughter' again. But then maybe it's been Kismet, all along the way. I'm inclined to think it has."

There was one other exalted thought on Jones's mind. After he left New York, he received a glowing letter from John Hall Wheelock. It inspired Jones to explain to Mitchell that "it's the first time I've ever seen in words just what I'm really striving to do in writing. [Wheelock] saw it and defined it, when I couldn't even define it myself. It's what I meant when I [told] you that I wanted to combine [Thomas] Wolfe and Hemingway in my writing."

John Hall Wheelock had galvanized Jones by praising *From Here to Eternity* with these laudatory words: "Without romanticizing anything there are moments when from reality itself, presented with fidelity, an exalted kind of poetry is wrung."

* * *

The "exalted kind of poetry" that Wheelock noted is vividly apparent not just on page one of *From Here to Eternity*, but on every page wherein a major or minor character is introduced (and elsewhere throughout the novel).

For the beginning, however, after innumerable revisions, Jones had perfected page one with a series of opening paragraphs that have the authority of Hemingway, but no echoes of the old master's patented style. Short, declarative sentences are not deployed. Paragraphs do not repeatedly begin with "And." No one is named right off.

There is, instead, a captivating sequence of paragraphs gradually shifting from an omniscient narrator's observations of the physical movements of an unnamed protagonist to the same narrator's evocation of the innermost thoughts of that unnamed character. The key tip-off to the reader is that Book I is subtitled "The Transfer." As such, Jones began *From Here to Eternity* with a military protocol common to millions of men, and also many women. It was one of his generation's well-known, demographic mass rituals:

When he finished packing, he walked out on to the third-floor porch of the barracks brushing the dust from his hands, a very neat and deceptively slim young man in the summer khakis that were still early morning fresh.

He leaned his elbows on the porch ledge and stood looking down through the screens and the familiar scene of the barracks square laid out below with the tiers of porches dark in the faces of the three-story concrete barracks fronting on the square. He was feeling a half-sheepish affection for this vantage point that he was leaving.

Somewhere along the line, he thought, these things have become your heritage. You are multiplied by each sound that you hear. And you cannot deny them, without denying with them the purpose of your own existence. Yet now, he told himself, you are denying them, by renouncing the place that they have given you.

John Hall Wheelock was surely not the only editor at Scribners to ascertain that any one of those paragraphs could be reconfigured, reformatted, and read as poetry in free verse. What mattered most, though, was that the opening paragraphs boldly revealed Jones's control over his material.

Without yet knowing the protagonist's name, the reader has met Robert E. Lee Prewitt. And Prew—as he is often called—will be the axis around which the narrative revolves.

With those paragraphs on page one, Jones deftly informed the reader that this universal soldier, an Everyman, this not-yet-individualized "he" is soon to depart; "he" is on a journey; a "Transfer" is underway. Reflections abound. And ruminations ("*Somewhere along the line, he thought, these things have become your heritage*") segue to Emersonian apercus: ("he" alludes to Prewitt a' la Emerson's "transparent eyeball of the universe," and "*You are multiplied by each sound that you hear*" echoes Transcendental ideas).

By the novel's second page, however, dialogue is prominent. One by one, names are introduced and by page three the reader knows the essence of the conflict that will launch the odyssey of Prewitt. He is leaving the Bugle Corps at his own request, after being demoted as First Bugler.

In the novel's opening chapter, Jones gives readers an anti-hero. A go-your-own-way enlisted man who has requested a transfer to the Infantry because his musical gift and personal integrity have been besmirched. And we learn quickly that it's not the first time Prewitt has transferred elsewhere, due to personal conflicts. This pattern of going against the grain is at the heart of Prew's farewell dialogue with a fellow soldier named Red:

"You had to leave the 27ᵗʰ," Red told him. "When you quit the boxing squad and refused to fight any more, you had to transfer out. Because they wouldn't let you alone, wouldn't let you just quit in peace. They followed you around and put pressure on. Until you had to transfer out."

"I did what I wanted to do," Prew said.

In an offbeat way, Prewitt is akin to Herman Melville's protagonist in "Bartleby, the Scrivener" —like Bartleby, Prewitt increasingly defines himself (and is more and more assessed by others) by what he will *not* do.

Which is precisely why Red sums up with resignation, using the word "bolshevik" in lieu of synonyms such as radical, rebel or rabble-rouser:

"It's a bad thing," Red said tentatively. *"You're gettin yourself a reputation as a bolshevik. You're settin yourself up for all kinds of trouble, Prew."*

All kinds of trouble, indeed. By the time Chapter Two ends, and Prewitt's background has been filled in with an abundance of details, Jones has created a rounded character whose hardscrabble life story is representative of millions in Americans who were children in the 1920s, and later suffered through the Great Depression of the 1930s. To detail Prewitt's pre-Army life story, Jones duly recycled tales Lowney often told about her father's family and its violent Kentucky origins. "My people were killers," she'd insisted. Her stories were transformed by Jones.

Prewitt is recalled as a young boy who "learned to play a guitar long before he ever learned to bugle or to box. He learned it as a boy, and with it he learned a lot of blues songs and laments. And this was long before he ever seriously considered becoming a member of The Profession." The references to long-term Army service as "The Profession" are often stated in a different way, a way that Prewitt is exceedingly proud of: He sees himself as "a thirty-year man."

When Prewitt reports to Captain Dana "Dynamite" Holmes, he has sworn off two areas that he excels in. He refuses to box anymore, having once blinded a sparring partner named Dixie Wells; a memory which torments him incessantly because, on her deathbed, Prew's mother made him promise never, ever to hurt anyone. And he refuses to serve again as First Bugler, because the only way Captain Holmes will grant him that post is if Prew, in turn, fights as a middleweight with Holmes's regimental boxing team. Meantime, in between Captain Holmes and Pvt. Robert E. Lee Prewitt, there is First Sergeant Milton Anthony Warden.

After Prewitt's mandatory first meeting with Captain Holmes sours because of his refusal either to bugle or to box, there's a reckoning—the first of many—between Sgt. Warden and Prew. Jones wrote:

They were like two philosophers starting from the same initial premise of life and each, by irrefutable argument, arriving at a diametrically opposite conclusion. Yet these two conclusions were like twin brothers of the same flesh and heritage and blood.

Warden broke the spell. "You haven't changed a bit, have you, Prewitt? Haven't learned a thing. All a man has to do is leave it up to you and you'll put your own head in a noose for him."

Warden unfolded his arms and proceeded to light a cigaret, lazily, taking

*his time. "You had a soft deal as a bugler . . . . You wont like straight duty in
my compny."*

"I can soljer with any man," Prew said. "I'll take my chances."

On the same day that Prewitt joins Sgt. Warden's G Company, the
First Sergeant meets the Captain's lonely, promiscuous wife, who comes
calling unexpectedly to see Captain Holmes. Here Jones borrowed from
Lowney's foolproof method of shocking local citizens, in order to give
Karen Holmes a sensual, flagrant mien:

*Warden watched the tall lean blonde woman get out of the car. The woman
moved on up the walk . . . her breasts always falling slightly, under the purple
sweater. Warden looked at them closely and decided she was not wearing a
brassiere, they moved too much and were too pointed.*

Soon, Warden and Karen plunge into a dangerous affair ignited by
their mutual contempt for Captain Holmes. First Sergeant Warden
detests Captain Holmes for his sloth, privilege, and mediocrity. Karen
Holmes despises him for personal reasons, including the fact that
she contracted syphilis from him on their honeymoon. (Some details
defining Karen and Dana Holmes derived from Lowney and Harry's
lives.) Then there is Angelo Maggio, whom Prewitt meets on his first day
at G Company. Maggio's stuck on Kitchen Police (KP) duty, and radiates
nervous energy:

*"Fine way to pass the time," the KP said, motioning with the speared spud
before he went to peeling it. "Good for the mind. You the new transfer?"*

"Thats whats the matter," Prew, who had never liked Italians, said.

"Ha," the KP said. "'You picked a helluva outfit to get into, friend . . .'"

"I aint no jockstrap," Prew said.

*"Then I pity you, friend," said the KP fervently. "That's all. I pity you.
My name's Maggio and as you can see I aint no jockstrap neither. But I'm a
spudpeeler though. I'm one helluva hotshot spudpeeler. I'm the best spudpeeler
in Schofield Barricks, T.H. I got a medal."*

"What part of Brooklyn you come from?" Prew grinned.

Thus begins one of the great man-to-man rapports in American
literature. Prewitt and Maggio have a shared destiny.

*   *   *

Against all odds, the shared destiny of Jones and Lowney unfolded. His progress on *From Here to Eternity* was steady and slow, the way it had been since he started writing it in 1946. And sometimes it would slow to a crawl. Six times in 1946-47, when weeks went by with no work on the novel whatsoever, Jones had used that time to create a handful of short stories. It was a wise choice. Although he was wholly rejected by *Esquire* magazine when he first submitted his new stories, the way he was rejected shone a light not just on Jones's talent but on the mood of the nation as reflected in the choices of a top-tier editor.

On the one hand, *Esquire's* Assistant Editor George Wiswell assured Jones: "It's unnecessary for me to tell you that you can write exceedingly well. I think you will no doubt succeed. I am sure sooner or later you are going to crack the publishing world wide open." On the other hand, Wiswell bluntly informed Jones: "We are rejecting all six of your stories not because they showed any lack of talent, but because . . . for the time being we are not running any war stories. Later we hope to publish a good many of them but at present the climate of reader opinion is against them. I like 'The Way It Is' the best of the lot. It was a beaut, very honest, real and carried a lot of punch." None of which mattered. The public had combat fatigue.

Jones knew that the "slick" magazines were not likely to care for his brooding, ultra-serious stories. But he did submit "The Way It Is" and several others to *Harper's* and *The Atlantic* in 1948-49.

Meantime, it was impossible not to notice that even if *Esquire* or other magazines temporarily boycotted war stories due to the postwar public's feeling of saturation with WW II movies, memories, and the sheer exhaustion felt by millions with the cataclysms of 1939-45, there were big new novels—first novels—by Norman Mailer and Irwin Shaw in the headlines. In May 1948, Mailer's *The Naked and the Dead* was published to enviable reviews and major sales. It was a bestseller for a year. At age 25, the previously unknown Mailer became the most celebrated "war writer" of his generation. His glacially paced and densely textured novel of one Army platoon's "long patrol" on a Pacific island, as they endure an interminable recon mission, captured the public with its powerful writing. Mailer cited James T. Farrell and his *Studs Lonigan* trilogy, as well as Hemingway, John Dos Passos, and John Steinbeck as the major influences on his style and vision in *The Naked and the Dead*. And then came Irwin Shaw with *The Young Lions*.

Since 1936, when his antiwar one-act play *Bury the Dead* was a *cause celebre'* in New York's theater milieu, great things were expected from Irwin Shaw. His short stories appeared often in *The New Yorker,* and his service in World War II was a monumental inspiration to his ambitious, Euro-centric, historically informed first novel. The *Young Lions* is an exhaustive narrative, recapitulating everything from the bewilderment of draftees to the D-Day landings at Normandy; then the ecstasies of the Liberation of Paris, and the ineffable revelations of the concentration camps.

The question dogging Jones was simple: Would there be any audience for his novel when he finally managed to finish it? It was a valid question. Indifference to short stories about the war epoch was a red flag. How could a long novel on the pre-war Army fare? Especially if it did not appear for a few more years? Jones brooded.

There was no going back. Besides, he had not only Scribners's faith in him but also the cash advances that verified the collective belief of the late Max Perkins, as well as Burroughs Mitchell and John Hall Wheelock. But the money from Scribners had been limited and intermittent. Overall, the spectrum of Jones's needs was still being financed by Harry Handy, who at the behest of Lowney kept the faith in the "shining dream" (as Jones described his quest to write *From Here to Eternity*).

Emotionally, psychologically and even spiritually, Jones's succor came not just from Lowney but also, to a degree, from John Hall Wheelock. When Jones wrote to Wheelock, it allowed him to share parts of himself that remained shielded from the world at large. Superficially, in the late 1940s, Jones still appeared to be a gruff, taciturn, moody ex-GI who was quick to anger and oftentimes ready to fight.

Yet, at any given time, he was also reaching out John Hall Wheelock in this vein:

"I looked up all of your poetry I could find in the local library. I read enough of them to see that you had done considerable reading in Eastern philosophy and its ramifications, like we talked about. There is something there that intrigues me, but I don't know exactly what it is. Anyway, there was a new book here for me when I got home [from the New York trip at the end of 1947], and I wanted to mention it to you. It's called *A Strange Language.* And it's by Pundit Acharya."

Jones skips any mention of who gave him such a book, but surely such a gift was handed over by Lowney Handy. At this time, Jones had yet to speak to Wheelock or Mitchell about his private life back in Robinson, Illinois.

"I think you'd like it," he told Wheelock, regarding his new book by Pundit Acharya. "There's wonderfully fine material in it. It's written in a very odd way, *a poetry in prose that is really excellent*" [emphasis added].

Thus in turn did Jones offer back to John Hall Wheelock some echoes of how Wheelock himself exulted, when he read *Jones's work in progress.* No matter what frustrations or bouts of despair now afflicted him, Jones could re-read whenever he needed to Wheelock's remarkable affirmation about *From Here to Eternity*: "Without romanticizing anything, there are moments when from reality itself, presented with fidelity, an exalted kind of poetry is wrung."

Economically speaking, reality was always "presented with fidelity" by the daily, weekly, monthly, and yearly costs of sustaining Jones and his "shining dream."

Not only for the fiscal boost but also for the national exposure, Jones was thrilled to inform Lowney and Harry and Mitchell and Wheelock that 1948 would mark the year of his debut publication in a national magazine. Edward Weeks at *The Atlantic* magazine sent Jones a telegram to confirm: **PUBLISHING TEMPER OF STEEL MARCH ATLANTIC PROOFS SENT AIR MAIL VENICE. KEEN TO SEE YOUR NEW WORK. REGARDS EDWARD WEEKS**

Translated: Jones's short story "The Temper of Steel" would appear in the March, 1948, issue of *The Atlantic* and "the proofs" of the final draft going to print were being air-mailed to Venice, Florida, for Jones's perusal and ultimate approval.

Once again, the dread Illinois winter had been escaped by Jones and Lowney. But now, they traveled in a way that was doubtless more economical and liberating.

Harry Handy had signed a note at a local bank in Robinson, and purchased both a jeep and a 26-foot Airstream trailer that allowed Jones and Lowney (separately or together) to roam the nation, keep on writing, not squander money on motels or cottages, and most of all be on the move and able to live in climates they preferred. As the 1940s came to a close and well into the 1950s, Jones and Lowney and their jeep and trailer would travel to Florida, Arizona, New Mexico, California, and elsewhere. It was a stunning act of generosity on Harry Handy's part; Harry and Jones had a rapport that was sometimes edgy, but more often warm and affable.

When "The Temper of Steel" appeared as an "Atlantic First" in March 1948 (along with the first-ever short story published by another veteran destined for literary fame: Joseph Heller's "Castle of Stone"), Jones was again devoting all his energies to *From Here to Eternity*. Meanwhile, Lowney not only worked on her own novel and her own stories, but she also took under her wing two more aspiring writers named Don Sackrider and Willard Lindsay. Both hailed from Robinson, Illinois, and had been introduced to Lowney through family or friends. This alliance inaugurated what would eventually emerge in 1951 as the Handy Writers' Colony.

By the middle of 1948 the embryonic beginnings of the Handy Writers' Colony and the gradual progress Jones was making on *From Here to Eternity* were equally reported on when he updated Burroughs Mitchell.

Jones was full of praise and high hopes for Lowney's widening of the circle:

"Lowney has been working with two fellows here, who want to write ... [she] started them out on copying, picking stories by different good writers, or even chapters out of their books.

"She had them copy 'Snows of Kilimanjaro,' I think, and then a story by Nancy Hale. She had them copy 20 [pages] from [Thomas] Wolfe's *Face of a Nation* that Wheelock edited, letting them pick their own sections.

"The point was for each to copy toward his weaknesses. For instance, if one loved poetry she put him to copying the tersest stuff she could find, like Cain, Raymond Chandler, William Irish. If he was a Hemingway addict, she put him to [Thomas] Wolfe. It's really intriguing as hell to watch how it works.

"I think I mentioned *Challenge of the Unknown* by [Louis K.] Anspacher to you when I was in NY. The theory used is based on his chapter entitled 'Psychic Manifestations in Art and Literature.' John Livingston Lowes tried to show the same thing in his massive tome *Road to Xanadu*, but he got muddled ... Anspacher does it better. It's a clear explanation of how an artist creates, although I've found that with me (and with all of them, I guess) there is still some X factor that is unaccountable."

This fixation on "copying" large swaths of content from the published works of great writers has been the single most derided aspect of Lowney Handy's ideas and convictions on how to help young writers develop their skills. And yet, at the same time, it's worth noting that there is a phenomenal similarity between the "copying" calisthenics that Lowney ordered Jones (and others) to perform, and the highly similar way that another evolving artist, in a different field, found his voice.

One decade earlier, in the summer of 1937, Charlie Parker was a fledgling alto-saxophone player gigging with a local dance band and other musicians in Kansas City; and he was already seized by an inner sense of great musical possibilities that he heard in the privacy of his mind. However, he lacked the technical skills and the essential knowledge of harmony required to execute the solo lines he heard in his head. At a crowded jam session one night at the Reno Club, young Charlie Parker was utterly humiliated when failing at his effort to play an improvised solo to the tune of George Gershwin's "I Got Rhythm" (a favorite for jazz players at competitive "cutting contests," where one's ability to solo in a personal style was at a premium). In the middle of his solo turn, Parker lost all control of the tune's rapid-fire chord progressions, and stumbled over what notes were apropos, as the up-tempo jam continued. In other words, he choked up. And there was no chart, arrangement or sheet music to fall back on. Parker's solo fizzled as the other players stopped dead after drummer Jo Jones (a local hero for his newfound success with Count Basie's Orchestra) took one of his cymbals and tossed it at Parker's feet: being "gonged" like that was mortifying.

So, he vowed to make it right. That summer in 1937, Charlie Parker retreated to a remote cabin in the Ozarks, near a resort where he played nightly gigs with a dance band that stayed safe by hewing to written arrangements. But, during his free time, Parker did something else. He obsessively played his new Decca records by Count Basie and His Orchestra, over and over and over again, on a Victrola that had a mechanism by which Parker could slow down his turntable. He intuitively knew that by slowing down certain newly released Count Basie records, he could learn "by ear" the exultant saxophone solos played by Basie's star reed-man: Lester Young. Hour after hour, for days and weeks and months, Charlie Parker wore down the grooves Count Basie's Decca records of "Swinging at the Daisy Chain," "Honeysuckle Rose," "Exactly Like You," and other tunes featuring Lester Young. By slowing down the speed of the turntable and mastering each phrase, every inflection, all the varied shades of color, tone, and nuanced mood that Lester Young articulated through his horn, Parker did more than improve his fingering technique and strengthen his tone. He instinctively used his own method of "copying" from a proven artist in order to catapult himself to a higher level – the only difference being that instead of learning the cadences of dialogue by "copying" Hemingway or mastering punctuation effects by emulating John Dos Passos . . . young Charlie Parker was ensuring that never again would he lose his place in a jam session on a familiar tune. Or any tune. By consciously absorbing the combined melodic, harmonic, and rhythmic elements of Lester Young's remarkable long-form solos on Count Basie's earliest hit records, the die was cast. Charlie Parker elevated all of his own skills simultaneously.

And in a short period of time, inevitably, Parker went beyond the profound lessons learned by mastering the recorded solos of Lester Young. Such "copying" was neither derivative nor exploitative. Instead, it fueled Parker's ability to break free and galvanize his own style. American jazz pianist Horace Silver once described his own artistic evolution in a remarkably similar way: "I got a harmony book from a music store and studied basic root positions. I used to take those Charlie Parker, Bud Powell, and Dexter Gordon records on Savoy and put them on an old wind-up machine and slow the speed down. That would put everything in another key, but I'd hear the chords that way and pick them out note by note."

That, too, was Lowney's fondest wish: for "copying" exercises to induce a young writer's artistic breakthrough.

* * *

Early in the winter of 1949, "some X factor that is unaccountable" dominated the lives of Jones and Lowney Handy. And dominance itself, as a life condition, caused them to experiment in a new way. Crosscurrents of toxic emotions and unresolved disputes created such chronic tension toward the end of 1948 that Jones cut short the time he spent in Florida as winter began. Despite his dislike of the frigid Illinois winter, Jones returned home (alone) to Robinson in January of '49. He and Harry Handy shared the house on Mulberry Street. Lowney worked on her novel, *But Answer Came There None*, down in Florida. While they lived apart for three months, their relentless epistolary binge functioned not only as a form of personal communication but also as a form co-counseling, psychological jousting and most of all a search for healing between Jones and Lowney. Each of them had upset the other with a dalliance. Lowney briefly made room in her life for a man named Jack, while Jones had more than a platonic interest in a woman named Doris. A truce was called after Lowney declared: "I think we can cancel Doris and Jack off as even."

In addition to rising tensions over roving eyes, there was the ever-present issue of Jones's quest.

Once again, as was the case back in the fall of 1944, when Lowney's "copying" dictums were dutifully applied by Jones to the bulk of *The Portable Hemingway* collection, the looming legend of Ernest Hemingway was a prompt. As usual.

Only this time, thanks to the January 10, 1949 issue of *LIFE* Magazine and a photo-essay entitled "Portrait of Mr. Papa" written by Malcolm Cowley, the latest burst of publicity for America's best-known writer was both a prompt and an irritant.

In the hagiography of "Portrait of Mr. Papa," it was obvious that Cowley had suspended his critical faculties. The essay was an exercise in myth-making. All aspects of Hemingway's persona were romanticized. His experiences in the two world wars (as a Red Cross volunteer in 1918 and as a *Collier's* correspondent in 1944) were transmogrified into swashbuckling heroic excursions. His Paris-in-the-Twenties hiatus was given a golden patina. His big-game hunting and deep-sea fishing and all other exploits (including the silly episode when he commandeered his famously photographed boat, the *Pilar*, ostensibly to hunt German submarines off the Cuban waters in 1943) were written up in a way that burnished his image.

Cowley's "Portrait of Mr. Papa" signified a transition of Hemingway's career. He was now the ultimate patriarch: burly, white-bearded, and iconic. Although he had not published a new book since 1940's *For Whom the Bell Tolls*, he was crowned as America's once and future literary king. And Lowney was miffed. She knew enough to be able to see through all of Cowley's royal flattery. Unlike the vast majority of *LIFE* Magazine's millions of subscribers and many millions of off-the-rack readers, Lowney perceived that Hemingway's image-control was now his ultimate priority.

His serial marriages, macho swaggering, and self-aggrandizement were anathema.

"READ AND RE-READ that article on Hemingway," Lowney advised, as she and Jones began a ten-day blitz of intense correspondence on January 20, 1949. "There but for the grace of God goes James Jones," she chided. "[A] King complex," Lowney said: "Won the war singlehanded, both on land and sea and air. Look at the change of his head in the different pictures—keeps widening out through the middle—appetites do that. I feel sorry to see such tremendous vitality WASTED," Lowney exclaimed. "He's repeating himself, developing recipes for drinks— first in France and now in Cuba. However, I note that none of them are original with him—he just makes them fashionable and gets his name stuck on."

She then surmised: "Of course the whole thing is nothing more or less than a plug for his next book. I hope you do not pattern yourself on him in anything at all."

The critical issue causing such acrimony between Jones and Lowney at this time was sex. As she furthered her Yoga studies and delved more deeply into her Eastern spiritual readings, Lowney preferred to minimize her sexual self-expression. She did not choose to be celibate, but in no way did she wish to keep sanctioning Jones's admittedly overwrought sexual cravings. Lowney dubbed his libido "goat cries."

"I like sex," Jones freely proclaimed: "In fact, I love it. I've always been oversexed. I am constantly fighting for control of myself not to think about it all the time."

Lowney understood this all too well. And though she was not happy to see Jones return to Illinois for the winter of 1949, she did appreciate the ways in which her newfound solitude brought forth fresh thinking. "I had a terrible time after you left," she confessed. And yet, it was because he was so far away that she could see anew.

"What I see in you is a great capacity for love," she concluded. "You are tender and kind and have a boyishness that men don't normally have. You have an honesty and a love that has nothing to do with . . . sex. However, you are more tender and adoring of someone who will give you this thing your passion demands."

Lowney's increasingly ascetic attitude toward her body and the realm of physical erotica was entwined with her deepening immersion into the literature of dreams, astral projections, reincarnation and other esoteric subjects. Thus she offered unto Jones the unexpected idea that he may very well be better off married to a younger woman, if he decided in the end not to try to sublimate his libido in his writing.

"It may be that your time on this earth is of many more lives," Lowney suggested, "and that you need to marry a [younger] woman. That I can't say, but if you cannot conquer the desire nor forget it—nor do not want to go through the great agony it might take—then I think the best thing for you to do would be to concentrate on the college girl in Indianapolis—or have Mary Ann [Jones's younger sister] look for you a group to choose from. At least go all out one way or the other. And don't after you get married delude yourself as Hemingway did—and keep switching them off—they are all the same. [Hemingway had four wives.] Make as good a choice as possible and then settle down to a wife—but give her a family because that is normal and if you go against nature for her you will only give her grief and unhappiness."

Although she was suggesting what would have been invariably a revolutionary alteration in their lives, Lowney never lost sight of their mutual commitment to writing and their shared passion for the evolution of *From Here to Eternity*.

"Me? I am going ahead," she vowed. "No compromise. No counting the cost. No taking thought of the morrow. I had to go on a three-day [liquid] diet in order to lose contact with the reality around me. My work goes fine. All I had to do was empty my mind—shake off the little irritations—and I'll write a great book. So will you. I know I never spent all that time for nothing. I'm with you all the way. And I'll be waiting." Then she signed off in her usual transcendent way: *"Forevermore."*

Back home in Robinson, Jones mulled over Lowney's suggestion about possibly marrying a younger woman in order to assuage his carnal appetites. In no way could he seriously see himself pursuing that option. After typing up page after page of thoughts regarding the shifting phases of their shared history, Jones circled back to the unique passion he shared with Lowney: "I had a piece [of ass] thrown in my lap last night, and turned it down right in front of me—not because I felt guilty about you but because I just didn't want it. It was not your body, your kiss, your anything."

Jones elaborated further on how he'd been out that night with an old friend from elementary school, Sylvanus "Tinks" Howe, and how "Tinks called me up and said he had a piece picked up for me, a girl from Iowa who was broke and on the bum, a pretty girl. I was reading Stendhal and almost didn't go. Harry and I talked about it a long time. I didn't really want to go. Harry thought it might make me feel better. I told him it was not sex I wanted but the contact of love without dominance."

The issue of "dominance" was paramount during this strained period. "I let myself too often be dominated," Lowney admitted. Jones reminded her: "Between us, we can conquer it, Lowney. We must. We must have love without dominating . . . There is no joy in life without love, everything is drab, meaningless. I'd just as soon not be alive, as not have your love. Write that you love me. I don't want sex. I want your love. Even without sex entirely, I want your love. Oh, Lowney. I'm all gone inside. Letters are bitches. Harry's gone to Findlay [Ohio]. I'm going to drive the jeep to Vincennes and call you. I won't be able to work if I don't."

Long-distance calls were a rarity for Jones and Lowney. And not just because long-distance charges were expensive. At that time, to place such a call, one had to dial the local operator and spell out to whom the call should be placed. Lowney knew and Jones understood that the gossiping in Robinson would intensify if the local operator blabbed that Jones was racking up Harry's phone bill placing long-distance calls to Lowney in Tampa, Florida. His decision to make the call from neighboring Vincennes, Indiana, was a matter of discretion.

Not that there was much doubt among the locals about the state of affairs. For years now, citizens in Robinson sneered as Lowney and Jones sunbathed together in shorts on hot summer days: long-legged, bra-free Lowney sporting a bare-shoulders halter-top, and Jones in all of his muscular fitness, looking ripped thanks to vigorous daily exercise; they made the front lawn of 202 West Mulberry Street their own spa. In addition, the local knowledge about Harry's philandering made all three of them grist for Robinson's gossip mill.

By this time in 1949, though, Lowney wanted to draw as little attention as possible to their unorthodox arrangement. She advised Jones to put Scotch-Tape on the envelopes of his letters to her, to make it as annoyingly difficult as possible for snoops at Robinson's post office to pry.

The long-distance call was appreciated, though. Lowney fell in love again with the sound of Jones's voice, writing: "I think the conversation, hearing the sound of each other's voices, did more than anything. Just to hear the low husky sure tone of your voice made me happy." Their commitment now took on a new depth of feeling.

"You can't imagine how the whole overall picture changes by a word or two," she wrote. "Just to know you are wanted. Are needed above everything else in the world. It's a strange thing about us ... I'm like you ... nothing bothers me now that I know. But the not knowing for some time was very bad. I know that our thoughts have been tearing back and forth across the miles and each one [was] upsetting the other. It's got to stop. If we're ever going to be on our own—have financial security to free us—we've got to learn to stop upsetting the other and work."

Lowney's projections of an unencumbered future together (presumably without Harry in the picture) collided with one essential role being fulfilled—because Harry continued to finance one and all, as he had been doing since 1944. During this time, Jones completed other short stories that he wrote when pausing now and then on his novel. Submissions were underway, with their inevitable periods of frustrated waiting. Lowney suggested that when Jones again sold a short story to a national magazine, he hand over the money to Harry: "If you get [any] money—Harry can [use] it on his notes at the bank to re-finance the jeep."

Then, having dispensed with practical matters, Lowney would segue to another of her mystical insights: "Annie Besant says," Lowney often reminded Jones, "that the mind is the only instrument by which you can create and re-create yourself."

What mattered most, however, is that after their conciliatory long-distance call, a long typed letter from Lowney to Jones arrived at the right time. Responding to her loving assertions, Jones overflowed with gratitude, grace, and epistolary ardor:

"That's where my faith is founded. I know now for sure you can never get over me, and that I can never get over you. It is as simple as that. Just as we are a man and his woman who love each other, a woman and her man who need each other. We are in love. Don't ask me why, or how. It just is, and must be accepted. We have loved through more than one eternity, to be able to love so much.

"Words just fail me, Lowney. I can't explain. It's just love, overpowering, all embracing ... You say: 'I need for you to need me.' There is no word to say my happiness at reading that. Because I need for you to want me to need you. Of course, you'll have to help with every other book I write, too. I will need you with me to begin something else. It just looks like I'm always going to need you, and there's no way we can get out of it . . . is there?"

Amid the joys of reconciliation, though, the nagging issues of sex and money remained. Jones flat-out concurred with Lowney: "You're right that we need to get a [new] light on sex. I'm beginning to think it's only our different definitions of it."

Lowney knocked Jones out of the ring with this statement: "To me one of the things about a predominantly sexual love is that it has a core of selfishness. You have a tendency to extract all of the meat of love— the delight and pleasure in the hours in bed. To me love exceeds this. It carries a thoughtfulness, a closeness, a warmth and thinking of one another that has no connection with sex. I have always thought of sex as a stealer from love. Lots of women get that feeling and there arises a sort of anger inside them, a feeling of thwart."

To which Jones replied:

"In the first place you say, 'a predominantly sexual love.' To my mind, there is no predominantly sexual love. No matter what I've said in the past or done . . . I say now that love cannot be predominantly sexual. That doesn't mean, though, that two people in love can't have sex every night, if they want it every night. You are right that 'you have a tendency to extract all of the meat of love—the delight and the pleasure in the hours in bed.' I did do that, but I did more because I was frantic for fear of losing you—I could *see* I was losing you—and I was grasping frantically at whatever straws I could seize. It wasn't that way at the very first with us, if you remember. I was ravenous, yet even so, [there] was a warmth there that heightened everything, like the way we would look at each other glintingly, when other people were around (especially Robinsonites), we knowing what we had had shortly before and would have again.

"Somehow, I feel we won't have much trouble with sex when we get together again. Somehow, now, I feel like it will already have ironed itself out . . . The thing with you is, nobody has ever been able to lull you with love enough to awaken the sex that is in you. I did maybe for a little while, or rather I was just beginning to (remember how I used to say relax your mouth?) . . . There is tremendous sex in you . . . sex as love and sex as nearness and sex as giving pleasure and taking pleasure, it hasn't been awakened yet with trust. I think it will be when we come together again, if only by the fact of my being true to you (not from willpower, but from being incapable of doing anything else but be true to you)."

Jones confirmed that Lowney's manifest effort to channel most of their libidinous energies into writing was essential. "I might very easily have killed myself by fucking," he admitted, "if I hadn't been forced to see that it was not an answer. Every sexual bout . . . consumes so much energy. Every bit of energy consumed thru sex is energy that cannot be placed elsewhere. [So], if I wish to write 6 hours a day, I can only take so much sex without taking energy from my work."

As for money, there was no getting around their continued dependence on Harry's largesse. Fortunately, Harry wanted to be left alone, by and large, to enjoy his own mistress, and his varied affairs; to earn his salary as the superintendent of the Ohio Oil Refinery in Robinson, Illinois; and most of all to be able to drink as much as he pleased without rancor. He did not want a divorce (being married was his shield against the overtures of any women who might want to be legally attached to his money); and his willingness to underwrite the literary quest of James Jones was, in truth, his way of compensating Lowney for her willingness to tolerate his philandering.

Still, money worries caused Lowney to fret. She warned Jones in a letter: "You musn't make Harry envious or upset. Even now [in 1949] he may be just biding his time until he can get us on our feet and live his own life. We'd be lost if he did. Neither of us can hold onto money or manage [it]. We'd be at each other's throats worse than we've ever been. The success of our greatness depends on Harry and I want you to make an all out effort to let him know. I think he's been hurt about the jeep. He did everything and not a word of praise has he had, hardly a decent thank you. He wrote me in one letter [that] he never saw much of you, that you stayed in your room working and writing and reading. That may be what he wants—but he also wants recognition for all he is doing."

As winter gave way to spring and summer in 1949, the three-month winter separation that Lowney and Jones had experimented with led to an intensified new commitment between them. It wasn't just a matter of reemphasizing the superficial looks attracting them to each other, although plenty of body heat was again in the air. "I go down to the beach every other day at least for an hour of sun," Lowney wrote. "I want to add to my tan before I come home and buy something white."

She added: "I've lost some of that bad fat and look better. In fact, Mrs. Mahlon told me the other day that her cousin said [I've] 'got the best figure in this town'—(mentioning how I looked in a bathing suit). Since I've been here alone I've felt bad that we didn't go out someplace and me wear my yellow dress. I have dressed up for you so little. I'll have something that makes me look nice when we meet and you'll be proud of me."

"And now," Jones remonstrated, "[you're] telling me about what Mrs. Mahlon's cousin said about your figure! What have I been trying to tell you all along? You have the most beautiful [body] I've ever laid my eyes on, and I mean that (IN or OUT of a bathing suit). Oh, if I could only see you now."

He had a far more in-depth reaction to Lowney signing off on one of her letters with these words: "Forevermore: and never doubt that I love you, I can't help myself."

Jones read and reread her typed words. He stared at her addendum: "*Yours forevermore, Lowney*" was handwritten in her flamboyant penmanship.

Then he replied with soulful, renewed devotion to Lowney, echoing her words:

"You closed with 'Forevermore: and never doubt that I love you, I can't help myself.' There is nothing you could say that could make me prouder, happier, or greater than that. So I repeat it back to you, as hungrily and sincerely as you said it.

"Forevermore: and never doubt that I love you, my darling, I can't help myself, you just can't get over some people . . . you meet them and there is a look between you, and you are bound together to the grave, and to beyond the grave. I love you."

*   *   *

Forty years later, in a 1989 Preface composed for an archival volume devoted to the Handy Writers' Colony, author and former colonist John Bowers wrote:

"One thing was apparent to all who saw them together—Lowney was the stronger in the relationship. . . . The major thing Lowney gave [Jones] —and at a most pivotal time in his life—was improbable understanding. She gave him succor when no one else could or did. She took him in, emotionally and physically . . . . Others in that classic Midwest setting wrote him off as a batty drunk, or, hard-drinkers themselves, could not fathom his tender artistic side. Everywhere he turned he faced misunderstanding and repression—except in the arms and care and psyche of Lowney Handy."

As 1950 dawned, postwar optimism lingered. Then the Korean War knocked America off balance. The Red Scare ignited furious anti-Communist witch hunts. No one could have predicted that by the end of 1950 President Truman would declare a State of National Emergency, after China's stunning entry into the Korean War. Still, throughout 1950 both Jones and Lowney pressed on. In tandem. Together. As always, Lowney's husband, Harry Handy, remained a central figure.

In a letter Lowney sent to Harry from Memphis on April 10, 1949, she said: "Yesterday I wrote you about the cabin. I want it at Marshall . . . on the Marshall lot . . . I love those woods and I love not being so easily reached. Back in a hollow and out of sight if possible . . . a home that is ALL MINE – I'd like that. Not a cabin for others. [Jones] has his trailer and I'm welcome. And you have the house in Robinson and I'm welcome – but let this be my home – and you will both be welcome."

9

" . . . a startling enigma to this day . . ."

It is impossible to think of the writing of Eternity . . . without the tutelary presence of this tough, courageous, unconventional woman who was 17 years older than Jones and had the encouragement of her husband in one of the strangest arrangements on record. She remains a startling enigma to this day . . . she was a powerful, magnetic presence in the first and undoubtedly most crucial half of James Jones's artistic life, a determined, "liberated" woman out of sync with her time and place, and she paid the bitter price.

~ Seymour Krim, 1986

Lowney Handy wasn't the only woman with whom Jones was preoccupied and consumed at this time. Female characters dominated much of *From Here to Eternity*.

Both Karen Holmes and Alma (aka: Lorene) emerge more and more forcefully as Jones's massive narrative unfolds. Their bold, audacious characterizations signified a breakthrough in American fiction of the mid-twentieth century. Neither woman fit the profile of a wholesome, all-American, homemaking, idealized married lady. That stereotype continued to be enforced (almost always) by the Production Code offices out in Hollywood. And it always, in a major way, permeated the national magazines in the years after World War II, when Rosie the Riveter was sent home. Women after the war were simply expected to marry, have babies, and make a nice home.

Scant other paths for adult women (except nursing or teaching) were affirmed or encouraged in those years. A great deal of advertising in the tonnage of national magazines was directed toward women's presumed wants: A new washing machine and a dryer, too. Better baby paraphernalia, and of course the elegant jewelry, new nylons, and snazzy dresses to please an amiable husband, whose brand new car and new postwar job would complement the Levittown agenda for happy new American homes; with room for rollicking children and the proverbial white-picket fence out front. In the ads, canned foods were as prominent as sketches of domesticated women running their vacuums, or washing the family's dishes, in high heels.

Contrarily, in the pages of *From Here to Eternity*, Jones was intuitively smashing these stereotypes and allowing his two principal female characters—Karen Holmes and Alma (aka: Lorene)—to engage the reader as forcefully as Prewitt and Maggio.

Even Jones, however, could not have foreseen how women all across America would not only celebrate his novel when it finally appeared, but would flock to see the major motion picture that his novel spawned. Against the array of obstacles presented by the rigidly powerful Production Code office in 1953, Hollywood managed to capture the essence of *From Here to Eternity*. And then and now, balancing the Army narrative, there's the audacious power of its women.

As the wife of career officer Captain Dana "Dynamite" Holmes, it is Karen Holmes who early on in Jones's novel proves herself a match for the overbearing men in her midst. Starting with her husband. Captain Holmes is interested only in the shrewd advancement of his Army career. Although he claims that neither he nor anyone in his company will pressure Robert E. Lee Prewitt to box for the company's team, it's understood by all that he's lying. Holmes will turn away and let "The Treatment" take its course. And "The Treatment" is nothing less than a brutal, all-encompassing pattern of hazing (day and night) intended to exhaust Prewitt, put him in his place, wear him down, and finally impel him to give in and do what the Captain wants.

And what Captain Holmes wants most of all is for his boxing squad to be champions. If they are, his promotion is more likely. Holmes never stops currying favor with Colonel Delbert in regard to the machinations of power and promotion. And he is just as manipulative on the home front. His marriage to Karen Holmes is now all for show. A chronic philanderer, Holmes transmitted syphilis to her at one time, and her subsequent hysterectomy (the removal of the uterus) ruined forever her chance to have another child.

They have one son, but the bitterness harbored by Karen is such that no matter what, she despises her husband. Yet, divorce is out of the question. For Karen, whose whole life is dependent on Captain Holmes's officer's salary and his prospects for further advancement, starting all over as a single mother with no discernible job history is out of the question. Unless she wants to start anew with nothing in hand, she is trapped.

Similarly, in the case of the Captain, a divorce on his Army record would threaten the prospect of promotions. At that time, just as presidential candidates were not considered acceptable if they had divorced (even though American history had its share of exceptions to that rule), an Army or Navy or Marine officer was expected to be married. Once. Happily married at that. Period. Case closed.

Jones obliterated such grand facades in his novel. And long before her love affair with Sgt. Milton Anthony Warden becomes a central force propelling the narrative, Karen's strength, emotional depths, and verbal pugnacity are on full display.

When Captain Holmes pleads with her to attend an officers' party that he believes requires her presence (he needs her to obsequiously flatter a senior officer), she refuses.

After Captain Holmes explains the expectations—"I saw Colonel Delbert this morning . . . He asked if we were coming to General Hendrick's party . . . We'll have to go . . . There's no way out of it. Also, his wife is having another tea, I got you out of that"—Karen snarls: "A smile, to him, is only an invitation to put his hands between your legs. He's got a wife. Why doesn't he take it out on her?"

Then Karen yields—"All right. I'll go. There I said it, now lets talk about something else." In short, to avoid wasting any more energy on their debate.

Meantime, her inner life remains a cauldron. Jones pays careful attention to the unspoken, interior monologues of Karen Holmes. While throwing away almost all the standard grammatical rules about the need for apostrophes for varied reasons, he also threw away the tendency of many male authors to avoid female perceptions.

After Karen Holmes is irked by her husband's patronizing remark that she ought to avoid fretting—"*Now, darling . . . take it easy. You'll have yourself sick in bed*"—her unspoken thoughts are elucidated:

"*Theres nothing wrong with me,*" she protested. "*I'm no bedfast invalid,*" thinking how he had no right to use that word with her, to call her darling. He *always did it, in these spells, and the word was like a skewer pinning her to the beaverboard among the other butterflies of his collection. In her imagination she saw herself rising up, telling him what she thought of him, packing a bag and leaving, to live her own life and earn her own way. She would get an apartment and a job someplace. What kind of a job? she asked herself . . . what training have you? Besides to be a wife.*

There must be more, there must be, something told her, someplace, somewhere, there must be another reason, above, beyond, somewhere another Equation beside this virgin + marriage + motherhood + grandmotherhood = honor, justification, death. There must be another language, forgotten, unheard unspoken, than the owning of an American's Homey Kitchen complete with dinette, breakfast nook, and fluorescent lighting.

* * *

The inner life of Karen Holmes is vivid. But the public life that Jones dramatized for the character named Alma (aka: Lorene) is unprecedented. She is a prostitute who does not make excuses for her choice to become one. She is a professional, in her view, who is earning the maximum amount of funds in the minimum amount of time. And she is not presented as society's victim a' la Stephen Crane's *Maggie: A Girl of the Streets*. In every way, she lives life on her terms and most of all on her timetable. Prewitt asks her: "How did you ever come to get into this racket?" Alma minces no words:

"I am a volunteer . . . Maybe you think that all whores are virgins who were kidnapped by Lucky Luciano, and raped, and then farmed out. Maybe you think . . . that all whores are inducted. Well they're not. Lots of them enlist. Some because they just like the life, and don't mind doing what they do to have to get the rest of it. Others because they are bitter against some man who took their cherry and maybe knocked them up and then left them, and now they are getting even in some funny way, or else just don't give damn, anymore."

After Alma (aka: Lorene) adds the remark that "there are lots of us who have enlisted," she then elaborates in an effort to help Prewitt understand her plan:

"Lots of them, like me, figure it all out beforehand. Get in for one hitch and clean up and then get out. Lots of them do that."

"Is that what you aim to do?"

"You don't think I mean to do this all my life? For fun? In another year I'll be back home, with a pile of bills big enough to choke a steer. And then I will be all set, for life."

"But what about home?" he asked . . . "What will the people back home say?"

"They will say nothing. Because they will know nothing. In my home town, where my mother still lives—on the money that I send her—I am a private secretary to a big, big shot in the Hawaii sugar trade. I am a hometown waitress who went to night school and developed herself and became a private secretary who is saving her money to come home and take care of her poor invalided mother.

"How can I get caught? In my little town in Oregon where I come from nobody but the very rich ever venture out as far as Seattle. When I come home wearing all my demure conservative private secretary's clothes and retire, on the modest 'nest egg' I will have, who is to doubt I am and was just what I say I am?"

Prewitt is just as startled by the social architecture of Alma's story, and her plan, which she explains without guile:

"I had a boyfriend . . . I was a waitress, working in the local chain drugstore. He was from one of the richest families in town. Old story, with no new twists. I didn't get knocked up, nothing like that. He just married the girl his parents thought was suitable for his position, after two years of sleeping with me.

"If prestige, position, money are what the good men need from their wives, why I will get them. The only way they can be got. With money.

"And after I go home with a stocking full of bills, after I build the new home for my mother and myself, after I join the Country Club and take up golf, get in the most acceptable bridge club . . . then the proper man with the proper position will find me as a proper wife who can keep a proper home and raise the proper children, and I will marry him. And I will be happy."

Alma is no less mercenary than any man. And she is especially simpatico with an enlisted man like Prewitt, who understands that his own options are limited:

What a possibility, he thought; man, man, what a possibility. But then why not? In this place, on this Rock [the island of Oahu], who else is it possible for a soldier to fall in love with, except a whore? This Rock, where the white girls, even the middle class white girls, were all little snobs and where there

were no white girls below the middle class. This Rock, where even with the
gook girls that were the lowest class it was a disgrace to be seen talking to a
soldier. So then why not a whore? It was not only possible, it was perfectly
logical. Maybe it was even sensible.

* * *

Just as "sensible" was Lowney's advice when she suggested to Jones that
he harness his energies and try to not only stick with the daily discipline
of writing, but to try his best to segment his writing hours in an effort to
quell his distracted mind.

"Mark your day off into sections," she advised while still in Florida.
Up in Illinois, Jones pondered her simple, direct agenda: "Make it
systematic," she counseled. "Time won't pass so slowly if you form a
routine. You've already learned that writing will get done that way. It's
the looking ahead that seems long. Don't do it. Look at a week at a time.
I measure [my time] by the two weeks [when] the laundry comes. It goes
by fairly fast and I get daily [writing] done. Just let the time move as
beads on a chain—let them slip through your fingers without crying
and complaint. Just be calm. Organize every day."

In turn, Jones kept Burroughs Mitchell informed of his progress and
his struggles:

"Nobody knows how much I want to get it done and out," he
informed Mitchell. "It's been so damned long I've been working on this.
Some damn fool is always asking me about 'that book' I heard you been
writing for the last three years . . . .

Nobody believes I'll ever finish it," Jones groused, as Books II, III, IV
and V of *From Here to Eternity* each became as long as a single novel.
Even Book I, which in published form is the shortest of the five "Books"
in *From Here to Eternity*, required 98 full pages in print, comparable to a
short novel.

But the other four "Books" in Jones's evolving magnum opus would
each take up hundreds of pages. Indeed, he was creating nothing less
than a detailed, comprehensively dramatized, realistically grounded
parallel universe.

"I just go on writing and writing," he told Burroughs Mitchell: "On
into eternity, a long line of typed pages stretching off like railroad tracks
coming together, right on to the Millennium, and beyond, on one book,

the same book, the forever book, the book that never has an end, only a beginning, the eternal serial."

Just when it seemed that his bemoaning tone was slipping into self-pity, Jones's self-deprecating humor arose. He reminded Mitchell that he was not *too* weary.

"I feel better now. I see I've slipped off into rhetoric, so I must be feeling better now. You know, you're a wonderful punching bag . . . you don't bounce back and slap me in the nose like so many punching bags are apt to do, both the actual and the simulated. I can beat you all day. Well, you write me." Jones hunkered down.

*   *   *

"I've done the next entire chapter—*right*," he assured Burroughs Mitchell at February's end in 1949. He was now deeply into the writing of Book IV: "The Stockade." But Mitchell knew by now what critics and readers would marvel at when the novel was published. Namely, that the immensity of *From Here to Eternity* was such that the motif indicated by each book's subtitle (e. g., "The Company" or "The Women" or "The Stockade") did not exclusively define that part of the novel. Case in point: "The Stockade" as Book IV of *From Here to Eternity* did not just delve into the unspeakably vicious routine violence inflicted on the Army prisoners in the subterranean realm of the guards and their superiors. The chapters illuminating and illustrating the dehumanizing mayhem in the grim underworld over which the sadistic officers and guards ruled were contrasted with equally hefty chapters carrying forward the mythic narrative, with all its major and minor players.

Nonetheless, Jones was up front about the challenges presented by writing "within the Stockade." He knew that Mitchell had great expectations for this section of the book and without qualms, Jones admitted: "I'm finding the Stockade part is about the roughest writing I've ever tried to do up to now."

That said a great deal. The depravities of "The Stockade" were superseding the excessive hazing of Prewitt that dominate the first half of the novel. And hazing is a wimp of a word for what Prewitt endured via The Treatment, all in an effort to break his spirit and compel him to yield to the Company's need for his skills as a boxer. The psychological pressures aside, Prew is hit with interminable hours on KP after being repeatedly tripped or otherwise physically harassed during Close Order Drill; although he marches with precision, he is called out time after time and dressed down for imaginary infractions; punishments all across the board include ditch-digging labor for no discernible purpose, exhausting ten-mile hikes up and down Kolekole Pass (under a blazing sun in headgear and uniform, with a full-field pack weighing him down and his rifle held chest-high at all times). The Treatment is a benign form of torture, but referred to at worst as "hazing" for its lack of violence.

Not so the netherworld of "The Stockade." But long before Jones guides the reader into a species of organized, hierarchical, officially sanctioned inhumanity, he takes the time to develop further the daily goings-on in the lives of his characters. Such methodical storytelling and its plethora of details about every little thing would inevitably reflect back unto the World War II generation its collective drama. Henry James's "novel of saturation" was James Jones's organic milieu.

In *From Here to Eternity*, it is Angelo Maggio who first blazes a trail to The Stockade. Having been charged with a slew of violations ranging from being drunk and disorderly to resisting arrest, compounded by insubordination and the more serious offenses of *"Disobeying a Direct Order... Striking a Non-Commissioned Officer in the Performance of His Duty ... [and] Conduct Unbecoming to a Soldier."*

Maggio is found *"guilty on all counts of all charges brought against him"* and thus sentenced *"to six months confinement at the Post Stockade, Schofield Barracks, T.H. and forfeiture of all pay and allowances for a like period.*

That's the official lingo, as reproduced by Jones in his italicized preamble to Book IV: "The Stockade."

Later, following another whole onslaught of violence and drama, Prewitt will also be sentenced to serve time in The Stockade. There he and Maggio will again be allies. Meantime, as Book IV begins, Maggio's doom has affected Prewitt, and he knows it:

Something changed in Prewitt after Angelo's one-man revolution. It was something The Treatment with all is refinements had not been able to touch. Something went out of him. The Treatment could never have taken it out of him. It was as if somewhere deep inside himself he could feel bone rubbing somberly against bone, changing gears. It sounded like a rough-edged file on stone.

Jones himself was undergoing a significant transformation as he wrote this part of the novel. Lowney and others remarked on how thin he had gotten. His exercise regimen was intact, but his dietary patterns and his chain-smoking caused him to appear wiry. Internal changes, however, were more profound and in Lowney's view the toll Jones's writing was taking on him was part of the plan: "You need have no fear," she reminded him. "Of anything." And she also reminded him of the degree to which his evolving novel was the result of prodigious efforts only *they* understood.

"Nobody but you and I will ever know what agony made the greatness of the book," she declared. "It's written out of your heart, blood and your very body tissue. No wonder [John] Dos Passos (who must have had a similar agony) could not agree within himself to go on with it—the cross was too much [to bear] and so he wrote 'Number One' and those others."

Lowney's critical insight was discerning. John Dos Passos achieved a mighty goal when completing his massive *"U.S.A."* trilogy (which consisted of three full-length novels published separately as *The 42nd Parallel*, *1919*, and *The Big Money*). Yet, his post-*"U.S.A."* work disappointed many. He had written himself out, as it were.

But John Dos Passos was well into his forties and Jones was now merely twenty-seven. It wasn't physical or mental fatigue oppressing him. It was ethics.

The easiest way out for Jones would have been to create a cadre of monstrous characters who make The Stockade into their hellish fiefdom. But that would have ensured a cheapening of his novel. He did not want one-dimensional, cardboard characters—be they good or bad. Honorable or evil. He insisted that his men and women in *From Here to Eternity* manifest the fullest range of human possibilities.

Jones eclectic reading included forays into the Greek and Roman classics. One playwright of the Roman Republic was Terence, whose statement "I am a man; nothing that is human is alien to me" served as an inspiration. That meant not merely presenting the guards as stereotypes or The Stockade as some inexplicable aberration. Instead, it's a fully functioning underworld beneath the Army's realm as a parallel universe outside of all civilian society. And it is a man-made world.

"It goes very slowly and very agonizingly," Jones alerted Burroughs Mitchell and John Hall Wheelock. And he clued them in on how ethics were now a challenge.

The problem wasn't just that Jones's imagination was taxed because "I was never actually in a Stockade per se, but only in a prison ward

in the [hospital] where they brought the boys after they beat them up."
The real problem was far more knotty.

"I don't know if I could ever explain it," he announced to his editors.
"Maybe I could give a rough idea of what I'm trying to hit on, though: All
the new books since the war are occupying themselves with the problem
of <u>Evil</u> with a capital E—like Buchenwald, etc."

Because of the photographs by Margaret Bourke-White published
in May 1945 in *LIFE* Magazine (along with the postwar publication of
several books about the notorious Nazi concentration camps, as well as
the extermination camps), Buchenwald was alluded to in many articles
and several books in the late 1940s.

As for "trying to understand it" (i. e., the emerging knowledge about
the Holocaust), Jones did not think the prevalent articles and books
succeeded. He told Mitchell: "They've all failed . . . the fallacy lies in
the concept of Evil with a capital E, and the attempt to understand it as
a thing outside oneself, not objective at all but subjective, which they
all are either unable or else ashamed-and-afraid to understand. What
I mean is, we are horrified at Buchenwald, yet every man if put in the
position of the guards and overseers would have ended in the same way
doing the same thing. Given the same place and position in History,
every man would be Hitler—or Shakespeare—or, to stretch it, Christ.
We all think we could have been a Christ or a Shakespeare, but we will
not all believe that we could have been a Hitler.

"We will not any of us believe that. So that, viewed from that angle,
there really isn't any Evil with a capital E. We just think there is and
torment ourselves with it."

The implications of this notion were enormous. Jones did not just
reveal the horrors of the programmed violence in The Stockade. He did
so in a way that ensures that the reader must grapple with the fact that
the guards, too, are also human beings. Lowney took note of this adroit
effort on Jones's part. And she reminded him that she was not alone in
her awe, when she alluded to "Mitch" (by this time Burroughs Mitchell
was regularly addressed as "Mitch") in one of her letters to Jones:

"I'll always be with you, behind you, beside you. You must work. I must
work. In that lies our chance of future happiness. Believe me, greatness
comes from understanding. As Mitch pointed out, it *is* in your book and
not in [Norman Mailer's] 'Naked and the Dead' – you care about your
characters – making the reader care – that is important – very much so."

* * *

The violence and the other patterns of dehumanization in The Stockade are so endemic that even during Prewitt's initial meeting with Major Thompson, who is The Stockade's senior officer, he is physically abused. Prewitt is told never to speak, unless answering a question. Of course, he slips. After examining Prewitt's service record, Major Thompson addresses him. Two guards are standing adjacent to Prewitt. Each guard holds a wooden hoe handle:

"I see you are from Harlan Kentucky," Major Thompson said. "We get quite a few boys from Kentucky and West Virginia here. I could almost say they are our chief stock in trade. Most of them is coal miners," he said, "but you don't look big enough to be a coal miner."

"I'm not a coal miner," Prew said. "I never was a ---"

The butt of a grub hoe handle thudded into the small of his back above the kidney on the left side and he was afraid for a second he would vomit.

"—Sir," he said quickly.

Lest anyone get the impression that the guards give Prew a mere poke, Jones adds details while omitting moralistic denunciations:

There are two kinds of grub hoe handles, curved ones and straight ones. The straight ones are longer and heavier than the curved ones. A pick handle is longer and heavier than any ax handle, and a grub hoe handle is longer than a pick handle. [This] makes the grub hoe a fine tool for clearing brushy root-matted ground.

It's also "a fine tool" for smashing the backside and pounding the kidneys of stationary prisoners who make the slightest wrong move, or say a word out of turn. And yet, the protocols are so entrenched that Prewitt is complimented by one of the guards, Hanson, after they leave Major Thompson's office:

"You done pretty fair," Hanson grinned, as they climbed in the thick-dusty back and he signaled the driver. "What was it, only four wasn't it?"

"Just four," Prew said.

"Hell, that's good," Hanson grinned. "I've seen them get as many as ten or twelve, during their first session. I've even seen a couple of them clean lost their head and had to actually be carried out finally they got so fuckedup. I think the

least I ever seen is two, and that was Jack Malloy who's a three time loser. You
really done exceptional."

    "That's good," Prew said grimly. "I was beginning to think for a minute
there I'd failed my first examination."

    "Naw," Hanson grinned. "I was real proud of you. Four is fine. You'll be
all right," Hanson grinned.

The maddening irony of this is intensified because Jones avoids any commentary on the fact that Hanson was one of the guards blithely rupturing Prew's kidneys, by violently using a grub hoe handle like a baseball bat.

*   *   *

Jack Malloy. The name comes up time after time in Book IV ("The Stockade"). And by the time the character is revealed to the reader, his paramount reputation amid The Stockade is enough to induce prodigious curiosity. The name Jack Malloy is spoken of by other prisoners with reverence. He is a legend in The Stockade for his meditative skills at defying the calculated efforts to break the human spirit. And his presence in the narrative of *From Here to Eternity* (the novel) is unforgettable.

    Jack Malloy is a mystic. Regardless of how much time he has spent in The Stockade, he is able to transcend the dietary abuses, the backbreaking hard labor, the brutal assaults, and the overwhelming atmosphere of deliberate spiritual deadening; and he can transcend such a panorama of dehumanized activity by invoking the power of his mind. Malloy is partly a Christ figure, in that he finds himself surrounded by disciples (the other prisoners) and his coping skills border on the miraculous. But he's also a repository for all the tenets and each of the lessons touted in the early 20th-century tract so beloved by Lowney Handy: James Allen's *As a Man Thinketh.*

    Another element helping Jones as he wrote "The Stockade" was his discovery of an undervalued novel that Jack London published in 1915: *The Star Rover.* In that novel, Jack London explored a medley of reincarnation themes through a death-row prisoner chained in his cell. That prisoner is the medium through which London projects astral powers of mind and the healing capacities of out-of-body journeys that allow one's soul not to be destroyed, even though one is physically locked up, deprived of all but the basics to survive, and soon to be executed by the State.

Jack Malloy is not just a symbolic character. Like all the major players in *From Here to Eternity*, he is a living, breathing, manifest presence who was written out of the film version of Jones's novel (as were two other major characters: the Jewish-American soldier Nathan Bloom, who commits suicide; and the Native-American called Chief Choate). In the novel, throughout the bulk of Book IV, the wisdom and the sage counsel of Jack Malloy buoy Robert E. Lee Prewitt, whose own endless curiosity is a match for Jack Malloy's lifelong study of comparative religions, historical movements, social trends, and spiritual mysteries. They vibrantly discuss everything from the evolution of Judaism and how it spawned Christianity, to the violent State repression inflicted upon the Industrial Workers of the World (IWW), when the so-called Wobblies were broken, in the era of the First World War. For a time, Malloy is Prewitt's mentor. In terms of invoking the idea that English poet John Keats defined as "the silent work of Imagination" to survive periods of solitary confinement, Jack Malloy is a master.

Jack Malloy is also the channel through which Jones transmits many of the Eastern spiritual precepts that he learned from Lowney. As such, even in the pit of The Stockade, there are dialogues and debates and genuine efforts to evolve beyond the limitations of one's immediate surroundings—if one chooses to do so.

Other choices lead to other fates, however. Witness Blues Berry. Nicknamed "Blues" after the American roots music identified with America's outcast poor blacks in the Mississippi Delta region (and elsewhere), Blues Berry was written out of the movie version of *From Here to Eternity*. Even though he's white. No film made in the 1950s could have dramatized Blues Berry's doom.

Prewitt is startled when a fellow prisoner ("an Indiana farmboy" named Murdock) begs someone—anyone—to deliberately break his arm, ensuring him time off from hard labor to convalesce. Finally, it's Blues Berry who does the deed. But he's seen from afar by a guard. That night, both Major Thompson and Sgt. Judson—nicknamed "Fatso" Judson by the prisoners—wreak havoc demanding that he confess. Blues Berry is savagely beaten, on Major Thompson's orders. He is tortured. All through the night, this horrific abuse goes on. It is a hellscape.

Jones sums up:

The occasional screams from the gym did not stop however, and there was not much sleep. But in the morning they were got up at 4:45 just the same.

At chow they learned that at one-thirty Blues Berry, unable to urinate and with his ears knocked half loose from his head, had been taken up to the prison ward of the Station Hospital for treatment . . .

He died the next day about noon, "from massive cerebral hemorrhage and internal injuries," the report was quoted as stating, "probably caused by a fall from a truck traveling at high speed."

*   *   *

In his memoir *The Education of an Editor*, Scribners veteran Burroughs Mitchell looked back at a career spanning over thirty years, and offered this praise: "We knew what we had in [Jones's] fourteen-hundred page [typescript]. That required no great publishing percipience. I wrote to Jones that I believed it to be a great book—the only time, I think, that I have said those words, so commonly thrown about."

The notion of "a fourteen-hundred page [typescript]" sounds hyperbolic. Or at the very least like an exaggeration. It was neither. To gauge the enormousness of Jones's work, all that's necessary is to understand is that Book IV (aka: "The Stockade") on its own consists of 16 full-length chapters. Furthermore, Book IV alone (in the published novel) runs from pages 405 to 677.

When it appeared in book form, the novel had 860 pages. By the time Jones let go of the book (and even after significant cuts were made) his narrative consisted of well over 400,000 words. *From Here to Eternity* has the heft of several novels.

All the more reason that Lowney declared: "This book will always mean so much to us—a million times more than we can estimate now— because it will be your heart and blood and your muscles, too. You're thin. I think of it a lot, how thin you are, and how much your very body is put into your work."

The physical exertions required for Jones to complete his novel were prodigious. But it was his imagination that was most galvanized. In the beginning, when he began to write *From Here to Eternity* under the aegis of Maxwell Perkins, it startled Jones to realize that contrary to his experience with his first novel, this time he had to exercise his powers of invention more. He was doing so on a vast scale.

Always, though, there were autobiographical milestones to anchor his work. He once wrote to Perkins about a grim memory he had about a fellow soldier back in 1944: "... beaten with pickhandles, his ears torn loose from his head (I saw this same thing, incidentally, when I was in the Prison Ward of the Station Hospital at Camp Campbell, [Kentucky]."

In the late 1950s, when interviewed by *The Paris Review*, Jones highlighted the convergence of his eyewitness experiences and his imagination when he was asked: "Do you draw your characters from life?" After alluding to several of his characters in different works, Jones summed up: "Sometimes ... it's an event that strikes me and then I try to imagine a character who would fit into that event. For instance, the man who was killed by Fatso Judson in the stockade, Blues Berry, I never knew him at all."

On the other hand, a great deal of Karen Holmes was derived from the sense and sensibility of Lowney Handy – and she flat-out urged Jones to take full advantage. Eventually, in the aftermath of their months of separation early in 1949, Lowney asserted: "I'm sure your work will ease up. And this last agony should really make a masterpiece out of the last of the book. *Put it all into Karen* [emphasis added] ..." To some extent, Jones did that. Lowney and Harry Handy's unorthodox marital "arrangement" was partly rooted in their early history as a couple. Lowney told Jones, and others, that prior to marriage she'd had an abortion, and, out of guilt over that, Harry agreed to marry her. Shortly thereafter, philandering Harry transmitted to Lowney a case of gonorrhea that led to her infertility. All of that was grist for Jones's mill.

But his imagination was so afire that he invariably also conveyed the essence of Lowney's esoteric spiritual and mystical beliefs, and harbored them within the consciousness of his character Jack Malloy. In a novel that would break new ground for its articulation of soldiers' profanities and also for its brazen presentation of sexual appetites considered illicit, immoral, and even illegal at the time of the book's publication, there's also a fundamentally humane, transcendental spiritual yearning.

Incarcerated in barrack Number Two of The Stockade, Prewitt converses with Jack Malloy. Their dialogues revolve arond Judeo-Christian tenets, mainstream Protestantism and Roman Catholicism, too. No matter what challenges arise, Jack Malloy preaches "Acceptance." Malloy says:

"You see what that implies? If God is Instability rather than Fixity, if God is Growth and Evolution, then there is no need for the concept of forgiveness. The mere concept of forgiveness implies the doing of something wrong, Original Sin. But if evolution is growth by trial and error, how can errors be wrong? Since they contribute to growth? Does a mother feel called upon to forgive her child for eating green apples or putting his hand on the stove? Did you ever truly love some body, or some thing? A woman; did you ever love a woman? If you ever really truly loved a thing, you never even considered forgiving it something, did you? Anything it did was all right with you, wasn't it? No matter how much it hurt you. You don't have to forgive something you love. You forgive the ones you don't love."

He came back to it again and again, later on. He couldn't stay away from it. It meant too much to him. But always it amounted to this same thing: that over the old God of Vengeance, over the new God of Forgiveness, was the still newer God of Acceptance, the God of Love-That-Surpasseth-Forgiveness . . .

* * *

On October 30, 1949, Jones mailed to Scribners the all-important Chapter 50. "Here is the piece de resistance, the tour de force, the final accolade and calumny, the climax, peak and focus. Here, in a word, is Pearl Harbor. From here on it is all down hill."

Indeed it was. After sending off his chapter-length re-creation of December 7, 1941, which still remains the greatest recapitulation in American fiction of that "date which will live in infamy," there were seven more chapters written to resolve the novel. The death of Prewitt was agonizingly dramatized in Chapter 52. And the denouement of the adulterous love affair between Karen Holmes and Sgt. Warden (who realize that though they fell deeply in love, there can be no future for them) is evoked in Chapter 54 with exquisite restraint: They do enjoy a last visit together, yet it's a platonic scene rife with honest words and tender emotions, without carnality.

The final chapters literally close the book at the end of 1941: America goes to war. Jones and Lowney had gone clear across America between the spring and fall of 1949, as the laborious completion of *From Here to Eternity* occurred. Hitching up the jeep and the 26-foot Airstream trailer that Harry had financed earlier that year (with its kitchenette, toilet, bed, and desk-and-lamp area, the trailer was a mobile home and suitable office), they traveled first to Memphis in May of '49 for a visit.

Following months of separation early in 1949, these seasons on the road were sure to be times of renewal and occasional conflict. After spending several weeks in Memphis, Lowney went back to Illinois and en route considered the possibility of checking into a big-city hospital for a battery of tests and to ask for help with health issues.

Jones wrote to her on May 29, 1949, knowing that she might visit Barnes Hospital in St. Louis, Missouri.

"I'm sorry to hear about Barnes," he let her know: "I find, looking deeper into myself, there is some obscure fear I have of having you go into a hospital, not because you will die (tho there is that fear too), but mostly because it seems to take you entirely away from me, out of my reach, into a social structure where you are, and perforce must be, Mrs. Handy. I've even imagined you falling back in love with Harry. I'm learning more and more to cover up tho, so that no one suspects how upset I may happen to be. I was hoping you'd get better, just resting, that it was only frustration here and nervous strain that was causing all of it, but I guess it's more than that. I guess I have to admit it . . . You ought to have a checkup, anyway, at the least."

Such words hint at the complexities of reconciliation, after months apart. Aside from the fact that it's possible that Lowney was in perimenopause at this time (she was now age 45), there is a distinct possibility that being in close quarters again with Jones was simply too much for her, as he finished his book in a white heat.

"There's a quality in you—a franticness—that comes through that is awfully upsetting," Lowney explained to Jones. "I'm sure it was this [type of] inner frenzy that caused the love affair of Aline [Bernstein] and [Thomas] Wolfe to break up. It's destructive. It's the thing that upsets me so that I eat too much and get sick."

Lowney opted not to visit a hospital and tended to her health by continuing her perennial regimen of vegetarian meals, regular enemas, and daily iron capsules.

She also bluntly conveyed to Jones how she needed their time together to be low-key, so their edginess would subside. "I went through agony in Venice [Florida] because of this franticness [in you] that was always around me. I need more quiet and a restful peace. The 'goat cries' of [Thomas] Wolfe is a perfect description. It's a thing that I can't handle—when I'm trying to keep peaceful and still myself. I need an inner stillness to what I do."

Back on the road, by October of '49 they had made their way out to Albuquerque, New Mexico, where they stayed for a month. It was there that Jones wrote, revised, and then polished his *"piece de resistance"* on the attack at Pearl Harbor. He made no effort to disguise his Olympian literary ambitions. Sending Chapter 50 to his Scribner allies, Jones finished off his letter with this rhetorical rodomontade:

"Well, anyway, here is Pearl [Harbor]. And I, personally, believe it will stack up with Stendhal's Waterloo [in *The Charterhouse of Parma*] or Tolstoy's Austerlitz [in *War and Peace*]. That was what I was aiming at, and wanted it to do, and I think it does it. If you don't think it does, send it back and I'll re-rewrite it. Good isn't enough, not for me, anyway; good is only middling fair. We must remember people will be reading this book a couple of hundred years after I'm dead, and that the Scribners first edition will be worth its weight in gold by then. We musn't ever forget that. If this note sounds overly enthusiastic, you must remember that I have just finished writing [Chapter 50]."

Later in November 1949, Jones wrote a thank-you note to Harry Handy that was sent from Tucson, Arizona. "We got the money of course, and it was very welcome," Jones assured Harry. On the road with no cash flow to speak of, Lowney and Jones hit bottom in Arizona, where Jones said: "I think we had about seven cents, all told. That noon, before [the money sent by Harry] came, we . . . needed a quart of milk and a loaf of bread, so we compromised and bought the bread and used canned milk in the gravy."

Oddly, given that his own obsession with his writing made sense to Jones, he exuded both jealousy and irritation with Lowney's increased passion for Yoga. It had become a transformative force in her life, about which she insisted to him: "Yoga has never taken me away from you. Without Yoga I'd have hated you long ago and you'd not have a chance today anymore than Jack or Harry will ever have another chance to sleep with me again. Not that either would want it—but that's the way it is. Instead of being standoffish and resentful of Yoga, you should be more than grateful. Try to grow calm, to subdue the wild franticness of your thinking."

From Tucson, Arizona, they drove straight out to California, where Jones, at age twenty-eight, finished writing his new novel in a trailer park outside of North Hollywood, California, on February 27, 1950. He did so alone. Lowney stayed at a motel in Hollywood. On the same day, from the Valley Trailer Park in North Hollywood, California, four years and two weeks after inducing Maxwell Perkins' interest with his suggestion of "a novel on the peacetime army," Jones typed a letter to Burroughs Mitchell, announcing the book was done. "I really feel very peculiar," he wrote. "Not elated. Not depressed. But peculiar. Maybe humble."

Despite their separate lodgings, Lowney's mystical belief in astral dreaming impelled her to write to Jones: "Try to meet me in your sleep." And she reminded him: "I'll love you to eternity and through all there are of them, just as I have loved you through many, many more before this time."

One year later, *From Here to Eternity* was the world's most famous new book.

10
JONES, LOWNEY, AND THEIR COLONY

You'll have to help me with every other book I write, too. I will need
you with me to begin something else. It just looks like I'm always going
to need you, and there's no way we can get out of it . . .
~ James Jones (in a 1949 letter to Lowney Handy)

One month after he finished writing his novel, Jones was still living alone
at the trailer park in North Hollywood. On March 18, 1950, he noted that
"Lowney has gone home now, due to a lack of funds," when he wrote to
Burroughs Mitchell "to ask a favor of you." Symbolically and otherwise,
Max Perkins was on the agenda.

Scribners was about to publish a book-length collection of Perkins'
correspondence with dozens of writers (the famous and the unknown).
Edited and with an Introduction by John Hall Wheelock, an advance
copy of the first edition had been sent to Jones by Wheelock. It was
Jones's request that Mitchell try to do the same for Lowney. In *Editor to*
Author: The Letters of Maxwell E. Perkins, three of the letters that Perkins
sent to Jones were reprinted toward the end of the collection. While
Lowney was still out in California, and Jones received his copy, he saw
that "she was as thrilled over it as I was. And I would like for her to have
a copy. If you could have Mr. Wheelock fix it up, just like he did the
one to me, with the card and the publication date written on, and then
address it to her at the Robinson address, and send it soon, before it
hits the stands, I know she would be very happy to have it. And I would
appreciate it greatly."

Jones did not shy away from admitting that for him there was "the
additional thrill of seeing my name in a <u>book</u> for the first time. It is not
the same as seeing it in a magazine, which is mentally and intellectually

a passing thing and physically is flimsy and destructible. There is such a sense of *perm*anence about an actual book."

Out in New York City, poet-editor John Hall Wheelock had been singing the same types of praises about the value of Jones's book. As everyone began preparing for the laborious business of line-editing *From Here to Eternity* and considering all the attendant issues of its profanity, its sexuality, its violence, and varied taboo topics (adultery, homosexuality, prostitution and binge-drinking and more), John Hall Wheelock could not restrain himself. Even before Jones mailed the final two chapters to Scribners, Wheelock drafted a letter that communicated his awe:

"I have just finished my reading of your novel, *From Here to Eternity*. And I can't resist telling you how deeply moved, and excited, I have been by this splendid, often beautiful, often terrible, book. It is an achievement of the first order and one that I believe will be so recognized. I know of no novel in which the comradeship of men has been so convincingly portrayed—a masculine book, sometimes harsh but always charged with a tremendous compassion."

There was still a long way to go, however. It would take months for Jones and Burroughs Mitchell and John Hall Wheelock and the lawyers at Scribners as well as Charles Scribner himself to finally concur on all the editorial conflicts at issue. Even before they began the process of assessing each page and considering any cuts, Jones cast himself in the role of the writer-as-fighter, with apt boxing analogies.

"To be frank," he told Mitchell, "I feel a little like the fighter who has climbed into the ring and is shuffling his feet in the resin, and hears the stir that means his opponent is coming down the opposite aisle, but does not turn around and just goes on scuffing his feet in the resin in the great deep silence."

Jones's "opponent" was neither Mitchell nor Scribners. It was the Zeitgeist. The mores of mid-century America. On television and even in films, married couples slept separately in single beds. Clark Gable's line--"I don't give a damn"—at the end of *Gone with the Wind* in 1939 was still the rarest of exceptions when it came to a curse word in major media. As recently as 1948, the GIs in Norman Mailer's debut novel were on the pages of *The Naked and the Dead* saying "fug" this and "fug" that and "fuggin' " whatnot, because a major publisher would not sanction the repeated use of "fuck" or "fucking" in print. Jones intended to break those barriers down.

With courtesy, tact, and great prescience, he put Burroughs Mitchell on notice:

"One of the things I would like you to remember is that the things we change in this book for propriety's sake will, in five years, or ten years, come in somebody else's book anyway, that may not be as good as this one, and then we will kick ourselves for not having done it, and we will not have been first with this . . . and we will wonder why we thought we couldn't do it. Writing has to keep evolving into deeper honesty, like everything else, and you cannot stand on past precedent or theory, and still evolve. You remember that," Jones advised Mitchell. He was firm about this.

"You know there is nothing salacious in this book as well as I do. Therefore," Jones declared, "whatever changes you want made along that line will be made for propriety, and propriety is a very inconstant thing." The rebel in Jones was afoot.

* * *

Burroughs Mitchell had a streamlined method in mind when it came to the editing of *From Here to Eternity*. He began mailing sections of the novel back to Jones. Only now the typescript from which Mitchell read showed the editor's penciled-in "cuts."

"[My] proposed cuts [were] marked with a penciled parenthesis at beginning and end," Mitchell later explained. "If one could leap over the marked passage without any difficulty or loss, I argued to Jim, then the passage needn't be there."

Yet, it was never as simple as that sounded in Mitchell's memoir. Right off the bat, at the end of March 1950, only one month after the novel's completion, Jones began to swing with both fists regarding sex, profanity, and other possible censorship issues.

"There are some [cuts] that I agree with entirely," he admitted to Mitchell, "others I agree with partly; some I do not agree with at all." That was Jones's diplomatic peak.

"Now as to the sex cuts," he informed Mitchell: "I agree with you in principle."

Jones yielded to Mitchell's notion that they had to remain cognizant of how the book might very well be banned if certain words, phrases and segments were not omitted. For the sake of sales and to avoid an obscenity trial, he was willing to try to be flexible. But the last thing Jones wanted was a text gutted by "propriety."

Instead, he preferred that "accustoming the reader gradually" be their strategy.

The word "fuck" was an issue from the get-go. Mitchell had suggested dropping its usage in the first chapter. Jones countered: "It is the only use of 'The Word' in that chapter, and it is not used at all in the second. I actually think the leaving of that one in, there, and then going on for quite [a while] before using it again will have a tendency to help prepare the reader."

But every variant of the word "fuck" was as nothing compared to using the word "cunt." Mitchell wanted it excised from Chapter 9, and Jones made a powerful case for how the word was not being deployed to stun the reader, but to dramatize one character's state of shock upon hearing it said by Sgt. Warden.

"The thing is," Jones argued to Mitchell, "to have used any other word there, such as 'snatch' or 'pussy,' or some other slang word for it would be to take away all the psychological shock that I want to show in the clerk Mazzioli. The paragraph after Warden says it . . . starts: 'Mazzioli was deeply shocked.' I have put a comma after 'deeply' and added the word 'profoundly.'

"I want that word to be left in there, Mitch. I am willing to sacrifice the use of it in Chapter 11 (though I definitely don't want to, unless I must), but in Chapter 9 it is necessary to the effect of the scene and the depicting of both their characters."

Jones buttressed his argument with a specific example. "As to the word itself, I have seen it published—in America. The word [cunt] is used once in Faulkner's *Wild Palms*, in one of those italicized stream-of-consciousness parts. If it can be published there, and that book circulates over most of the country, surely it can be printed in *Eternity*."

As for Chapter 11, it was a masturbation scene with Prewitt that raised red flags and inspired Mitchell's pencil-marks. Jones vigorously defended that scene's integrity.

"The positive mention of that . . . is necessary. You see, Prew is a proud man. He would not do it unless forced so completely to the point that there was absolutely no escape . . . on account of the loneliness and frustration . . . on account of the fact that guys are *forced* to masturbate in the Army. Have you done any reading in Kinsey's book? That is the point of the scene; not simple frustration and loneliness and that."

Jones's allusion to Dr. Alfred Kinsey's 1948 surprise bestseller, *Sexuality and the Human Male*, was savvy. In that academic compendium of research conclusions and statistics derived from hundreds of contemporary personal interviews, the universal practice of masturbation was written up as a fundamental fact of life. In Jones's *From Here to Eternity*, lack of access to women (most of the time) was dramatized as a form of torment for most of the enlisted men, often inspiring fierce masturbation, wet dreams or periodic encounters with the "queers downtown."

Ultimately, it was his novel's authenticity that concerned Jones. Already the combined forces of Hollywood and the major magazine editors had patented what he knew to be a sanitized, unrealistic, holier-than-thou, choirboy image of GIs in World War II. Even amid the need to kill or be killed, they spoke like Boy Scouts.

Jones deftly reminded Mitchell that their very different wartime backgrounds might be contributing to the problem. "I don't know if I can make you understand," Jones admitted. "You think I put those things in arbitrarily, just for simple shock value. But it isn't that. You see, you were an officer. Officers are inclined to be a little more polite about such things."

The whole society was "inclined to be a little more polite about such things." No one had ever suggested that the famous WW II "pin-up" photos of actresses Betty Grable and Rita Hayworth were obscene. Nor were they dubbed pornographic. Or smutty.

But that didn't make it advisable (from a publisher's point of view) to explicitly, repeatedly present in prose fiction the actual way that the soldiers talked about such pictures. Yet the glossary of profanity replicated by Jones was prodigious.

Nonetheless, he continued to make the case that his novel's realism demanded it.

"For instance," Jones exclaimed, "the word 'cunt-pictures' in Chapter 11. That word is as much a common term in the Army as 'latrine' or 'chow down' instead of 'eat' . . . to be crude . . . [it's] 'cunt' that us men of the lower classes, especially in the Army, are interested in. It isn't love; the love only comes later, if at all. In fact, in a great many cases it only comes grudgingly and with great reluctance on the part of the male. But that term ['cunt-pictures'], and not the term 'pin-ups,' was the term used in the Army. The use of it implies a whole host of things that are absent when it is left out."

It was just as important to Jones that there remain in his novel a vivid illustration of something else that Dr. Kinsey's tome reported on with statistical evidence. Namely, the ubiquity of wet dreams. But in Kinsey's book-length research report (a stunning bestseller throughout 1948 and into the early 1950s), everything was anonymously described in the dry, heavily footnoted prose of a medical professional. Until Jones.

"Then also, in Chapter 11," he chided Mitchell, "you cut out the little thing about Red having a wet dream. I want that to stay in. I saw that, with my own eyes—with very little variation—I saw it a great many times. If it is illegal as written, then maybe I can cut it inside, a word or two here and there, to make it a little more palatable, but I want it in. Christ, Mitch, the people of this country don't know what the hell goes on in it. Maybe that's why they're such sanctimonious bastards. But if [James] Joyce can have Molly Bloom [in *Ulysses*] remember how she tossed him off into a handkerchief, then I can have that about Red's wet dream."

Except that "Red's wet dream," as Jones duly noted, might be "illegal as written." On most of the language questions, "propriety" remained the snag. And Jones remained vigilant regarding those subtleties. "You have cut absolutely every place where the phrase 'piece of ass' is used," he sharply observed: "Yet I have read plenty of times the phrase 'piece of tail' in other writers."

Months of this editorial jousting ensued. All along the way, Jones and Mitchell kept their strong sense of commitment both to the book and to each other. A united front was necessary once Scribners lawyers entered the fray. The attorneys raised many concerns and pointed out a whole new set of problems in terms of censorship.

Before the lawyers were part of the debate, though, Jones pinpointed his chief concern to Burroughs Mitchell. Regarding the many "cuts" proposed by Mitchell, Jones summed up: "You see, if you take it all out like that, the whole things is going to sound like a historical novel of the [*Forever*] *Amber* ilk, which cunningly hints at everything but never has the guts to say anything. You understand me."

Mitchell understood very well. "We did a certain amount of trimming of the manuscript and clarifying here and there," he explained decades later to former *Harper's Magazine* editor-in-chief Willie Morris, who became Jones's closest friend in the final years of Jones's life. "But the big job didn't come until the lawyers had read the galleys. Remember, at that time Mailer had found it necessary to use the word *fug* in *The Naked and the Dead.*"

In 1948, the same year that *The Naked and the Dead* was published, Gore Vidal's third novel appeared. Titled *The City and the Pillar*, it was eviscerated by critics for its presentation of a same-sex love affair between two men. In Vidal's case, the so-called "f-word" was not the problem. *The City and the Pillar* did not have a text even remotely profane. It was the story itself that made critics apoplectic.

Similarly, in 1949, when John Horne Burns (whose first novel, *The Gallery*, was a huge success two years earlier) published *Lucifer with a Book*, his second novel, the critics snuffed him. Burns wrote a satirical, febrile narrative about a New England prep school in which homoerotic overtones were anything but subtle. And then of course there were his characters' all-too-human foibles, many of which revolved around the author's sympathetic presentation of gay and lesbian allusions. To broach such topics in a novel filled with teachers and adolescents doomed Burns. He was dismembered by the critical establishment, and exiled himself to Italy.

Now came *From Here to Eternity* with its 800-plus pages of viscerally evoked adult drama written in the tradition of Theodore Dreiser's "saturation" novels, and replete with expressions and exclamations ranging from "Godammit!" to "suck the Captain's ass." And then there was the novel's adultery, whoring, boozing, brawling, the Stockade's brutalities, gay cruising, grim hazing, masturbation, and more.

None of this intimidated Jones. When Scribners lawyers called for a meeting, he was ready. And set. So was Burroughs Mitchell.

*   *   *

Meantime, later in the spring and during the summer of 1950, a new and highly industrious aspect of the vision shared by Jones and Lowney vividly took shape.

For years they had imagined the possibilities. What they envisioned was remote enclave for serious writers that was in no way affiliated with anything academic. In the immediate postwar years (1945-1950), the number of graduate-level creative writing programs increased at colleges and universities all across America. Writing degrees of were soon available at every level of the academic enterprise. Most prominent was the Master of Fine Arts, which morphed over decades into a cottage industry and MFA-networking phenomenon for thousands of literary aspirants in the second half of the twentieth century. The loquacious, workshop-oriented MFA programs were the opposite of what Jones and Lowney envisioned at The Colony.

Their goal was to create an isolated, self-sustaining community of serious writers who were willing to live, work, and interact with all the others according to the rules and regulations laid down by Lowney. Her conviction was such that she believed in no uncertain terms that anyone could be transformed into a powerful, unique, true author. On one condition: They all had to adhere to Lowney's Spartan agenda.

And that meant rising at 5:30 and practicing silence in the company of the other writers (unlike the verbose critical commentaries in MFA workshops). They drank Instant Coffee and had a silent breakfast of raisin toast and juice. Then the "copying" from Lowney's list of approved authors dominated the morning, before they worked on their own material. Eating meals that she often prepped, they cut themselves off from the outside world at large. No TV, no radios, no newspapers, no magazines. And no girlfriends nearby cluttered the lives of Colony members. Real attention, full concentration, all focus and energy were devoted to cultivating a monastic discipline and a committed vocation as a writer. As Lowney would say to skeptics crossing her path: If she could help Jones, she could help *any*one. Periodically, Lowney dispensed cash for colonists to binge-visit Terre Haute's red-light bars and cheap brothels.

At this time, before more money was advanced to Jones by Scribners (they would always be exceedingly conservative with financial disbursements), and before any royalties had been earned or any film rights sold, there was no cash flow in Jones's life. Expectations were high that *From Here to Eternity* might possibly enjoy a wide readership, but in the meantime it was Harry Handy (again) funding things.

Once Jones's novel earned big money and especially after the film rights brought him a windfall, then *he* began years of financing all that The Colony required. Now, though, throughout 1950's spring and summer, he offered his labor and his great enthusiasm. Lowney and Jones had relocated by this time to Marshall, Illinois, twenty-eight miles north of Robinson. It was there, on five square miles of cow pasture owned by Harry Handy's mother, that construction began on what Jones, Lowney, and Harry would incorporate as The Handy Writers' Colony in September 1951. Jones lived in his trailer; and Lowney commuted between Robinson and Marshall. Harry conscripted local contractors for varied, specific projects; and also brought in, as needed, hired hands from the Ohio Oil Refinery where he remained Superintendent. Thus a vision began coming to life. A collective vision.

Before inaugurating any writing regimens for future students, an infrastructure was required. Lowney's vision involved building a barracks-type dorm and small cabins for single-minded writers (so small that only a cot, desk, and chair could fit inside), plus the *ramada* with its full kitchen, screened-in porch, a few bookshelves, and a large table for community meals. Jones explained this to Burroughs Mitchell, while Scribners lawyers examined all of *From Here to Eternity*. Wrote Jones:

"The 'Marshall Plan' is coming along pretty well. We've about reached the place of having enough necessities done now that we can relax somewhat and stop working on it mornings, just afternoons now, because what remains to be done will be a long time in the doing anyway. Water and sewer lines are in now, and the electricity, and we've got enough old brick laid into patios for the two trailers . . . the drainage still isn't right, but that's the next big job.

"Well, to get water and lights . . . we had to dig a 2 ½ ft. ditch from an outside faucet over at [Mrs. Handy's] house clear down one hill across the half-swamp in the bottom and up the other hill. I did that part, me and Bob Smith, a boy who quit school at the U. of New Mexico to come up here, after meeting us out there last fall. The wiring, which required the setting of poles and other professional stuff—such as having to run our line under the power line which runs down through the bottom, and then over a phone line which goes across the hill on this side, both specified requirements of the electrical code—the wiring was done by some of Harry's boys from the plant."

Harry Handy continued to live at 202 West Mulberry Street in Robinson. Jones, however, now preferred to stay in his trailer in Marshall. And Lowney's life was evenly divided between Robinson and Marshall. A private cabin was being built for her on the Colony grounds, as Jones explained to Mitchell, outlining in detail his support and enthusiasm: "The cabin itself, which is being refinished entirely in plywood inside, won't be done for quite a while yet. The cabin is Lowney's, hence she is still down at Robinson and drives up three or four times a week to see how things are going . . . I'm in my trailer, and the other trailer belongs to Alma Isley Akers and twin daughters June and Jane (aged 12), who are from Oklahoma City, and whom we all met in Colorado Springs last year. It was Mrs. Akers whom I wrote Jack Wheelock about several months ago ... Well, the typewriters are really going mornings, as you can imagine. We've even got the twins working, copying fairy tales. Alma is copying Hemingway, and Bob [Smith] a mixture of Hindu Yoga and Hammett and Raymond Chandler. You would be amazed what this copying system, which I wrote you about a long time ago, does for them. And the twins—god, man! If I had only had somebody to get on my tail and put me to work when I was twelve! It makes me sick to think about it, what I've missed. And they are [all] quite serious about becoming writers, too. The copying, of course, is interspersed with periods of working on their own stuff—except the twins. The whole thing is Lowney's invention, and it is to her whom the entire credit belongs."

Much credit also belonged to Jones, who was formidable in his effort to help Lowney realize her dream. The Colony marked the beginning of Jones's lifelong willingness to offer generous support—financial and emotional—to struggling young writers. He was particularly excited about the cross-section of individuals who were already likely to head for The Colony: "Don Sackrider is expecting to get out of the Army any time now, and come up. And a boy named Dan Towns from Ft. Worth .. . And then there is Warren Pearsley of Rapid City, S. D., one of the most erudite individuals with whom I have ever corresponded; he is expecting to pull in some time this summer for a month or two." The vast majority of the Colony members would always be male. Yet, she did allow for a few exceptions in addition to Alma Isley Akers. In the early 1950s, Mary Ann Newlin Crank was at The Colony, as was Jones's only sister, Mary Ann.

Born in 1925, Mary Ann (Jones's younger sister) was traumatized early on. In 1942, not long after their mother's death, when Dr. Ramon Jones committed suicide by gunshot as he sat in the dental chair of his clinic, it was Mary Ann (age 17) who discovered his lifeless corpse after school that day. In subsequent years, she lived with older brother Jeff and his family; then other relatives and friends; she also had a brief, abusive marriage. When Mary Ann moved to the Colony at the end of 1951, she was at work on a novel titled *The Third Time You Killed Me*. From the get-go, Mary Ann's talent was strongly encouraged by Lowney Handy. In a letter from Lowney to Mary Ann dated September 3, 1951, "copying" is highlighted:

"Here's something I've discovered. Hemingway is usually thin for copying. Beyond getting the knack of doing dialogue, he [doesn't] offer much. But if you want perception, depth . . . for thinking and developing richness in your book . . . then I suggest you slowly and carefully and THOUGHTFULLY copy [parts of] Fitzgerald's *Tender is the Night*. It's in the Portable . . . you should buy yourself a set [of the Viking Press Portable series] – HEMINGWAY, WOLFE, STEINBECK, FITZGERALD, FAULKNER – Copy [Of] *Mice and Men* from Steinbeck and some from Faulkner – "The Bear" – [it's] a good story. That should give you plenty for a while. I am positive you are really going to break them down next Spring. I'm betting on you with all I've got. We've got to get some women writers to press."

When Jones alluded to Don Sackrider, he spotlighted another local about whom Lowney had high hopes. Sackrider's mother was acquainted with Lowney, and Don received encouragement through Lowney's correspondence while he was in the military. As always, Lowney stressed her fundamental beliefs. In one 1950 letter to Don, she concluded: " . . . Try getting little short skits down in your notebook – no matter if they are only a line or two or a paragraph or a page or an incident. I had [Jones] do this for years before you came along. He's got marvelous notes tucked away." Her advice echoed Maxwell Perkins' index-card method of idea storage.

She corresponded with handpicked, striving writers, to whom she was willing to give her time, share her ideas, and whose efforts she strongly encouraged. African-American writer Charles Wright, whose three novels were republished in a one-volume omnibus by Harper Perennial in 2019, had real kinship with Lowney; he came and went at The Colony for a number of years. Wright eventually migrated to New York, making Greenwich Village his home. In a 2008 PBS documentary by Dawn Sinclair Shapiro, *Inside the Handy Writers' Colony*, there's interview footage of Wright toward the end of his life, recalling Lowney with passion: "Oh, you'll never meet no one else like her—even if you're lucky!"

Strongly endorsed by James Baldwin, who dubbed it "a happening" as well as a vital book, the debut novel of Charles Wright (*The Messenger*) appeared in 1963. Three years later, *The Wig* followed, and early in the 1970s, a third novel by Wright caused a stir. His innovative hybrid blend of autobiography and experimental fiction has been celebrated by esteemed author Ishmael Reed and a new generation of literary critics and scholars. It is to Lowney's credit (along with Jones) that in the ghastly era of Emmett Till's lynching, amid the atrociously racist status quo of America in the 1950s, Charles Wright found a place to come to and a haven in which to write at The Colony.

Eventually, nearly one dozen Colony writers placed books with distinguished New York publishers. One of the best of those writers was Tom T. Chamales, a Chicago-born Greek-American three years younger than Jones. A standout issue in Chamales' background is that he survived the oft-ignored China-India-Burma theater of World War II. But he wrote about more than the war.

His two novels (1957's *Never So Few* and 1959's *Go Naked in the World*) are laced with spiritual yearning, psychological complexities, and meticulous details about various milieus. He first moved to The Colony in summer 1954. Unlike Jones, who described his own writing process as one of "slowly, and painfully" composing, Chamales had the rare Stephen Crane-like ability to burst forth with pages that were almost already finished.

On July 13, 1954, in a letter to Scribners editor Burroughs Mitchell, the innate gifts of Chamales were spotlighted: "We have a new guy here," Jones reported to Mitchell, "who is writing like a house afire. His name is Tom Chamales and he has led a fabulous life . . . at nineteen [he] commanded the largest guerrilla force in the Far East. He has been here less than a month and has already done over three hundred pages on a novel of the Far East [*Never So Few*], all of which is excellent writing . . . only a very small portion will need any structural changes."

It's no surprise that Chamales and Jones bonded over books, writing, booze, athletics, wartime experiences, and the ineffable mysteries of women. They were bound to be allies. And Lowney? More than any other Colony member, Tom T. Chamales intuitively, emotionally, and psychologically yielded to Lowney Handy's personal interest in the literature of Hinduism and Buddhism, meditation, and other forms of spiritual discipline. Like Jones, however, Chamales waged a war within, aspiring to his Higher Self impulses (reading, meditating, writing diligently) and often losing to his Lower Self (binge drinking and violent outbursts). But neither Jones nor Lowney Handy misjudged matters when it came to the writing gifts possessed by Chamales. He was a born novelist, a shooting star, and doomed.

*   *   *

"It's really an amazing thing," Jones exulted on June 28, 1950, when writing to Burroughs Mitchell about the evolving Colony, "And of course, behind it all, is the guiding-light, whip-cracker, and guardian-angel which is Lowney. Keen Rafferty, head of the Journalism School at the U. of New Mexico, who has been in town for a short stay and has been up a few times and who will probably be here himself for a while next summer, and is almost wildly enthusiastic about the whole thing (Bob Smith was more or less one of his protégés), said last night that he thought Lowney has the most intelligent, and demanding, and yet most feeling eyes he has ever seen in a human being. I guess that would describe them. *Anyway, I know I never would have written neither what nor as much as I have, had she not stood over me with a club, like the mother standing over the future concert-master as he sits at the piano with one eye on the clock.*" [emphasis added]

*   *   *

In September 1950 Jones returned to New York City for a series of three critical meetings with Burroughs Mitchell and Scribners lawyers. Plenty was on everyone's agenda. A number of literary agents were introduced to Jones, because the editors at Scribners thought that he might want a Manhattan-based representative handling his business affairs. Now it was clear to Jones—"they treated me royally, while I was there" he told his brother Jeff—that he was a rising star at Scribners.

"I met everyone in the editorial staff, all of whom are fine people," he wrote in a letter to his brother Jeff, "and [even] old Mr. Scribner, the one they call CS. 'Young Charlie,' his son, has been called back into the Navy. Several times Mr. Scribner stopped me to ask if I had enough money, that they wanted me to enjoy myself while I was there, as well as work. And if I didn't I was to ask for more. I was bucking for this [additional] $2000 advance, which I've later got, so I did not ask for too much."

Jones's allusion to "Young Charlie" being "called back into the Navy" shone a light on the rapid escalation of the grim Korean War. Back in June 1950, after Communist North Korea invaded South Korea and nearly vanquished it, President Harry S. Truman committed America's military forces (in league with the United Nations) to the defense of South Korea. Overnight, the United States was again at war. Only this time, it was in a remote corner of northeast Asia that many Americans could not find on a map. The nation was bewildered at being mobilized for war again, only five years after the end of WWII. Perhaps the most shocked were the veterans who kept their commissions or who'd opted to stay in the reserves. They were called up in staggering numbers, and often had their newly-married-with-kids-and-jobs postwar lives disrupted. The Korean War dragged on for three disconcerting years.

Jones's conflict was now with Scribners attorneys. He was briefed on the crucial elements by Burroughs Mitchell, who recalled that the "painful, taxing job, almost submerging us in matters of propriety, came with the galley proof, after the lawyers had read it." In publishing parlance, the "galley proof" is the next-to-last copy of the pages that will go to print, once final corrections or changes have been made.

"The issue was obscenity," Mitchell recounted, "the fucks and shits and explicit details that could endanger a book in those dim, faraway days when Norman Mailer spelled the word 'fug.' We did not misspell it, but we were instructed to ration it."

The instructions came from two of Scribners's lawyers named Horace Manges and Jack Raskin. Their consensus was that eliminating a large quota of profane words and ostensibly vulgar expressions would, at the very least, minimize the ability of anyone to bring a suit against the publisher in regard to obscene or lewd material.

"Mitch and I had three sessions with the lawyer, Manges, who [was] a sharp boy," Jones recalled, "and went over the 50-odd galleys he had pulled from the whole that he felt would cause trouble . . . the love scene between Prew and Lorene [aka: Alma], well a large part of that had to be cut . . . And there were five or six other places . . . One thing we had to cut was all mention of 'one-way, two-way, and three-way girls'."

It is mind-boggling to ponder that Jones thought he might retain *any* passage about "one-way, two-way and three-way girls" (meaning vaginal intercourse only; or vaginal and oral sex; or oral, vaginal, and anal allowed) when the word "sex" could not be said on TV or in films. Then there were Jones's gay-friendly passages.

"The scene with the queer Hal," Jones remembered, "the part [with] his pornographic picture sitting on the desk had to be cut out completely—just the picture, not the scene. All in all I think we patched it up pretty good . . . I think they were all quite pleased with my reaction; I think they were scared I would blow up and go temperamental, but I didn't."

Instead, as Mitchell noticed, "he began to treat the dreary job as a game, and I believe that he even got a certain amount of fun out of it." That rings true. All his life as an adult, Jones loved games involving concentrated, strategic thinking. Chess, in particular, absorbed him a great deal. Poker galvanized him, as did other card games. He also loved darts. "He began to treat the job as a puzzle," Mitchell once remarked, "and was delighted with himself when he found solutions."

Jones evinced some of that delight when recalling this: "[In] some places I was even able to twist the cutting to my advantage and give a whole new twist to particular scenes." Oftentimes, though, there was tension. Mitchell finally described it as "an especially difficult task because Jim's ear was so exact that to change a word in dialogue would throw the line out of kilter. Jim went at it doggedly, getting to his feet from time to time to pace around in torment. He never took the easy way out."

He also never lost his sense of humor. According to Jones, attorney Horace Manges "had a 'score sheet' [that] he kept while reading, and there were 259 fucks, 92 shits, and 5 pricks. He did not count the pisses for some reason. Well, Mitch and I . . . cut the fucks [to] 146, the shits to 45. This was all subject to Manges' approval, and after I left [Manhattan] he agreed to everything but [specific] words, and Mitch and he cut the fucks down again to around 106 and some shits; Mitch says he does not know how many, he is tired of counting small words. I can sympathize."

Back home in Illinois, as early autumn arrived, the process finally ended after Jones and Lowney and Harry and two friends had one last crack at the galleys.

Helen Howe was newly married in 1950 to Jones's childhood schoolmate Sylvanus "Tinks" Howe. "Tinks" was friendly with Lowney and had once dreamed of being a writer. In an interview for a 1984 PBS documentary entitled *James Jones: From Reveille to Taps*, Helen Howe laughingly told of how "Lowney called us one evening and said [some] galleys had come from 'From Here to Eternity' and they only had a few days to get them proofed and back . . . [she] asked us if we would come in and proofread galleys . . . [Jones] had to remove a certain number of four-letter words . . . And we worked until about three o'clock in the morning. [There was] a case of beer, Lowney cooked hamburgers about midnight . . . And we got them done. Every time we came to one of Jim's fantastic four-letter words, we'd say: 'The sentence says so-and-so. Can we take that one out?' [And Jones often replied] 'Hell, no!'"

With an air of professional resignation, all this came to be seen by Jones "as a practical problem, not an artistic one which, if it were, I should balk on . . . [but] if you are going to print a book and sell it you have to get it under the wire as legal."

In the end, Burroughs Mitchell gratefully noted, "[despite] some cries of shock and outrage, only one threat of censorship arose, in the Post Office Department, and that did not develop into an action against the book."

Jones was grateful, most of all, to Charles Scribner. Even after all the edits and the rewrites and the elisions by the score, the lawyers' quota was not acceded to. So, as autumn progressed, Burroughs Mitchell simply went to Mr. Scribner's office to aver that they had done their best. Further cuts would hurt the book. Mitchell vouched for Jones's good faith, and Charles Scribner signed off. The novel was now ready.

And so was the most astounding kind of pre-publication boost. The word getting around was so vibrant regarding Scribners's new writer and *From Here to Eternity* that on December 16, 1950, Jones's picture adorned the cover of *Publishers Weekly*.

It was brilliant publicity. Looking like a younger James Cagney and radiating the confidence of a middleweight contender, Jones's photo on the cover of *Publishers Weekly* broke the rules. A new suit? No. A silk tie? No. A dress shirt? Not a chance. Jones sported a French nautical T-shirt, his famously chiseled jaw on full display.

"Was there ever such a face," fellow novelist William Styron later wrote, "with its Beethovenesque brow and lantern jaw and stepped-upon-looking nose—a forbidding face until one realized that it only *seemed* to glower, since the eyes really projected a skeptical humor that softened the initial impression of rage."

Scribners placed a big ad in that issue of *Publishers Weekly*. The novel appeared on February 26, 1951, more than two months later. Whetting the public's appetite worked. The book had buzz. And the large ad bought by Scribners was akin to the tribute the esteemed publishers paid to Jones, on the inside cover of his new book:

"The publishers believe that the appearance of this novel is of comparable importance to the publication of *This Side of Paradise* or *Look Homeward, Angel*. For like the first novels of Fitzgerald and Wolfe, *From Here to Eternity* introduces a writer who will take a commanding place in American literature."

* * *

Six years earlier, James Jones had been an insolvent ex-GI who'd barely escaped an Army court-martial and who had the courage (because a woman named Lowney Handy believed in him) to appear, uninvited, at Scribners's offices, quietly in search of Maxwell E. Perkins. Six years later, in 1951, his debut novel made him famous overnight; an American Phoenix.

Influential literary critic and cultural historian Malcolm Cowley, in 1954, singled out Jones in *The Literary Situation:* "There are a few individualists among the new authors: notably there is James Jones, who is the only one to write about the Army as an institution and a permanent way of life."

And yet, life would have been quite different for James Jones if not for his fateful meeting and perennial kinship with Lowney Handy. "[Others] may have great will power and strength of character, I do not, and I need somebody to look after me and keep me from killing myself drinking and fucking, somebody who has common sense, like Lowney," Jones once explained in a letter to writer Norman Mailer.

Author John Bowers, in his 1971 memoir *The Colony*, recounts listening and observing as Lowney and Jones recapitulated their odyssey. Wrote Bowers: "Jones is leaning back against a kitchen counter . . . sipping from a hot mug of Instant Maxwell House. Lowney putters around in a loose peasant skirt and blouse without a bra, nibbling at food and directing that utensils should be carefully washed to prevent diarrhea – or 'the shits' as she puts it. . . . 'But if I hadn't come between him and this sweet-talking woman from St. Louis, he'd be married now, like a truck driver, with twelve kids. You know what she had [this] stupid bastard believing? That she was a virgin. She used to tell him, 'Ohhh, isn't it nice, Jamie, being alone by the fire like this, just the two of us? That's all I ever want in the world, just the two of us together like this." [Jones] didn't know a goddam thing'."

Bowers also recorded Jones's reply: "Awwww, shit."

*   *   *

More formally, in the Acknowledgment that Jones placed on the final page of the first edition of *From Here to Eternity*, he paid tribute to the memory of Maxwell Perkins, and sang the praises of Burroughs Mitchell and John Hall Wheelock. Most of all, he highlighted "Mr. & Mrs. Harry Handy of Robinson, Illinois, without whose initial impetus I would never have started out to be a writer at all, and whose material and spiritual expenses over a period of seven years provided me with necessary nourishment."

11
"THE MOST FAMOUS BOOK IN THE WORLD"

I don't think you have any conception of how completely Lowney works with these writers here [at The Colony]. And she does all this without ever impinging on what the writer himself wants to say. I know of only one editor who was able to do that kind of thing with writers, and that's Max Perkins.
~ James Jones (in a 1956 letter to Norman Mailer)

The word "stunning" does not begin to describe the level at which *From Here to Eternity* succeeded when it was published on February 26, 1951. Even the word "astounding" will not do. The novel was a blockbuster from the get-go.

It sold 163,000 copies in hardcover within three months of its publication. And it continued to sell after that at a steady rate of four thousand copies per week.

All the usual obstacles that doom most new authors' debut work (minimal advertising or none at all; a small print run; scant reviews—if any) went missing.

Scribners allocated a budget of $10,000 for first-run advertising (this at a time when a brand new two-bedroom house in the suburbs went for under ten thousand dollars), and they followed their full-page ad in *Publishers Weekly* ("A prediction! A great new career in American fiction will begin with...") with yet another publicity bonanza. Famous writers who were critically esteemed received copies of the novel in advance, with a request by Scribners to offer a blurb. One by one, as the publisher rolled out its expanding ad campaign, there were more and more encomiums available to complement the expensive, larger-than-life new novel.

Serious readers who may have had justifiable reservations about parting with five dollars for a new writer's book (note: a diner breakfast of ham and eggs, with bacon, toast and coffee then cost fifty cents; weekly issues of *TIME* and *LIFE* often ran close to 200 pages in length and cost twenty cents per issue off the rack; a paperback book was usually priced at a quarter) had reason to believe that they'd get their money's worth paying $4.50 (plus tax) for Jones's novel, once John Dos Passos sent a blurb declaring that in *From Here to Eternity* the characters were evoked in such a way that they "reach something of the greatness of figures of tragedy because their hopeless dilemma expresses so glaringly the basic human dilemma of our time."

The praise from John Dos Passos indicated, in a way, a passing of the torch. The new generation of war writers was already receiving an enormous amount of attention, year after year, and had been since 1946. Nonetheless, several writers of who were identified almost always with either the Twenties in general or as post-World War I authors in particular were still very much alive, and on the scene. Dos Passos was one of them (he would continue publishing until 1970). William Faulkner and Ernest Hemingway were also still writing and publishing, but neither one of them contributed a blurb. Faulkner rarely gave quotes. And Hemingway? He shared his thoughts about *From Here to Eternity* in private correspondence to Charles Scribner, Sr. Nothing Hemingway wrote illuminated anything other than Papa's raging envy.

Meanwhile, when making *From Here to Eternity* an Alternate Selection for its vast readership, the Book-of-the-Month Club's editorial board proclaimed that Jones's novel ought to be considered "with the best of such American realists as Dreiser, Wolfe, Hemingway, [and] Faulkner," and after warning its readers about the raw violence and rough language to be found throughout the novel, the BOMC mavens assured their subscribers that the arrival of James Jones "marks the advent in American letters of a young writer who, thoughtfully and with a born talent, is following in the great tradition of the novel."

If John Dos Passos and his praise represented the endorsement of the First World War's literary generation, then the good words of Norman Mailer served notice that one of Jones's famously published Second World War peers agreed with Dos Passos. Mailer's blurb asserted that

From Here to Eternity was doubtless "one of the best of the 'war novels' and in certain facets perhaps the best."

Mailer knew that Jones had written "a big fist of a book, with powerful virtues and serious faults" about the old-time Regular Army; a novel so dense with telling detail, so authentic, and so evocative as a parallel universe, that it stood in a class by itself. Many years later, in 1999, Mailer spoke eloquently about how personally affected he was by *From Here to Eternity*: "I truly suffered. I suffered because it was too damn good. So it was an extraordinary experience reading that book. I think it was better than *The Naked and the Dead*, because it went into the taproot of Army experience. [Jones] hadn't had a successful career life as an adolescent and a young man, so he went into that Regular Army ... his book, I felt, went deeper into the nature of what it was like to be a soldier ... it was a better book than I had written."

Reviews from coast to coast in major and minor newspapers and magazines were often ecstatic. And even when reviews were not laudatory, respect was paid for a variety of reasons. The amount of space granted to Jones was unusually generous. There was a cover story in *The Saturday Review of Literature*, a lengthy review in the daily *New York Times*, coverage in the *Chicago Tribune*, the *Cleveland Plain-Dealer*, the *Des Moines Register* and the *Los Angeles Times*; plus extended pieces about the novel in the *New York Herald Tribune*, as well is in the highbrow monthlies like *Harper's* and *The Atlantic*.

Although novelist John P. Marquand had openly chastised the *New York Times Book Review* for not providing page-one coverage to Jones's book—describing *From Here to Eternity* as "a piece of news in the literary world that will not repeat itself for a considerable period of time"—there was compensation in the form of critic David Dempsey's assessment. If the *New York Times Book Review* cast a wide net, they could not have snared a more enthusiastic reviewer than Dempsey, who said:

"To anyone who reads this immensely long and deeply convincing story of life in the peacetime army, it will be apparent that in James Jones an original and utterly honest talent has restored American realism to its pre-eminent place in world literature. Make no mistake about it, 'From Here to Eternity' is a major contribution to our literature, written with contempt for the forces that waste human life, and out of compassion for men who find love and honor and courage in the lower depths."

In March 1951, Scribners doubled their budget for advertising *From*

Here to Eternity and by April the novel was the nation's number-one bestseller. As the rave reviews—and, increasingly, some not-so-rave reviews—kept accumulating, Jones stayed away from New York City. He and Lowney were again wintering in Florida.

A note from Burroughs Mitchell reminded Jones that Manhattan was "sizzling" as *From Here to Eternity* exceeded everyone's expectations, but Jones veered away from the celebrity capital of the world and had already begun making tentative efforts at what would emerge in 1958 as his second novel: *Some Came Running.*

Something else happened in March 1951. It would have momentous consequences for Jones's life and career in every way, although at that time no one foresaw such an impact. Against the advice of Hollywood insiders who believed that the novel could never be successfully transposed into a major motion picture, the film rights to *From Here to Eternity* were bought for a then-staggering sum of $82,500. The buyer was Harry Cohn, the infamously gruff, crude, and dictatorial head of Columbia Pictures. For the rest of 1951 and all through 1952, Hollywood's grapevine referred to "Cohn's folly," on the assumption that the movie would never get made. Even as Harry Cohn purchased the movie rights to Jones's book, he was warned in a memo that there were no fewer than "four major sources of potential trouble: military, censorship problems, political, and religious." The task of converting the novel into a screenplay seemed dubious. Perhaps impossible.

Cohn gambled anyway. He was a tall, overbearing, cigar-chewing autocrat whose behavior resembled Lyndon B. Johnson's elbow-twisting Master of the Senate histrionics. Jones received a down payment of twenty thousand dollars, and would acquire an additional payment of $20,000 (plus change) on January 2nd of the next three years: in 1952, 1953, and again in 1954. It was a gargantuan payday, mostly donated by Jones to finance building six Colony barracks, plus a well-furnished Ramada, where members of the Handy Writers' Colony took turns cooking and eating communal meals. Jones also purchased vast quantities of everything from designer shoes and rare knives to rifles and chess sets; as well as fine men's tailored clothing, expensive tools, a new car, new motorcycle, and huge numbers of books.

The primary reason that the Book-of-the-Month Club made *From Here to Eternity* an Alternate Selection was that they feared trouble from the U.S. Post Office if they distributed the novel to all its members by choosing it as a Main Selection. Yet, the BOMC's editorial board also released a unique statement to its subscribers, calling Jones's book "one of the most impressive novels they had read in many years." In short order, however, they rationalized (without alluding to the Post Office) their reticence about offering *From Here to Eternity* as a Main Selection: "In spite of its unusual quality, we decided to present it to our members as an alternate, instead of as a regular selection, for reasons which will be clear to all who read the book. It is not the kind of novel to be put in any reader's hands without warning. Its barrack-room language is unvarnished, and some of the episodes will come as a shock to readers who have led sheltered lives."

In the meantime, a review written for the *Washington Post* by critic Robert P. Jordan—appearing beneath a headline saying "It Makes You Sick But Proud"—underscored the book's relentlessly tough-minded dramatic evocations:

"It is Jones's faithful reporting, of which these [profane] words are a part, that gives the novel its extreme and, at times, terrible realism. It, too, is Jones's deep understanding of the Army and the men in it that makes the novel human and appealing. It is his communication of the brotherhood of man and man's inhumanity to man that brings the novel close to greatness."

Contrarily, there were dissenting voices. But even most of the critics who did not believe the book to be a major achievement still saw something of value in it. For every rave review like that in the *Library Journal*—where the reviewer found the book to be "powerful and substantial" and prophesied that "this is an outstanding novel of enduring worth"—there was a naysayer like Bernard De Voto, a fixture for decades at *Harper's*, whose review was headlined "Dull Novels Make Dull Reading."

And that headline was the friendly part of Bernard De Voto's critique.

Ernest Jones, writing for *The Nation* magazine, denounced *From Here to Eternity* as a novel that was "preposterously overpraised." An equally harsh critical salvo came from critic Leslie Fiedler, whose long essay in *Commentary* bore the title: "James Jones's Dead-End Young Werther: The Bum as Cultural Hero." Fiedler's essay was far more exploratory than any status quo book review. In his usual pugnacious, incisive, acerbic style, Fiedler instead published one of the earliest essays to attempt a comprehensive overview of where and how *From Here to Eternity* fit within the larger scheme of American literature.

When it first appeared in September 1951 in *Commentary*, Fiedler's essay ignited a whole new round of arguments for and against Jones's colossus. Even at the other end of the decade, in the Winter 1958-59 issue of *The Paris Review*, which featured what is arguably the greatest interview Jones ever gave (#22 in *The Paris Review*'s "Art of Fiction" series), the theme of Fiedler's critique still cast a shadow.

Jones was reminded by his interviewer during that colloquy: "Another critic, Leslie Fiedler, has written a more ambitious essay on *From Here to Eternity* . . . 'The Bum as American Culture Hero' . . . and his point was that the Ishmael figure [Melville's narrator in *Moby-Dick*], which is almost constant in American literature, was recast in the novels of Steinbeck and Dos Passos as the man on the bum. He goes on to say that Prewitt the bum turns up again, this time at the end of his wandering, in the army. But in the army he is recognized as an artist. The army gave him his bugle, but it was being on the bum that made him an artist."

That made Jones bristle. He said: "I don't agree that it was being on the bum that made Prewitt an 'artist.' What made Prewitt an artist, in my interpretation, was that his old man used to beat up his old lady, as well as himself; and that his old man, like so many human male animals, didn't give a damn about him one way or the other. He was always competing, in a sense, with this image of his father that he was always trying to please. But as for the bum heroes of Steinbeck and Dos Passos, whether they're the inheritors of Ishmael or not—and I guess they are— the main point about them is that they were all involved in the social revolution that came in the Thirties. What's interesting is that if Prewitt is *their* heir, Prewitt as the wanderer had no place left to go *except* into the army—where he became, artist or not, a ward of the government. Which is what is happening everywhere, today, even with businessmen."

Although the Fiedler critique was not full of glowing remarks, there still emerged a deep appreciation for elements in *From Here to Eternity* that even a dissenter had to admire. There was, for example, "the authority of the documentation that is forever saving the book from its own ambitions," Fiedler noted with a backhanded compliment. He also stressed that the novel's "value as literature . . . lies in redeeming for the imagination aspects of regular army life never before exploited, and in making of certain of those aspects (the stockade, for instance, our homegrown concentration camp) symbols of the human situation everywhere."

That was certainly more thoughtful than the denunciation offered up by the editors writing for *San Francisco News,* who dubbed Jones's magnum opus to be "A Second Rate, 800-page, Rotten Bundle of Filth."

Far more prevalent, though, were overviews like that of critic Gene Baro in the *New York Herald Tribune:* " 'From Here to Eternity' is in some ways a difficult book for it faces squarely the agonies of our time. It has a directness, a force, a vigor that cannot be described. Many will think it too brutal. It has no more brutality than a daily newspaper. It is a work appropriate to our age, a novel in the tradition of free inquiry."

The most vicious assessment of *From Here to Eternity* was not in the form of a book review. It came in the form of a letter seen worldwide in 1981, when *Ernest Hemingway: Selected Letters ~ 1917-1961* was published.

"About the James [Jones] book," Hemingway declared to Charles Scribner in a letter dated March 5, 1951: "It is not great no matter what they tell you. It has fine qualities and greater faults. It is much too long and much too bitching and his one fight, against the planes at Pearl Harbour [sic] day is almost musical comedy."

Right off the bat it's clear that Papa had an ax to grind. Six months earlier, in September 1950, Hemingway's first new novel in ten years appeared. *Across the River and Into the Trees* was a bestseller, due to the loyal readership Hemingway had cultivated for decades. But almost all critics and reviewers (with a few notable exceptions) not only shrugged off the book, they mocked it.

Across the River and Into the Trees, the toughest critics said, revealed a washed-up Hemingway whose once lean, spare prose had given way to discursive, self-absorbed, hopelessly contrived murk. The novel began well, with a duck-hunting scene that reminded some reviewers of the power of Hemingway's early stories. But unlike 1940's *For Whom the Bell Tolls,* which also found Hemingway manifesting a much more long-winded, big-breathed prose style (yet somehow retaining control of his material), his new novel was chided by many as not really being a novel at all. (Princeton professor Carlos Baker, in a discerning scholarly article published in 1952, argues that *Across the River* is akin to a book-length prose poem.)

Nonetheless, the knives were out and Hemingway was attacked by reviewers who considered his 1950 novel autobiographically transparent, semi-coherent, atrocious self-parody. Telling the story of a 50-year-old Army officer whose heart condition is so precarious that he expects to die within a week or so, *Across the River and Into the Trees* revolves around static scenes of dialogue between the aging soldier and his 19-year-old lover in Venice, Italy. The narrative unfolds over a span of twenty-four hours and Hemingway did himself no favors by having his 50-year-old sage of a Colonel dispensing pearls of wisdom and subjective summaries of World War II, while repeatedly referring to his 19-year-old lover as "Daughter." Critics pounced.

Strong sales did not serve as a balm to Hemingway. He expected big sales. But to be derided and written off as has-been was unthinkable to him. Always perceiving the writing world as a sports arena where one and all were forever compared (in his letters, interviews, and casual remarks) to famous boxers, bullfighters or baseball players, the glee with which some reviewers scorned his new novel was not just anathema to Hemingway, it was a license to kill.

Having been Scribners's top gun since 1926, all the attention being showered upon Scribners's new star made Hemingway want to kill the very idea that *From Here to Eternity* had merit. So, after receiving a complimentary copy of Jones's novel, which was officially published on February 26, it took Papa all of one week to explode in his March 5th letter to Charles Scribner. Hemingway went berserk.

"Probably I should re-read it again to give you a truer answer. But I do not have to eat an entire bowl of scabs to know they are scabs; nor suck a boil to know it is a boil; nor swim through a river of snot to know it is snot. I hope [Jones] kills himself as soon as it does not damage his or your sales." That was one of the three eerie references to suicide that Hemingway made in this letter, written ten years prior to his own violent suicide in 1961. "Things will catch up with him and he will probably commit suicide," Hemingway also ranted, adding also that "[Jones] has the psycho's urge to kill himself and he will do it."

Actually, Jones was fated to die of congestive heart failure (a disease inherited from his mother's side of the family) at the age of 55 in 1977. Hemingway, in the manner of his own father and also Jones's father, committed suicide by shooting himself.

The anger, belligerence, contempt, and cynicism pouring out of Hemingway, as he wrote out his wrathful remarks to the distinguished publisher who now had a new superstar author representing the Second World War's demographic, peaked with this tirade:

"If you give [Jones] a literary tea, you might ask him to drain a bucket of snot and then suck the pus out of a dead nigger's ear . . . To me he is an enormously skillful fuck-up and his book will do great damage to our country . . . I am glad he makes you money and I would never laugh him off. I would just give him a bigger bucket on the snot detail."

Charles Scribner took issue with the "malice" he found in Hemingway's diatribe, but debating was futile. Like an exhausted heavyweight fighter on the ropes, it was clear that Hemingway felt vulnerable, threatened, insecure, and overwhelmed. His blustering rancor and the scope of his fury nakedly revealed his own inner demons.

Later in 1952, after wisely extracting a novella-length piece of work from the bulk of a massively ambitious (and never completed) postwar novel, Hemingway enjoyed a mythic renaissance with the success of *The Old Man and the Sea*. All the hostile verdicts heaped upon *Across the River and Into the Trees* were forgotten, and Papa's comeback was topped off when he won the Pulitzer Prize in 1953. He was then awarded the Nobel Prize in 1954. Yet he never published another book while he was alive. Alcohol, depression, mental illness, and declining health did him in.

Contrarily, as the 1950s unfolded, Jones was never stronger or more radiant. The sales of *From Here to Eternity* were so robust that, shortly after its publication, orders were placed by Scribners to finance one reprint after another. And the occasional negative reviews were more than balanced out by the plethora of positive commentaries. This pattern continued throughout the decade. Later in the 1950s, when Harvey Swados began his nasty review of Jones's second novel with a look back at *From Here to Eternity*, he summed it up as "sentimentally conceived and crudely written." On the other hand, in a piece entitled "A Second Look at *From Here to Eternity*," not only did critic Richard P. Adams call Jones "a major talent," but he celebrated the author's bedrock integrity: "[Jones] penetrates to the very center of the most important cultural, political, and philosophical questions of our day."

It was in *LIFE* Magazine's editorial "From Here to Obscenity" (in the April 16, 1951 issue) that the dual reaction to the book was best consolidated. Although not endorsing the novel's profanities or many of of its characters' proclivities (alcohol, sex, violence) *LIFE* still went on to tell its millions of subscribers and innumerable newsstand buyers: "Its vigor, its sincerity, and a fundamental understanding of the respect for the Army set this novel apart from such insidious slime as 1948's *The Naked and the Dead*."

Less than a month after *LIFE*'s "From Here to Obscenity" editorial, the magazine published a long, richly illustrated photo-essay entitled "James Jones and His Angel." This made Jones and Lowney household names and swiftly induced an avalanche of letters from aspiring writers who wanted to migrate to Illinois to be at The Colony.

It's difficult to say what is more amazing: The runaway success of Jones's debut novel and the fact that *LIFE* Magazine boosted its fame with such a royal dash of publicity; or the degree to which Lowney and Jones stage-managed the journalist who wrote the article. The essay was written by A. B. C. Whipple, who traveled to Illinois to interview Jones, Lowney, and Harry Handy. The truth of their triangle could *never* be revealed. Not in 1951. So, it was agreed that Lowney would be dubbed a "foster mother" to Jones. And Harry would be the generous benefactor.

As for Jones, his role was an admixture of Boy Wonder and New Hemingway.

In short, *LIFE*'s staff writer A. B. C. Whipple had more than his unusual byline to deal with. In the end, he wrote a rags-to-riches tale with a Freudian twist. By and large, the *LIFE* story is as much about Lowney as it was about Jones. It features a passel of quotations from Lowney and Harry (who appear in one photo as Mr. and Mrs. Harry Handy, smiling in front of their house in Robinson, Illinois), plus a vivid panorama of pictures stressing Lowney's widening of her circle with a quartet of other aspiring writers for whom she functioned as teacher, tutor, den mother, and disciplinarian. The story of her being James Jones's "foster mother" dovetails with the expanding agenda of The Colony as a one-of-a-kind writers' boot camp. *LIFE*'s five million-plus subscribers (and innumerable others who purchased the weekly magazine off the rack) read Lowney version of events, courtesy of A. B. C. Whipple.

Result? Lowney mopped the floor with Whipple.

The PR value was beyond category. First and foremost, there was the banner headline to the right of the magazine's famous all-caps *LIFE* title on the cover:

The Unknown Story Behind "From Here to Eternity" the readers were promised.

But before anyone even got to the photo-essay beginning on page 142, they were reminded in the Letters to the Editor section that Jones's novel was the talk of the nation. Ironically, in this issue dated May 7, 1951, the magazine featured eight letters from readers who wrote in response the *LIFE* editorial "From Here to Obscenity" that ran in the April 16 issue, three weeks earlier. Some of the eight letter-writers shared the editors' disdain for the number of so-called "four-letter words" in the book. The magazine had declared that "*From Here to Eternity* has more of them ["four-letter words"] per page than any other novel ever published for general reading in this country" and that impelled one reader to exclaim: "I could not honestly try to teach my children decency and have the book in my home—therefore we will not purchase it."

And yet, the same editorial had grudgingly averred the "vigor" and "sincerity" of Jones's novel, about which another letter-writer proclaimed: "I believe that Jones's novel is entirely a sincere and honest effort."

As for the article entitled "James Jones and His Angel," it was a triumph of spin. In a nutshell, Whipple composed a slice-of-life feature story that was fundamentally accurate about basic aspects of Jones's biography; and Lowney's, too. There were, however, large parts of Whipple's narrative that fudged facts, sentimentalized or sanitized details, and offered summaries that were too pat. One prime example: After recapitulating the story of Jones meeting Lowney for the first time in November 1943, Whipple wrote "both Lowney and Harry fell for him hard." Almost everything in the article was geared to generate the illusion that Harry and Lowney "adopted" Jones—or, as Whipple put it: "Together they set out to rehabilitate him."

In the end, what mattered most was to present a unique story without the true story being all too obvious between the lines. Hence the strong emphasis placed upon Lowney and Harry as loyally married couple; and the relentless focus on Lowney's lifelong history of maverick, help-the-downtrodden initiatives. Most of all, Whipple shone a light on the presence of not just James Jones in the lives of Lowney and Harry Handy, but also the omnipresence (in 1951) of Willard Lindsey, Bert Bliss, Don Sackrider and Robert Smith— four of the eight young men working on novels and stories under Lowney's tutelage, with Harry's sponsorship. Sharing the limelight helped whitewash Jones's off-the-record, intimate history (eight years' long) with Lowney. They sustained their cover story. For now.

Yet, some honesty emerged. Surprisingly, *LIFE* chose to print a quotation from Jones with the word "goddam." It's startling that *LIFE* printed that blasphemy in 1951, given the magazine's wide family readership and reputation for propriety.

Reported Whipple: "One day a visitor asked Jim if he were at work on a new book yet. Jim was already into the second chapter of it, but he glanced Lowney's way, grinned and said, 'Naw, I'm goin' be a goddam celebrity for the next six months.' Without a word, and only half playfully, Lowney lifted an uppercut from the floor that caught Jim flush on his outsized jaw, smashed his head against the wall and made the whole trailer quiver. 'Wonderful target, that jaw,' she muttered, licking her knuckles."

However theatrically staged that may have been, the reportage was still raw by the standards of the day. Especially because *LIFE's* photographer was on hand and he caught the moment when Lowney very much appears to be punching Jones in the face. Beneath *that* photograph, the *LIFE* attribute repeated the blasphemous word:

"JONES'S FAMOUS JAW is a perfect target when Lowney loses her temper. Here she gives her reply to his statement, 'I'm goin' to be a goddam celebrity.' "

That expansive photo-essay in *LIFE* inspired perennial letters of inquiry from writers all over the country, hoping to persuade Lowney to invite them to The Colony. It was an authors' milieu unlike any other. Burroughs Mitchell said as much after his late-summer visit to Marshall; he stayed at the Colony, witnessing what Lowney and Jones created. In his note of thanks, Mitchell wrote:

"Dear Lowney: I've been having a difficult time. A good many people have been asking me what the colony is like, and I can't answer them with a few well chosen words. (They ask, too, what you are like, and I can't answer that with a few well chosen words either.) The fact that I can't is good; it means that the colony has not set like its new concrete, that it has freshness, that it is a group of individuals rather than an organization. I can say that it is a good place to live and to work, but that is not saying what it is like. I can say I was impressed. But I think I will have to tell all these people to go out and see for themselves. This past summer, eight men have been enabled to write. That's good. The place is there, for writers to come to and work. You've done this thing, *and there is nothing else like it* [emphasis added]."

For the remainder of the 1950s, editors and publishers in New York inquired about aspiring Colony writers, and welcomed Lowney's periodic submissions. It's clear from the text in Whipple's *LIFE* article, and the content of Burroughs Mitchell's note, that when necessary Jones and

Lowney played their apropos roles. They willed themselves to perform on their best behavior. Other visitors to The Colony observed more dramatic behavior. When Norman Mailer visited Jones in Marshall, he relished the histrionic atmosphere. Decades later, Mailer recalled:

"There was so much going on at the Colony. There was Jones, who was now kind of like a pirate captain of a renegade company. And then there was Lowney Handy, who was the worst and toughest drill sergeant-major you could ever hope to encounter. And Jones had this intense relation with Lowney that consisted mainly of incredible, prodigious fights. When they disagreed, they were like two animals. It wasn't sexual, it wasn't carnal, it was mental. 'How dare you have an idea that's different from my idea!?' They were two extraordinarily powerful people always fighting each other all the time."

Meantime, in January 1952, Jones returned to Manhattan and this time not just to deal with business or editorial matters over at Scribners. This visit signified a new echelon of acclaim. Jones had won the National Book Award for Fiction.

*   *   *

At the Commodore Hotel in New York City on the night of January 29, 1952, James Jones sat on an elevated dais with other winners of the National Book Awards for 1951. He was flanked by iconic poet Marianne Moore (decked out in her patented ensemble of black on black; her petite physique topped off by her Colonial-era hat) and nonfiction author Rachel Carson. Jones was in good company, indeed. Moore won the National Book Award for her *Collected Poems* and Carson (ten years prior to the publication of her book *Silent Spring*, which catalyzed the Environmental Movement that blossomed in the Sixties) had won for writing *The Sea Around Us*.

The citation presented to Jones as he accepted the National Book Award for Fiction on that night paid tribute to the "passionate feeling and profound honesty" found in *From Here to Eternity*. The award represented the apex of critical appreciation by the leading lights of the book industry. But it was not a prize easily arrived at. Two other very highly regarded novels were heavily competitive: Herman Wouk's *The Caine Mutiny* and J. D. Salinger's *The Catcher in the Rye*. None of the nominated novels had a unanimous vote from the award committee. Different judges preferred one or the other for subjective reasons. Arguments were vigorous. And Jones won.

By now, *From Here to Eternity* had sold more than 250,000 copies in hardcover and there was no foreseeable end to the book's success. It wasn't just an American phenomenon, either. Foreign rights had been sold to more than a dozen publishers and the novel would also do spectacularly well on the international market. Already it was being translated into French, German, Italian, Japanese, and other languages.

In Manhattan, especially after the National Book Awards ceremony, Jones was a bona-fide celebrity. The much-circulated *LIFE* Magazine photo-essay from May 7, 1951, had generated a kind of heat that publicists can only rarely engineer. Jones had on his hands not only a critically acclaimed debut novel that had just won a distinguished prize, but he also had a commercially successful blockbuster that showed no signs of fading away. It was now almost one year since his novel had been published. In most writers' lives, if they're able even to see a novel through to publication, the following year is when they resign themselves to having their book remaindered. Instead, Jones now had what his fellow novelist William Styron once called "the most famous book in the world." Everyone wanted to meet him.

He entered now a whole new phase of professional acceptance and appreciation. The leading figure at that time in terms of networking and socializing in literary circles was novelist Vance Bourjaily. In a few short years Bourjaily would be superseded by George Plimpton, in terms of being the premier party-giver for Manhattan's literati. But in the winter of 1952, it was Vance Bourjaily whose invitations were coveted. And there was a powerful reason for Bourjaily and Jones to want to cross each other's paths. They had Maxwell Perkins in common.

Before the end of World War II, through a series of personal connections that led straight to Miss Irma Wyckoff, the all-important gatekeeper of a secretary in the office of Max Perkins, a play written by Bourjaily had been read by Perkins as a favor. As always, Max's sense of discovery was on high alert. Talent galore was on display in Bourjaily's play. So, Max suggested that he try writing a novel and within a year Bourjaily had completed *The End of My Life*. Scribners published it in 1947, and as one of the first "war novels" by a newly discharged veteran (Bourjaily was twenty-four when the book appeared), it received some fine reviews and two solid complimentary blurbs from Ernest Hemingway and James T. Farrell. But it was no bestseller. It was, however, given a new lease on life in 1951 when critic John W. Aldridge published the first book-length assessment of the new postwar writers.

In *After the Lost Generation: A Critical Study of the Writers of Two Wars*, Aldridge created a niche as a commentator. He boldly stepped forward and cast himself as the Malcolm Cowley of the post-WW II literary generation. In 1951's *After the Lost Generation*, Aldridge not only reassessed the works and days of Hemingway, Fitzgerald, and Dos Passos, but he also put forth chapter-length critiques and across-the-board analyses of the new works (mostly first novels) by Norman Mailer, Gore Vidal, John Horne Burns, Alfred Hayes, Robert Lowry and others, including Vance Bourjaily. (*After the Lost Generation* appeared too soon to include James Jones.)

In fact, after Aldridge proclaimed Vance Bourjaily's *The End of My Life* to be comparable to Hemingway's *A Farewell to Arms* and Fitzgerald's *This Side of Paradise* in terms of its wrenching coming-of-age motif, and the ways in which Bourjaily dramatized one's loss of innocence amid war's inexplicable lunacies, the novel was reprinted and enjoyed more success than it had when Max Perkins and Scribners published it back in 1947.

It was Vance Bourjaily who threw the most smoke-filled, booze-soaked, jazz-inflected all-night parties then. He and his first wife, Tina, had an apartment in Greenwich Village and during the winter of '52, as Jones strode like a lion on the loose in the streets of New York, one bash followed another. Vance was amiable, witty, very well read (after his military discharge, he completed his degree at Bowdoin College in Maine) and had a knack for bringing people together. He was not plagued by the jealousies and backbiting furies that made many of the young male authors of that era conceive of themselves as rhetorical gladiators. Vance's primary interest was in creating a community of writers, artists, actors, and also musicians (Bourjaily, like Jones, was a jazz buff who adored traditional New Orleans-style Dixieland music most of all). For a brief time, Bourjaily and John W. Aldridge co-edited a new literary periodical that was unique because it was never published as a magazine. Instead, after culling through a tonnage of submissions, Bourjaily and Aldridge published the best new fiction, poetry, and drama they could find in a paperback book format. Aptly entitled **discovery**, one of their significant selections in 1952 was William Styron's novella *The*

Long March, one of the few distinguished literary works ever written about the era of the Korean War.

Within a matter of weeks, as February 1952 unfolded, Jones was invited time after time by Vance Bourjaily to parties that raved on until dawn. The drinking was non-stop, and that suited Jones fine. These all-night literary soirees were top-heavy with overflowing ashtrays, emptied bottles, and chronic ego jousting. Such marathon parties invariably transformed any locale into an alcoholic arena. "It was a period," novelist William Styron once confirmed, "when whiskey—great quantities of it—was the substance of choice. We did a prodigious amount of drinking, and there were always flocks of girls around." That was understatement.

"Moving about at night with Jim was like keeping company with a Roman emperor," Styron recounted. "The man had such raw magnetism and took such uncomplicated pleasure in his role as the Midwestern hick who was now the cynosure of Big Town attention that I couldn't help being tickled by the commotion he caused."

Away from Illinois and beyond the reach of the long arm of Lowney, inevitably Jones cut loose. At one party hosted by Vance, both Norman Mailer and William Styron mingled with Jones as if the Three Musketeers were reborn. "In those days Jones was an avatar of energy," Norman Mailer once recalled. "The success of *From Here to Eternity* had given him huge stuff. His presence could certainly fill any small room. The variety of his small-town personality was not only uncanny and overbearing, but also as warm as your best buddy. It felt like a great new kid had just moved onto the block. And on the rise of this good musketeer spirit," a brief period of brotherly goodwill ensued. "I liked him much more than I thought I would," Mailer later remarked. "I sort of half-loved the guy as a buddy." And yet, an air of cold competition was always discernible. More than once, as the boozy mania peaked, Mailer and Jones ended up in arm-wrestling bouts and push-up contests; each one always ready to rise to the challenge. Their triumphs made them rivals.

It hardly mattered that Mailer's second novel (*Barbary Shore*) had fared poorly in 1951. The success in 1948 of *The Naked and the Dead* had been so robust that it allowed Mailer to comport himself as a heavyweight novelist for the duration. And after William Styron's first novel (*Lie Down in Darkness*) won the prestigious Prix de Rome prize in 1951, his star was ascendant. Mailer, Jones, and Styron had all had a rare kind of literary luck: Each one watched as his first published book caught fire.

Furthermore, each one enjoyed critics' approbation, as well as hefty sales. Plenty of naysayers also denounced all three, but that only drew them closer together. "We almost thought of ourselves more as talented athletes than writers," Norman Mailer once noted. "We probably would have *preferred* to be talented athletes," he added.

"We had that same fundamental love of competitiveness. We were drawn to our fellow competitors, but—there was no question—we each had to be the best."

For a brief golden phase of camaraderie, Jones, Mailer, and Styron were a trio to behold. It was as if they were three brothers, all nursed by a shared muse. In the twilight of his own career many years later, William Styron wistfully conjured up his memories of that halcyon period: "When I first met Jim ... [my novel] 'Lie Down in Darkness' had recently been published, and we were both subjected to a considerable amount of not unpleasant lionization. Jim was a superlion; his book, after these many months, was still riding high on the best-seller lists. He had achieved that Nirvana which, if I may tell a secret, all writers privately cherish—critical acclaim *and* popular success. My book, on a much more modest level, had also done well critically and commercially ... but Jim's celebrity success was extraordinary, and the nimbus of stardom that attended his presence as we tripped together from party to party around Manhattan was testimony to the appeal of [his] unforgettable looks but also to something deeper: the work itself, the power of a novel to stir the imagination of countless people as few books had in years."

Once, after leaving one of Vance Bourjaily's bacchanals together, the three of them stood on a street corner after midnight, warmed by whiskey and basking in the glow of each other's fraternal validation. Suddenly, Styron threw his arms around the shoulders of Jones and Mailer, declaring: "Look at this! The three best writers of our generation—and here we all are together!" Jones was thirty; Mailer had just turned twenty-nine; and Styron was twenty-six. In their milieu, they were like movie stars.

*   *   *

Jones blended right in with film stars when he met them. And in that season he met plenty. Actor Montgomery Clift was a guest one night at a party hosted by Bourjaily. Monty Clift became a sensation on stage in New York's theaters in the mid-to-late 1940s. Then, after only two films, he appeared on the cover of *LIFE* in December 1948. Hollywood was bedazzled. Between 1948 and 1951, Montgomery Clift delivered strong performances in three movies that are still discussed today for their cinematic élan: Fred Zinnemann's *The Search,* Howard Hawks' *Red River,* and George Stevens' *A Place in the Sun.* Jones told Clift that he hoped he would be cast to play Prewitt in the film adaptation of *From Here to Eternity.*

Columbia Pictures was still trying to develop a screenplay that would transpose the novel and maneuver it past the censors ruling the Production Code. Clift was skeptical about his chances of even auditioning for the role. Actor John Derek was now being talked about as the most likely candidate for the role of Prewitt.

Nonetheless, after nearly two years of what is laughingly referred to in Hollywood as "development," Jones's wish and Fred Zinnemann's authority came to fruition. From the get-go, director Zinnemann agreed with Jones, explaining that "I wanted Clift because the story was not about a fellow who didn't want to box: it was about a man who resists all sorts of pressure from an institution he loves, who becomes an outsider and eventually dies for it. It was clear to me, if difficult to explain, what Clift would make of that character."

At the very end of 1952, Jones rejoiced after receiving a note that Montgomery Clift dashed off from Rome: "Dear Jones," Monty wrote, "I guess you know I'm going to play your boy Prewitt. I never believed it would happen when I met you. I'd like to know where the Hell I could reach you when I get back to the States—which will be early in January. I don't care where you are—I'd like to talk with you . . . I'd like to impose on you to the extent of plaguing you with questions for a day. Please write." Jones wrote back. And the two of them did more than talk for a day.

Jones invited Monty to visit him out in Tucson, Arizona, where they spent four days and nights sharing thoughts, comparing ideas, ruminating on the vagaries of a character like Prewitt, and enjoying each other's company. One time, stoking the gossip that Jones enjoyed bisexuality in league with his macho swagger and posturing, he flabbergasted a mutual acquaintance by declaring: "I would have had an affair with [Montgomery Clift], but he never asked me!" What Monty did ask was to be allowed to closely observe Jones's every move. All conversations aside, those four days in Tucson were really all about the way Monty Clift studied Jones's body language and mannerisms. Monty modeled his performance as Prewitt on Jones's persona. In one biography of Clift, author Michelangelo Capua summed up that "Monty was carefully observing [Jones], paying particular attention to his gestures, his movements and his nervous tics, which were the result of a long training period spent in the Army that built his character. Monty was awed by Jones the writer, as well as Jones the military man." Jones and Clift remained friends until the actor's death in 1966.

Originally, Jones had worked on a film script for *From Here to Eternity*. But he realized that the protocols of screenwriting were not his métier. No two writing modes could be more disparate than the heavily textured, old-fashioned, lengthy paragraphs that Jones favored, as opposed to the visually cued, conversationally restrained requirements of a first-rate screenplay. Contrary to the faulty notion that scripts are usually medleys of dialogues, the true secret of every great screenplay has been summed up by film director Sidney Lumet as follows: "Dialogue should be like embroidery on the hem of the skirt of action."

It fell to Daniel Taradash to extract from Jones's 860-page novel the essence of a cinematic storyline, and though it represents a fraction of the book's scope and eliminates more than a few of its most compelling characters (Chief Choate, Jack Malloy, and Corporal Nathan Bloom have no presence in the film), the screenplay that Taradash wrote managed to convey the novel's passion, anger, and sensuality.

James Jones had hit it off very well with the studio chief of Columbia Pictures, Harry Cohn, and as the script development and the casting calls ramped up after New Year's Day in 1953, Jones was in the loop. His advice, input, overviews, and opinions were always welcome by producer Buddy Adler and director Fred Zinnemann. Because Zinnemann's *High Noon* won the Academy Award for Best Picture of 1952, he was in a position of power and control. Although Harry Cohn had wanted *From Here to Eternity* to be a vehicle for actors who were contracted by Columbia (John Derek and Aldo Ray and Glenn Ford), the cast that was eventually assembled was determined by Zinnemann and Adler, not by the studio's mogul.

For each lead actor on board, it was a monumental film. Cast as

Sgt. Milton Anthony Warden, Burt Lancaster (a former circus acrobat who had trained as a ballet dancer and had the body of a Greek statue) was already a matinee idol, but *Eternity* would propel him to the very forefront of Hollywood's leading men.

Similarly, after his work in tandem with Elizabeth Taylor in *A Place in the Sun*, Montgomery Clift, playing Robert E. Lee Prewitt, was at his zenith as a serious actor and as a romantic lead. The combination of Lancaster and Clift guaranteed that the film would have major box-office appeal. Provided that the actresses and the actors had chemistry. All the more reason that Zinnemann's final decisions about Deborah Kerr playing Karen Holmes and Donna Reed being cast as Lorene (aka: Alma) caught Hollywood by surprise. Deborah Kerr was perceived as a British matron (though she hailed from a Scottish family) and her roles had been those of elegant, prim ladies. To be playing the bold, adulterous, chain-smoking Karen Holmes was a big risk to her career. Equally audacious was Donna Reed, who had played wholesome, chipper all-American girls in a number of movies, but who now signed on to play against type as the runaway prostitute saving her money to return to Oregon.

Oceans of ink have been spilled in an effort to ascertain the fiction and the facts in relation to the casting of Frank Sinatra as Maggio. In *The Godfather*, novelist Mario Puzo fictionalized a variation on the theme of the Mob-sponsored crooner whose failing career and falling star are restored thanks to an unusually savage mode of intervention. In the case of *From Here to Eternity*, it was Jones's text that had more influence than anything. Harry Cohn did not countenance the idea that Sinatra was a real actor. He was a song-and-dance man, whose three musicals with Gene Kelly represented his best screen work. Sinatra's other films were not distinguished. But he was built *exactly* as Jones describes Maggio in the novel: bony shoulders, wiry, lean, slight, underweight, vulnerable, and yet still vigorous. The key issue was that the viewers had to side with the underdog (Maggio) when his doom is sealed by Sgt. "Fatso" Judson, the Sergeant of the Guard in the Stockade. When stage actor Eli Wallach tried out for the part of Maggio, his solid, husky, muscular body did not square with the way that Jones presented Maggio. One thing led to another. Eli Wallach opted to work with Elia Kazan on a play instead. A screen test that Sinatra agreed to evoked very promising results. And Sinatra's wife, Ava Gardner, who was at the peak of her stardom, lobbied heavily on behalf of her husband. For a paltry $8,000 salary, Sinatra got the part. Lancaster and Clift were paid $150,000 for their two months of work on *From Here to Eternity*, which indicates both the degree to which Sinatra's career was in the tank (his record contract had expired; CBS had canceled his TV show; MGM had cut him loose; and he hadn't had a hit record in years) and also the degree to which he was willing to do *any*thing to play Maggio.

Harry Cohn, in his own way, was willing to do anything to gain the necessary cooperation of the Pentagon to get his movie made. In order to have access to Schofield Barracks, authentic Army uniforms and equipment, as well as the highly necessary participation of a retired Army general as a Technical Advisor, certain concessions had to be agreed upon.

One: The entire Stockade portion of the story had to be eliminated. Instead of the Stockade being presented as a realm of Army-sanctioned quasi-torture, the script presented Maggio and Sgt. Judson as being caught up in a predatory grudge match, in the aftermath of a barroom brawl. Thus when Maggio is sent to the Stockade for drunkenly walking off Guard Duty, his personal war with "Fatso" Judson triggers the beatings that eventually kill him. No such beatings are ever shown in the film. But the way that "Fatso" Judson brandishes a billy-club hints at Maggio's violent fate.

And two: In the movie, the script had to indict Captain Holmes and find him dressed down and demoted by noble superior officers in the end. Contrarily, in the novel, in spite of all his grossly unethical abuses of power, Captain "Dynamite" Holmes is protected and promoted.

The shooting script was finally approved, and the movie was filmed in a 41-day blitz during March and April of 1953. Two weeks of shooting on sound stages in Hollywood, followed by three weeks on location at Schofield Barracks, plus other locations in Hawaii. Jones was quietly present throughout the filming, and was treated with great respect by all of the cast members and director Fred Zinnemann, too. He mingled easily, never interfered, and drank and ate heartily with everyone.

Just as easily as he formed a trio with Mailer and Styron back in New York, Jones and Sinatra and Montgomery Clift became a troika during the filming of *From Here to Eternity*. Alcohol was their nectar. The three of them had dinner together most nights, and boozed up until all hours. By this time, Sinatra and Ava Gardner were divorcing. So, at dinner,

Jones and Clift would listen to Sinatra bemoan his lost love, and they got more and more plastered in each other's company. Oftentimes, Burt Lancaster was summoned to manually lift Sinatra first, and then Clift, out of their chairs. Lancaster carried them to their hotel beds. Somehow, they managed to work during the day. However, things did devolve to the point where in certain scenes the filming was done despite both Clift and Sinatra being intoxicated. Chances are that added to the movie's verisimilitude.

American society trembled in the summer of 1953. The ongoing saga of Julius and Ethel Rosenberg reached its fatal denouement when the convicted spies were electrocuted at Sing Sing on June 19, even as protesters begged until the last minute for President Eisenhower to intervene for the sake of the Rosenbergs' two small children. An equal number of demonstrators supported their executions.

In July 1953, President Eisenhower fulfilled his campaign promise to resolve the Korean War. After three grim years in a war of attrition that Ike believed could not be "won" unless he authorized the use of atomic weapons, an armistice was signed that ended the war with the opposing sides glaring at each other, back where it all began, on the 38th parallel dividing North and South Korea. They're still glaring.

Hundreds of American prisoners of war would eventually return home, as would hundreds of thousands of Korean War veterans. There were few victory parades.

And on August 5, 1953, with nothing but a single full-page ad in *The New York Times* announcing the new film, Fred Zinnemann's *From Here to Eternity* opened at the Capitol Theater in New York City. Nowhere else. Harry Cohn was testing the market and he knew full well that an early-August opening (when many media critics are on vacation) was not prime time. Yet, his famous gut instincts kicked in and not only did he intuit that the public was ripe for this film, but, he did something he'd never done for any advertisement: He signed his name to the ad in *The New York Times*.

It started all over again. Late in the evening on August 5, long-distance calls were made from New York to Los Angeles alerting Harry Cohn and his colleagues at Columbia Pictures that in order to accommodate the lines forming all around the block of the Capitol Theater, an extra showing at 1 A.M. would be added. It did not even matter that the Capitol Theater lacked air-conditioning.

That year, August 5th was on a Wednesday. And it made no difference that the film opened on a Wednesday, instead of a Friday. From morning until midnight and beyond for the rest of the summer and through the fall and right into the spring of 1954, when *From Here to Eternity* swept the Academy Awards and garnered eight Oscars (including Best Picture, Best Director, Best Adapted Screenplay, Best Supporting Actress for Donna Reed as Alma/Lorene and most famously Best Supporting Actor on behalf of Frank Sinatra as Maggio), the film captured the public's imagination and played to packed theaters from one end of America to another. Although heavily sanitized when compared to the novel, the movie still broke new ground, pushed the envelope, and scandalized more than a few viewers with its lovers' "beach scene" and its evocation of an unhappy marriage, hazing in the Army, illicit love affairs, excessive boozing, and adults behaving like real-life adults, as opposed to the idealized projections for which Hollywood was famous.

So deeply did America's masses connect on a gut level with the cinematic version of *From Here to Eternity* that *LIFE* Magazine (which in 1951 published a "From Here to Obscenity" editorial) featured, without qualms, a striking photo of Donna Reed on its August 31, 1953 cover. There was no doubt about who she was.

LIFE's cover headline, in the lower-left corner below Donna Reed's sultry face, said it plainly: **DONNA REED AS JAMES JONES'S ALMA.** This was nearly twenty years *before* Jane Fonda's *Klute* won her an Oscar for playing a prostitute. And in the upper-right hand corner, another headline read: **LIFE'S MOVIE OF THE WEEK: FROM HERE TO ETERNITY.**

LIFE's review of the film was ultra-positive. And millions of the magazine's readers, like millions of others around the world, were enthralled. James Jones's triumph validated Max Perkins's instincts, and vindicated Lowney Handy's faith.

In January 1958, when Jones's next novel—*Some Came Running*—was published by Scribners, its publicity reminded readers that Jones's *From Here to Eternity* had sold 500,000 hardcover copies and more than three million paperback copies.

Mere numbers, however, don't answer the one lingering question: *Why?*

Why did *From Here to Eternity*—the novel in 1951 and throughout 1952; then the film in 1953 and well into 1954—transfix American culture and become utterly beloved? How could such a profane, erotically-charged, anti-authority narrative conquer the culture at the height of the McCarthy Era? Indeed, how did a novel that hammered home a severe critique of the U. S. Army become iconic amid a new "hot war" on the Korean peninsula?

What did James Jones tap into back then? To answer that question, it's essential to override the idea that the novel succeeded because it was released "back then." It's too simplistic to conclude that the timing of the novel's publication made it a big hit. Doubtless it is a candidate for the Great American Novel shelf. Its epic scope retains what it always possessed: a Biblical density fully supporting the epochal, mythical, narrative panorama that James Jones was uniquely destined to evoke.

As the World War II generation fades away, *From Here to Eternity* remains. It is a timeless novel that some critics mistakenly think became a blockbuster merely because the once-young WWII generation was there to receive it barely one decade after "their war" ended. A more perceptive understanding is succinctly offered by cultural commentator James Norton, who wrote: "If the mark of a truly great author is the hewing of a new cosmos from the insubstantial dross of the imagination, James Jones is among the best we have seen."

From Here to Eternity still engages serious readers because its star-crossed men and women are enmeshed in overlapping, agonizing human conflicts roiling "the deep heart's core" that poet W. B. Yeats alluded to. Jones's monumental debut novel (despite any weaknesses) is nothing less than a vast, soulful, epic lamentation for humanity. Joan Didion summed it up best when she wrote "that James Jones had known a great simple truth: the Army was nothing more or less than life itself."

12
TRANSITIONS GALORE

There is no structure [you] can build strong enough to keep out this
self-knowledge.
Or: the structure [you have] built becomes so stifling,
so lonely, so false,
and acquires such a violent and dangerous life of its own,
that [you] can
break out of it only by bringing the entire structure down. With a
great crash, inevitably, and on [your] own head, and on the
heads of those closest to [you].
~ James Baldwin, 1961

On November 6th, 1956, his 35th birthday, young James Jones was no
longer so young. Never married; not yet a father. At 35, he was ready for
life-transforming new directions.

After six years of Illinois-based, extreme concentration devoted to
the writing of *Some Came Running* (while supporting the Handy Colony
with generous annual cash donations), he went to New York City after
the holidays. Multiple editorial meetings at Scribners in January 1957
dominated Jones's Manhattan agenda. Until Gloria. That changed
everything. While staying in New York at the apartment of his friend and
fellow writer Budd Schulberg (whose Oscar-winning *On the Waterfront*
screenplay triumphed at the 1955 Academy Awards), Jones met Gloria
Mosolino.

A native of Pottsville, Pennsylvania, and a part-time actress-model in
Manhattan who worked as a stand-in for Marilyn Monroe during the
making of *The Seven Year Itch* in 1955, Gloria Mosolino was single, book-

savvy, brazen, and a woman of staggering beauty in the eyes of James Jones (and many others). Her blonde bombshell aura came naturally. And Gloria's ability to match Jones drink-for-drink enhanced their fervid chemistry; she also smoked as heavily as he did.

Seven years younger than Jones, Gloria graduated from Syracuse University in 1949. Harboring a flair for evoking glamour, she impressed others as a style-maven whose fashion sense, make-up skills, physique, wardrobe, and personal ease in most celebrity circles dovetailed perfectly with Jones's persona.

New York author Budd Schulberg made the introductions; he'd met Gloria when she worked as a stand-in for Eva Marie Saint in *On the Waterfront*. Instinctively, Schulberg predicted correctly that Jones and Gloria would inevitably marry. After they met in January 1957, their whirlwind romance exploded. They married in Port-au-Prince, Haiti's capital, on February 27, 1957.

Although not shocked by these transitions, Lowney Handy was jolted.

Lowney almost always said she'd never leave Harry; and at times she remarked to Jones that she expected, at some point, he'd find a wife. In 1947, in a conversation with colonist Don Sackrider (who successfully maintained a friendship with both Handys, even after his ambitions to write fizzled), the topic arose when Lowney told Don she assumed Jones would someday leave her, and his Illinois life, behind. Lowney and Jones had also broached the subject in letters.

The popular success of *From Here to Eternity* peaked after the 1954 Academy Awards; then the decade's mid-point passed in 1955, and soon thereafter 1956 concluded with Jones's plan to visit to New York and begin assisting Scribners editor Burroughs Mitchell, and his editorial team; prepping *Some Came Running* for its much-anticipated publication. They had their work cut out for them. When finally published in January 1958, *Some Came Running* stacked up, then, as the longest novel yet published in America: 1266 pages. It's a gargantuan narrative.

* * *

Elsewhere, as 1957 began, Lowney Handy was looking toward her 53rd birthday in April. She also, however, had a list of other new priorities as the year unfolded.

After years of wondering if the Handy Colony would ever yield some breakout newfound authors, with their debut novels acquired and published by top New York houses, a surge occurred between 1956-1958. Lowney and the Colony (plus Jones by association) were in the media spotlight as Gerald Tesch's *Never the Same Again,* and then Edwin "Sonny" Daly's *Some Must Watch,* and Tom T. Chamales's *Never So Few* received significant national attention: both negative and positive.

TIME Magazine's anonymous write-up in its November 12, 1956, issue exuded derision. Titled "Housemother Knows Best," the unsigned article in *TIME* has a tone of ridicule in its headline, and in the first paragraph. Here it is verbatim:

"Writers are passing strange, and those who herd together in writers' colonies are apt to be stranger still. Perhaps the strangest writers' colony on the North American continent is located in rolling corn-hog country on the outskirts of Marshall, Ill. (pop. 2,960) and looks rather like a struggling boys' camp, with two rows of barracks, a central cookhouse-cum-library and a pond swimming pool. Its founder and reigning queen is a bright-eyed, single-minded housemother of the literary arts named Lowney Handy."

With that as the lede, it's unsurprising that the new novel being reviewed was eviscerated. The unidentified *TIME* writer (or committee of re-writers) followed with this: "Lowney's only sorrow was that in the five years since the [Handy] colony was founded, it had produced no published book to follow Jones's *Eternity.* Last week, Lowney could boast of a second, with the publication of *Never the Same Again* by Gerald Tesch." With that sneering tone, *TIME*'s review laid out its case:

"Its unsavory subject is a homosexual affair between a 13-year-old boy and his 30-year-old seducer, a gas-station attendant. Tesch borrows from Jones the neo-Dreiserian conviction that life itself is a four-letter word. Among Tesch's victims and vermin: a girl who commits incest and goes mad, a wife-beating lush, an aging sadistic homosexual. The most defenseless victim is the English language. Some might argue that Tesch was a born bad writer. But Gerald, an off-and-on Handy colonist since 1952, has apparently been trained to write this way."

Never the Same Again tells a discomfiting story that'd raise hackles in any era, regardless of its publication year. It's surreal to think its launch coincided with Eisenhower's re-election. Yet it speaks well of Jones and Lowney, that they'd encouraged such freedom of expression.

A thoughtful, less contemptuous review by George Adelman in the November 15, 1956, issue of *Library Journal* praised the talent of Gerald Tesch, in regard to his controversial subject matter. George Adelman wrote: "This very powerful first novel has much to recommend it but regrettably also has objectionable aspects that would preclude it being wanted by most public libraries. Subject matter of this sort requires a masterful touch. Remarkably enough the youthful author does have this masterful touch. His treatment of the confused boy and the lonely invert is Gide-like in its perceptiveness and sensitivity."

Four months later, in the *Saturday Review* dated March 23, 1957, the Handy Writers' Colony was highlighted anew in a sidebar essay, plus two book reviews. The sidebar piece was titled "Lowney's Boys," and reads like a sequel to *TIME*'s "Housemother Knows Best." Once again, a skeletal history of the Handy Writers' Colony was duly outlined, and yet again a snarky tone was palpable from the get-go. But at least it's a signed article. Critic Walter Wray opined:

"Now it begins to look as if the faith and matriarchal urge of Mrs. Handy, fifty-two, unpublished novelist, childless wife of an oil refinery manger, is going to pay off handsomely. The second book by a Handyman, twenty-four-year-old Gerald Tesch's 'Never the Same Again,' produced a dull thud when Putnams published it last fall. But this spring, Scribners is offering two more that seemed destined to fare better: 'Some Must Watch,' by Edwin Daly, twenty-one-year-old Yale junior from Illinois, about a college boy's summertime return to the world of his parents . . . and 'Never So Few,' by Tom T. Chamales, thirty-two-year-old native of Chicago, who studied briefly at Northwestern and Iowa, served as a captain in the Burma campaign, [and] has wandered from place to place and job to job ever since . . ."

In the same issue, book reviewer Oliver La Farge balanced his tough-minded critique of *Some Must Watch* with a tip of the hat to its author: "This is exceptional work for so young a writer and it earns Edwin Daly that good old label 'promising.' Much of the actual writing, I gather, was done at the Handy colony . . ." After citing critical reservations about the novel, Oliver La Farge admitted: "This review is pretty harsh. We have a potential writer too good not to criticize honestly." At least his review of

Some Must Watch was criticism rooted in literary integrity.

Never So Few, published by Scribners in March 1957, found Tom T. Chamales on the March 23rd *Saturday Review* cover (a replay of how Jones and *From Here to Eternity* had been heralded in 1950 by *Publishers Weekly*). Esteemed critic Maxwell Geismar declared that "Tom T. Chamales has written an extraordinary first novel . . ." Geismar also stated his reservations, with a slew of critical insights; then ended on a majestic note: "Now that Mr. Chamales has dealt with war so brilliantly, he will have to come to terms with peace and with art." In the *Los Angeles Times*, Chamales was lauded for "one of the best novels to come out of World War II."

Anticipating another *From Here to Eternity*, the film rights to *Never So Few* sold to MGM for a staggering $300,000, but director John Sturges' 1959 adaptation of *Never So Few* did not match filmmaker Fred Zinnemann's achievement with *Eternity*. Paying the ultimate tribute to his mentor, Tom T. Chamales wrote glowingly of Lowney Handy in the dedication of his bestselling first novel: "THIS BOOK is respectfully dedicated to Mrs. Lowney Handy of Marshall, Illinois, who with infinite patience taught me the meaning of: 'to have the faith of a grain of a mustard seed,' and without whose spiritual and critical help this book would never have been written."

*   *   *

Meantime, the newly married author of *From Here to Eternity* had convoluted issues of his own making to confront: both positive and negative.

The good news was that as the days and weeks and months passed by in 1957, Jones was convinced he had found his perfect life partner. And when Gloria and James Jones eventually moved late in May 1957 to the large house that Jones had built on the edge of The Colony grounds in Marshall, Illinois, they were warmly welcomed by Lowney and Harry Handy.

Soon, though, and not surprisingly, all hell broke loose.

Predictable issues of jealous competition (in other words, Lowney vs. Gloria) were not the only problem. Somehow, Jones had persuaded himself that it'd be best not to tell Gloria the truth about his personal history with Lowney Handy.

In the swirling delirium of their three-week Manhattan courtship, and then throughout their subsequent adventures as they escaped New York's freezing winter for the tropical heat and exotica of Haiti, Jones opted to stick with the well-known tale written up in *LIFE* Magazine back in 1951, when the article "James Jones and His Angel" put a long-lasting glow on the success of *From Here to Eternity*, and the founding of the Handy Colony.

Despite his tangled, wildly unorthodox, knotty fourteen-year history in the private realm of Harry and Lowney Handy, the truth was not yet admitted, and the tall tale was repeated. Again and again. In short: Lowney and Harry Handy had been like "foster parents" to Jones, in the aftermath of his Army service and his parents' demise. Literary patrons and devoted surrogate parents: *The End*.

Provided that Jones and his new bride honeymooned for months, distant from Illinois, that story remained intact. Money was not the obstacle it had been for Jones in years past. The imminent publication of his next novel generated such confidence that, based on his track record with *From Here to Eternity*, lines of credit were at his disposal. And then, at pivotal moments in 1957 and 1958, the paperback rights and the film rights to *Some Came Running* proved to be lucrative.

Throughout March, April, and May of 1957, Jones and Gloria enjoyed their high life of continuous honeymooning, compounded by their heavy drinking. They would always be high-consumption drinking partners, until the end of Jones's life, when he finally tapered off with wine in lieu of hard liquor. (He then minimized the wine, as congestive heart failure led to his death in 1977.) Gloria's boozing routinely began during or after lunch. Jones always preferred to wake early, eat little, and sequester himself for hours, writing diligently. When his daily regimen ended, all bets were off. An alcoholic haze settled over late afternoons and most evenings. It requires neither medical expertise nor deep psychological research into alcoholism to see the total denial Jones tried to sustain about his intimate, personal history with Lowney.

It couldn't last.

Yet, until July 1957, his riff remained the same: He had been quasi-adopted by Harry and Lowney Handy in 1944. End of discussion. Gloria questioned none of this, until as a married couple they settled in Marshall, Illinois, and Jones attempted to resume his life in the capacious home that he'd spent a small fortune building to specifications. As Gloria tried adapting and adjusting to married life with Jones, while living nearly one thousand miles from New York City, their house of cards violently collapsed.

Here's what finally happened. On July 4th weekend in 1957, Gloria and James Jones welcomed two young nieces of Gloria's to the big house in Marshall for a holiday visit, and Lowney Handy snapped. In a raging fit of anger, jealousy, and myriad emotional and psychological crises, Lowney barged into Jones's kitchen and, with a knife in hand, screaming curses, she physically attacked Gloria.

It was a spell of madness. Fortunately, for Gloria's sake, Jones was home.

He heard the disruptive commotion detonating in his kitchen, and Jones immediately intervened. He took Lowney's knife, separated the two women, and, assessing the homicidal fury in Lowney's eyes, Jones then ordered Lowney out of the house. Foul language filled the air. Graphic profanities. Gloria's two nieces were petrified, after seeing their aunt assaulted by an enraged Lowney, recklessly brandishing a Bowie knife.

Gradually, however, things simmered down. No one called the police. This insane incident was more than an episode of madness. It was a reckoning. Also an ending. And a beginning.

The next day, sending Gloria's visiting nieces back home as swiftly as possible, Jones and Gloria loaded his car with clothes and essential items for travel, hit the highway, and never looked back.

In one life-transforming breakaway, conducted amid others' rage, bewilderment, confusion, and disbelief, James Jones discharged his past. He broke with Lowney Handy, Harry Handy, their Colony, and the Illinois milieu defining his life (when not in uniform for years, or on the road).

Jones walked away from an $85,000 custom-built home; his Harley-Davidson motorcycle, a library of 3,500 books, including innumerable rarities and first editions; his inventory of power tools and twenty-seven hand-crafted knives, plus $6,500 worth of guns and rifles; some rare artifacts (a Meerschaum Pipe collection), dozens of chess sets, and varied art works (paintings, pottery, sculptures) of great value. Also, a wardrobe dominated by hundreds of items: suits, ties, shirts, and shoes. His books and some of his guns were later retrieved. Everything else he off-loaded in estate sales arranged from afar, and handled by trusted locals. Eventually, Jones's house was sold. He let it all go. He had other problems now. Big problems.

As they drove out of Illinois, the truth finally came out. Jones admitted to Gloria that he and Lowney had been lovers ever since they'd met each other. And that their entire history from 1943 to 1957 had been intimate and conflicted, as well as ambitious and literary and economic.

One bombshell followed another. More than once, Gloria insisted that Jones pull over onto the shoulder of the highway, to let her out. She simply had to get out of the car and walk a mile or two, in order to calm down.

After getting back in the car, they traveled on. Truths were told. Bitter words spat out. Bellowing and screaming. Accusations. Excuses. After which, they punished each other with hours of "the silent treatment," and then exploded again when cigarettes and silences were exhausted. Furious words were sputtered. Growled. And then shrieked. Gloria had good reason to be outraged.

Shortly before Gloria's nieces arrived for the July 4th weekend, in a nasty bit of dismissal, Lowney made a public display of her own wrath by throwing all of Jones's personal items out of the small cabin Lowney lived in on Colony grounds: everything from his toiletries to underwear, and other blatant indicators of their relationship.

That display of raging discontent made it clear to Gloria that the oft-told tale of Lowney Handy being like a foster mother was a lie. Only in the car, however, as they stayed on the road with Illinois receding in the distance—then, and only then, did the worst of it finally spill out.

Not only had Jones been lying to Gloria about his history with Lowney, but, during a short interlude in the winter just past, after Gloria had agreed to marry him, Jones and Lowney again bedded each other. That devastated Gloria.

What happened was that after the wildfire Manhattan courtship enjoyed by Jones and Gloria, prior to their Haiti getaway, he briefly left New York behind, and returned to Marshall. Because it was the dead of winter, Lowney was already in Florida on her own. Jones immediately traveled to Florida.

At the time, he explained to Gloria that he was obligated to confer with Lowney Handy about getting married, because business-related issues in regard to the Colony had to be sorted out. Taxes. Debts. Bank loans. That was all true.

The Colony had been incorporated. Yet there was more. Much more. Once he was back in Lowney's realm as she wintered in Florida, even after clearly articulating his imminent wedding plans, Jones and Lowney reunited as lovers. To make matters even worse, Gloria then traveled to Florida to visit Jones. But he had prevented her from meeting Lowney at that time.

Gloria absorbed the awful fact that such deceptive gamesmanship occurred scant days before marrying Jones. Suddenly, their jet-setting Haiti elopement did not seem so perfect after all. Making it worse was the sorry fact that on February 11, 1957, in the middle of their three-week febrile romance and wedding plans, a brand new photo-essay (prepared in autumn 1956) appeared in *LIFE* Magazine, highlighting the completion of Jones's next novel. Artful subterfuge was duly repeated in the CLOSE-UP feature titled "The Good Life . . ." A new photo of Jones and Lowney sitting at the table in his elaborate kitchen was accompanied by these words: "In his kitchen, [Jones] talks to Lowney Handy, Illinois housewife who, with her husband, 'adopted' him 13 years ago, encouraged him to write . . . then founded a writers' colony where Jones lives and which out of gratitude he helps support."

Now, in July of 1957, trapped in a moving car that was in far better shape than their relationship, Jones and Gloria realized that they had one option. Back and forth they argued about their personal histories, with Gloria's promiscuous past dissolving in the murk of Jones's recent bald-faced lies.

At an impasse, they decided for once and forever: They would never, *not ever*, discuss Lowney Handy again. They would forgive and forget. And everything Jones left behind in Illinois, every aspect of his life pre-Gloria? All gone.

Jones and Gloria made a crisis-oriented vow and a mythic, all-consuming decision that was no less life-transforming than what had occurred between Jones and the Handys back in 1943.

Arriving back in New York City, Jones's marriage began anew. He turned his attention to the January 1958 publication of *Some Came Running*. Life began all over again. For half of 1958, they lived in Manhattan. Come summer, Jones and Gloria (buoyed by the sale of the film rights to *Some Came Running* in a six-figure deal) moved once again: a summer '58 sojourn in London was followed by their ultimate decision to settle in Paris in January 1959. They lived there full-time until 1974.

Jones bought an apartment on the Ile St. Louis, overlooking the Seine river. He strolled past Notre Dame regularly. Most importantly, he retained his discipline as an author, continuing to write the books he felt called to create.

Jones and Gloria returned with their two children (Kaylie and Jamie) to America in 1974; and he taught for one year at Florida International University. They settled on Long Island in 1975, in the writer-friendly enclave of Sagaponack. It was there, against all odds, as his congestive heart failure wore him down between 1975 and 1977, that Jones completed almost all of his final novel *Whistle*, the last volume of his WWII trilogy: *Eternity, The Thin Red Line,* and *Whistle*.

All of that is another story, belonging to another book. The final twenty years (1957 to 1977) in the life of author James Jones are a separate epoch.

* * *

As for Lowney Handy, everything came full circle. She kept offering her energy, advice, and insights to uplift others; a pattern which defined her life.

In the autumn of 1957, two photo-essays in prominent Black magazines highlighted the Handy Writers' Colony. Recently written books by Black authors William Duhart and Charles Wright (both of them quoted in articles and seen in photographs in the company of Lowney Handy and other Colony scribes) were highlighted. *Ebony* magazine's November issue featured a piece titled "Writers' Colony." The article showed that in that 1957 fall semester, as the racist mayhem at Little Rock's Central High School in Arkansas exploded (President Eisenhower had to order U. S. Army troops to escort and protect nine Black students integrating a public high school, as mobs of howling white haters demonstrated daily), the school of Lowney Handy was already integrated. *Ebony* eloquently stated: "Among writers' camps scattered over America, few encourage the entry of down-and-outers and, so far as is known, none has produced a successful Negro author. But the Handy Colony, in the small (population: 2,960), conservative and almost lily-white town of Marshall, Ill., is an exception. The downtrodden are grist for the mill of Lowney Handy, the camp's energetic 54-year-old leader, and two Negro youths are currently among her most prized proteges." The article spotlights "Charlie Wright, 23-year-old, Missouri-born ex-GI . . . [who] has written a stirring novel set in wartime Korea which he calls *The Highest Tension*.

[And] Bill Duhart . . . has written a novel called *Deadly Payoff.*"

William Duhart's mystery novel *The Deadly Payoff* was, indeed, published in 1958 by Gold Medal Books. Unfortunately, the fate of *The Highest Tension* by Charles Wright is less than clear. Literary scholar George Hendrick ascertained in one study that Wright's Korean War novel, had, in fact, been placed with a New York publisher.

According to Hendrick, however, the novel was withdrawn, at Lowney's urging, for further revisions by Wright. He set aside *The Highest Tension. It* wasn't published.

Three novels published by Charles Wright between 1963-1973 (*The Messenger, The Wig,* and *Absolutely Nothing to Get Alarmed About*) are collected in a 2019 one-volume edition, with an Introduction by Ishmael Reed; perhaps *The Highest Tension* will be exhumed and finally issued one day. Wright was an Army veteran, served in Korea circa 1953, and no doubt wrote a compelling novel worthy of attention.

After the *Ebony* magazine feature, one month later in December 1957, a similar photo-essay appeared in *Sepia,* another vital periodical tailored for America's Black readership. Pictured again in photos with Charles Wright and William Duhart, *Sepia* praised Lowney for her bold anti-racist trailblazing.

Throughout 1958 both William Duhart and Charles Wright continued to live and work at the Handy Colony. Wright chafed at the rules and regulations imposed on residents, and though he often left of his own accord or was ordered off the grounds by Lowney, in the end, Charles Wright returned—again and again.

In 1959, Scribners published a new novel written by Colony author Tom T. Chamales. *Go Naked in the World* dramatizes the family conflicts of a WWII combat veteran now at odds with his status-conscious Greek-American father, who scorns his son's prostitute girlfriend. It's a strong follow-up to *Never So Few,* and in 1961 a Technicolor MGM film of Chamales' second novel followed its successful launch. In the generous spirit of the Acknowlegments that Jones wrote for *Some Came Running* and *From Here to Eternity,* the Acknowlegment in Chamales' *Go Naked in the World* expressed a heartfelt tribute: "To Lowney and Harry Handy without whom I never would have become a writer at all."

A death by fire, suffered by Tom T. Chamales in his Los Angeles apartment on March 20, 1960, grievously affected Lowney. His lit cigarette fell between two sofa cushions, and Chamales (who'd passed out drunk) did not wake soon enough. When finally roused, blinded by heavy smoke asphyxiating him, he failed to find his way out. Chamales' black-sooted hand-prints were found on walls nearest the door.

Ex-colonist John Bowers still actively sought Lowney's succor in the very early 1960s, and her advice in letters is revelatory. On December 16, 1962, she wrote:

"I believe in telepathy, although I don't know the hows and whys of it, but about a week before you wrote me, you kept coming into my mind . . . There is so much I just can't tell you. I don't have the strength to do what I used to do – I had a stroke last winter – not a bad one but a warning – and the doctor said I just had to cut down on my work. Where I used to write to anyone who wrote to me – and try hard to write and sell – today I am not doing that – I am picking my people. You know – THIS IS IMPORTANT –life runs in cycles every seven years, and you change and have peaks at certain times. I used to love history and read it all the time . . . YOU KNOW WE ARE COMING INTO A NEW AGE OF WRITING – and all creative arts . . . I will write you more later – am very very tired."

Living in New York, Bowers often brooded on his 1952-53 Colony excursion. He annoyed Lowney by waxing nostalgic over long-ago Colony highlights. In a letter dated January 7, 1963, Lowney lowered the boom:

"Your trouble as ALWAYS is still living in the past – CHRIST SAID, 'Let the dead past bury its dead.' You need to think about that a lot. It is astonishing how much your letter is involved with the past. I can't remember what [Mailer] looks like – . . . That was another life. This is the key to success. I have no sentimentality. Good luck to you John – I wish you the best – I have loved you in my way – because I think I knew you in other lives . . . So if you write – or don't, isn't up to me – BUT YOU. We can never work worth two cents until we get free of our personality – stop chit-chatting – That is not working."

John Bowers created a career mainly as a nonfiction author. Two Civil War-related books published by Bowers (*Stonewall Jackson ~ Portrait of a Soldier* and *Chickamauga and Chattanooga: The Battles that Doomed the Confederacy*) followed his 1971 memoir *The Colony*. Teaching at creative writing programs, he has mentored many students.

The Colony ceased being an on-site, active community by 1960. Jones's sudden departure in mid-1957 meant no more cash infusions. Without Jones funding it, The Colony deflated overnight. To further complicate matters, aging Harry Handy had been downsized in 1954; a new superintendent took over the Ohio Oil Refinery, and Harry was made general manager at a refinery subsidiary in Robinson. After 1960, in retirement, Harry's health failed. He died of lung cancer on March 29, 1963.

Except for author Jere Peacock (a Marine Corps veteran whose important Korean War-era novel *Valhalla* was published by Putnam's in 1961), and African-American novelist Charles Wright, who came and went frequently before moving to New York City, the Colony in the early 1960s no longer had authors living there, writing full-time. That is, until Jon Shirota appeared in April 1963.

*   *   *

It's fitting that Jon Shirota was one of the last of many hopeful faraway writers who wrote to Lowney Handy. Their story is valedictory. They corresponded regularly between 1959-1963. By his count, Shirota received some 300 letters from her. And Jonathan (Jon) Shirota was destined to be the Colony's final student. His story, in many ways a twilight episode, reinforces much of Lowney Handy's legacy.

Born in Hawaii in 1928 to parents who moved there from Okinawa, Jon marveled at his homeland's historic transition in 1959, when Hawaii became America's 50th state. By that time, Shirota had earned his bachelor's degree at Brigham Young University in Utah, before going to work for years at an IRS office in Los Angeles. For two years, however, he served in the U. S. Army in the 1950s. Stationed in Hawaii, he was posted at Schofield Barracks, where James Jones's youthful milestones in the peacetime Army took place.

Like many other men in uniform in the 1950s (and beyond), Jon Shirota was transfixed when he read *From Here to Eternity*. Yet, the novel's staying power has never been limited to males: young or old; in any decade. Nor to readers in military uniforms. Joan Didion commemorated Jones, when concluding her medley "In the Islands," a portion of her landmark 1979 essay collection *The White Album*.

A vivid sentence by Jones was highlighted by Didion. She wrote:

"I have never been sure whether the extreme gravity of *From Here to Eternity* is an exact reflection of the light at Schofield Barracks or whether I see the light as grave because I have read James Jones. *'It had rained all morning and then suddenly cleared at noon, and the air, freshly washed today, was like dark crystal in the sharp clarity and somber focus it gave to every image.'* It was in this somber focus that James Jones rendered Schofield, and it was in this somber focus that I last saw Schofield, one Monday during that June [in 1977]."

Jon Shirota's reaction to reading Jones's debut novel was as visceral as Didion's.

When interviewed by Dawn Sinclair Shapiro for her 2008 PBS documentary *Inside the Handy Writers' Colony*, Shirota explained: "The book *From Here to Eternity* came out. When that book came out, I read it, and I thought: 'Wow!' Because I was in the Army. I was stationed in Schofield Barracks, where the story takes place—and the whole story takes place on Oahu. And I thought—wow, if a white person can write about Hawaii the way that this guy [James Jones] did, why can't I do that someday?"

One thing led to another. Inspired by the tribute to Lowney Handy on the very last page of *Eternity*, Shirota took action. He wrote to Lowney, introducing himself. By the time Jon Shirota began corresponding with Lowney, he was an honorably discharged ex-GI, writing alone, and employed full-time as a junior-level civil servant on track to becoming a career Treasury agent.

Jon's correspondence with Lowney evolved over time, and her harsh words of severe criticism about his rookie efforts segued to occasional affirmations. His first novel (*Lucky Come Hawaii*) was confounding him, and Lowney finally agreed to read Chapter One—then, gradually, several more chapters.

Time after time, she returned pages to Jon in the mail with her abundant comments written in the margins; above and below paragraphs, and on back pages. Brutal critiques (she wrote "SHIT!" on the title page of his novel's first draft) were balanced, as always, by encouraging notes about what she thought effective. Some of Lowney's correspondence enriches the anthology *Writings from the Handy Colony*, a valuable collection published in 2001. In a letter dated April 21, 1959, Lowney wrote this to Jon Shirota:

"Yesterday I marked your manuscript, rather severely, and returned it. Today, I began thinking you might feel all the markings on the manuscript meant you were a bad writer. Which they did not mean at all. Actually, you write a smooth well-constructed sentence, and I can see that you are groping toward a good style, and have much to say. As Pope once wrote: 'He moves easiest who has learned to dance,' and this is true in writing. The ease of handling a scene – thew know-how of writing one – or getting in and out – the transitions into a scene or a chapter sometimes are as important as the chapters or scenes themselves. The first thing to learn is SELF-FORGETFULNESS – not to be self-centered – for self-centeredness means – hate, love, fear, anger, sorrow, self-love, self-hate, self-seeking, ambition, all the many things that are connected with you personally as an individual. A GOOD WRITER RISES ABOVE THESE THOUGHTS . . . It is this rising above the everyday existence – above time and place—that you seek to learn concentration. Without it you cannot be a great writer. And anything that increases your ability to concentrate or to forget yourself is . . . beneficial and promising for a future as a writer."

Time after time, Shirota read (probably in a public library archive, where magazines were bound in orderly chronological volumes) the 1951 *LIFE* Magazine profile "James Jones and His Angel," and eventually took a giant step. On March 31, 1963, Lowney unburdened herself in a letter to Jon Shirota, admitting how disorienting it was to be a widow; she invited Jon to the Colony grounds to use its facilities, and its isolated locale, to focus exclusively on completing a salable draft of *Lucky Come Hawaii*. Already she'd renewed contact with New York literary agent Ned Brown, and Lowney touted Shirota's first novel vigorously. Right away, Jon hit the road.

Although he'd ascended in the bureaucratic ranks, Shirota left his safe, steady California job as an IRS Treasury agent, despite being next in line for a promotion. He quit his former life. With his first novel as the Holy Grail, he jettisoned a whole raft of all-American elements (secure job, pension plan, insurance benefits, and so on) and drove across the country to meet Lowney Handy in Marshall, Illinois.

When Shirota arrived on Colony grounds in April 1963, he saw a faded handmade sign hanging at the gate: "THE LAST RETREAT." James Jones gave the Colony that apt sobriquet years earlier.

Jon stayed in one of the Colony barracks until September 1963, writing three hours a day. When he had a newly revised chapter or a lengthy section of a chapter ready to be seen, he'd slip his pages under the door of Lowney's cabin. After her close reading of his latest efforts, Lowney and Jon would meet to discuss her ideas and suggestions. Shirota had discipline. And much of the time, he was left alone (although Lowney cooked him meals now and then; and they often walked all over the Colony grounds, talking). Jon decompressed from his writing by regularly mowing the vast swaths of lawn across the Colony's acres.

One last time, Lowney's instincts proved sound. In 1965 Jon Shirota's novel was launched by a New York publisher, in a deal made by Lowney's ally, Manhattan literary agent Ned Brown.

It is uncanny that Jon Shirota's *Lucky Come Hawaii* takes place in 1941 at Pearl Harbor. The last man standing at the Handy Colony in 1963 wrote a debut novel with a primary setting and a time scheme in alignment with James Jones's *From Here to Eternity*. Jon Shirota closed the circle.

Shirota's narrative, however, is from another perspective entirely. In *Lucky Come Hawaii*, the build-up to and then the aftermath of the attack on Pearl Harbor is experienced by a Japanese family that years earlier left Okinawa for Maui.

When it was published, one book critic (Saburo Kido for the *Honolulu Star Bulletin*) declared: "As far as I am concerned, *Lucky Come Hawaii* is the most exciting and mature novel written and published by a fellow Japanese-American."

*   *   *

In June 1977, author Joan Didion honored the memory of James Jones— he died one month earlier: on May 9, 1977. Heavy media coverage and a large, celebrity-studded memorial service had followed Jones's death. Didion sidestepped all that.

Instead, she made a solitary Hawaiian pilgrimage. Writing about it, the novelist-essayist-screenwriter-memoirist offered effulgent, precise, commemorative words published first as an article ("Good-bye, Gentleman-Ranker") in the October 1977 issue of *Esquire* magazine. It was published anew in 1979, as the final section of "In the Islands" for *The White Album*, Didion's second book of essays:

"I have never seen a postcard of Hawaii that featured Schofield Barracks. Schofield is off the track, off the tour ... and to leave Honolulu and drive inland to Schofield is to sense a clouding of the atmosphere, a darkening ... I wish I could tell you that on the day in May when James Jones died someone had played a 'Taps' for him at Schofield Barracks, but I think this is not the way life goes."

* * *

It is definitely not the way life goes. Yet, in lieu of musical lamentation, there is memory. In 2007, over fifty years after visiting Jones and Lowney at the Colony in 1953, Norman Mailer praised her in one of his final interviews, articulating what Lowney Handy believed: "[T]hat a new literary phenomenon was coming out of the Midwest; she was going to lead it; it was going to be incredible—and it was going to improve American literature. And she succeeded and failed, like we all do."

Ten books written at The Colony were published by major New York houses.

Lowney's health problems intensified, although chronologically she was never elderly. Born in 1904, her 60th birthday quietly occurred on April 16, 1964.

After Jones's pulverizing 1957 exit, compounded in 1960 by the demise of Tom T. Chamales, and then Harry Handy's 1963 death, she withered.

In her sleep on June 27, 1964, Lowney Turner Handy died.

No Colony writers attended her funeral.

EPILOGUE

"I had to be *broken*. And boy, I mean broken. Lowney cut the ground out from under me until I had absolutely no place to stand. I was completely lost. Every way I turned for aid or escape, Lowney was there and cut me off. Until in the end I had to either face myself or die. And I mean that."
    —James Jones (in a letter to his brother)

*   *   *

"It was, of course, a tremendous decision for both our literature and our popular culture: no one before or since has written with such feeling about the American Army from the inside. An entire world that had been hidden from most educated Americans before World War II was brought to such unexpected life that it remains indelible, both for the generation that fought the war and for the national memory."
    —Seymour Krim, "James Jones: Novelist of the Enlisted Man"

*   *   *

The typescript of *From Here to Eternity*, presented by James Jones to Lowney Handy in 1950, is now in the Rare Book and Manuscript Library at the University of Illinois (Urbana-Champaign). In 1990, it was acquired by the university from heirs of Lowney Turner Handy.

*   *   *

From Here to Eternity is on Modern Library's list of the twentieth-century's 100 Best Novels.

AFTERWORD

A few thoughts. Briefly. And quickly.

Poet and memoirist David Ray graduated from the University of Chicago in 1952. He journeyed to Marshall, Illinois, after gaining admission to the Handy Writers' Colony. Ray soon decided it was a bizarre milieu for which he was ill-suited. Embittered, David Ray left The Colony in summer 1953, and later wrote two blistering critical articles: "Mrs. Handy's Curious Colony" appeared in *Chicago Magazine* in September 1956 and "Mrs. Handy's Recipes for Writers" was published in *The New Republic* in April 1957. Ray claimed Lowney threw bricks at University of Chicago friends visiting him, as she chased them off The Colony's grounds, with James Jones standing nearby and laughing uproariously. It's possible that things ended that badly. Maybe. Maybe not. One thing I'm certain of, though, is that in his memoir *The Endless Search*, David Ray describes a childhood and adolescence of multiple complex traumas. As a student in the University of Chicago's classrooms, he found a haven. Temperamentally, though, like plenty of others, he was simply ill at ease in Lowney Handy's domain.

A contentious issue in all accounts of the Handy Writers' Colony is the methodology of "copying" that Lowney Handy touted to one and all, from James Jones to Jon Shirota and everyone else who resided at The Colony or corresponded with Lowney. I was fascinated in 2006 when Joan Didion explained in an interview that on her own, intuitively and instinctively, her evolution as a writer involved "copying" in a way that was identical to the protocol Lowney considered imperative. Said Didion: "Hemingway ... There was just something magnetic to me in the arrangement of those sentences ... they're deceptively simple because he always brings a change in ... I thought that I could learn—because they felt so natural. I could see how they worked once I started typing them out. That was when I was about fifteen. I would just type those stories. It's a great way to get rhythms into your head."

One of the last major novels to emerge from the realm of the Handy Writers' Colony was Jere Peacock's *Valhalla* in 1961. Highly praised by David Dempsey in the *New York Times* ("This is a strong novel ... a ruggedly honest point of view") and blurbed by Norman Mailer ("*Valhalla* is the best novel I've read about the Marine Corps"), Jere Peacock's final page offered this tribute: "In Gratitude —The author, for the writing of this book, expresses his deeply felt thanks to Lowney T. Handy— for her firm belief in my work and her remarkable creative understanding and editorial advice."

That's a legacy worth noting.

Notes of Gratitude

There are no fabricated statements, reconstructed dialogues, or imagined conversations anywhere in this book.

The extensive autobiographical passages in James Jones's 1975 nonfiction book, *WW II ~ A Chronicle of Soldiering*, are a superb resource for anyone writing about American civilians entering military service shortly before, or during, World War II.

I gratefully acknowledge not just the words I've quoted from *WW II ~ A Chronicle of Soldiering*, but also the vivid, essential, sometimes pulverizing passages quoted from *To Reach Eternity: The Letters of James Jones* (edited by the late George Hendrick and published in 1989).

Professor George Hendrick taught American literature at the University of Illinois (Champaign-Urbana) between 1967-1999. He was a charter member, a generous benefactor, and a guiding light for the James Jones Literary Society, which he co-founded in 1992. In *To Reach Eternity*, the 115 letters that Hendrick selected for publication galvanized my fascination regarding the literary legacy and rebellious life of James Jones; especially the crucially formative years of Jones's life with Lowney Handy, between 1943-1957.

I wish also to express my gratitude to scholar and biographer J. Michael Lennon (author of *Norman Mailer: A Double Life*), who offered his enthusiastic assistance when this book was in its embryonic stage.

As an English professor in Illinois at Sangamon State University —now renamed the University of Illinois (Springfield) -- J. Michael Lennon researched his 1985 PBS documentary film: *James Jones ~ Reveille to Taps*. He interviewed dozens of fascinating individuals, from obscure small-town figures to famous authors Joseph Heller and Irwin Shaw, all of whom knew James Jones at different times of his life. Barely any of those interviewees are now alive. Yet, their words echo profoundly in Lennon's transcripts of the interviews he conducted in the early 1980s.

Xeroxed copies of those interviews by Lennon were generously shared with me, and they are priceless. For example, Jones's elementary and high school acquaintances; the woman (Vera Newlin) who presided over the Carnegie Library in Robinson, Illinois; and various relatives in the family of Lowney Turner Handy— all quotations by such individuals, in my book, were discovered in Lennon's transcriptions.

I'm also indebted to retired librarian Thomas J. Wood, who worked (as an archivist) with J. Michael Lennon as regards the Handy Writers' Colony Collection housed in the Brookens Library at the University of Illinois (Springfield).

My book would not have been possible without the resourcefulness of Thomas J. Wood, who shared rare letters and other crucial materials that helped bring this unusual love story into focus.

Furthermore, I am grateful for the archival volume titled *James Jones in Illinois: A Guide to the Handy Writers' Colony Collection*, which Thomas J. Wood and Meredith Keating created in 1989. It is a trove of vivid information about young James Jones and his maverick mentor Lowney Turner Handy. The Preface by former Handy colonist John Bowers, and the detailed Introduction written by Thomas J. Wood, are mutually fine models of memoir and scholarship.

Finally, my thanks to three allies at the University of Illinois (Springfield), whose kind assistance made possible the use of a rare color photograph of James Jones and Lowney Turner Handy for the cover of this book: Associate Professor Pamela M. Salela, John Laubersheimer (Chair - Library Instructional Services Program), and Dean Pattie Piotrowski were all generously helpful.

CODA: Special thanks and deep appreciation to Kaylie Jones, the keeper of her father's flame.

BIBLIOGRAPHY AND OTHER SOURCES

Adams, Richard P. *"A Second Look at From Here to Eternity."* College English 17 (January 1956: 205-10).

Aldrich, Jr., Nelson W. *"James Jones" in Writers at Work: The Paris Review Interviews.* 3rd Series, edited by Malcolm Cowley, 231-50 (New York: Viking Press, 1967). Also available in The Paris Review 20 (Spring 1959).

Aldridge, John W. *After the Lost Generation: A Critical Study of the Writers of Two World Wars.* (New York: McGraw-Hill, 1951).

--------------. *In Search of Heresy: American Literature in an Age of Conformity.* (New York: McGraw-Hill, 1956).

--------------. *The Devil in the Fire: Retrospective Essays on American Literature and Culture 1951-1971.* (New York: Harper's Magazine Press, 1972).

Allen, Frederick Lewis. *Only Yesterday: An Informal History of the 1920s.* (New York: Harper & Row, 1931).

--------------. *Since Yesterday: The 1930s in America.* (New York: Harper & Row, 1940).

"The Art of Fiction XXIII: James Jones." *Paris Review 20* (Spring 1959): 35-55.

Baker, Carlos. *Ernest Hemingway: A Life Story.* (New York: Charles Scribner's Sons, 1969).

Baldwin, James. *Nobody Knows My Name.* (New York: The Dial Press, 1961).

Baker, Carlos (Ed.). *Ernest Hemingway ~ Selected Letters: 1917-1961.* (New York: Charles Scribner's Sons, 1981).

Berg, A. Scott. *Max Perkins: Editor of Genius.* (New York: E. P. Dutton, 1978).

Besant, Annie. *The Ancient Wisdom: An Outline of Theosophical Teachings.* (Wheaton, Illinois: The Theosophical Publishing House, 2001).

Boorstin, Daniel J. *The Seekers: The Story of Man's Continuing Quest to Understand His World.* (New York: Random House, 1998).

Bosworth, Patricia. *Montgomery Clift: A Biography.* (New York: Bantam Books, 1980).

Bowers, John. *The Colony.* (New York: E. P. Dutton, 1971).

---------------. "Preface." *James Jones in Illinois: A Guide to the Handy Writers' Colony Collection in the Sangamon State University Archives,* by Thomas J. Wood and Meredith Keating. (Springfield, Illinois: Sangamon State University, 1989).

Campbell, James. *Talking at the Gates: A Life of James Baldwin.* (New York: Viking, 1991).

Chamales, Tom T. *Never So Few.* (New York: Charles Scribner's Sons, 1957).

---------------. *Go Naked in the World.* (New York: Charles Scribner's Sons, 1959).

Carter, Steven R. *James Jones ~ An American Literary Orientalist Master.* (Urbana, Illinois: University of Illinois Press, 1998).

Cohen, Mark. (Ed.) *Missing a Beat: The Rants and Regrets of Seymour Krim.* (Syracuse, NY: Syracuse University Press, 2010).

Commins, Saxe, and Robert N. Linscott (Eds.) *The World's Great Thinkers ~ Man and Man: The Social Philosophers.* (New York: Random House, 1947).

Cowley, Malcolm. *After the Genteel Tradition.* (Massachusetts: Peter Smith, 1959).

---------------. *The Literary Situation.* (New York: Viking Press, 1954).

--------------. *Think Back on Us: A Contemporary Chronicle of the 1930s* . . . (Carbondale, Illinois: Southern Illinois University Press, 1967).

Cowley, Malcolm. (Ed.) *The Portable Hemingway*. (New York: Viking Press, 1944).

Cranston, S. I. and Joseph Head (Eds.). *Reincarnation: An East-West Anthology*. (Wheaton, Illinois: The Theosophical Publishing House, 1985).

Crews, Nathan. *"There is Nothing Else Like It": The Innovative Personality of Lowney Turner Handy*. (Masters Theses/Eastern Illinois University/ Charleston, Illinois, 2020).

Dearborn, Mary V. *Mailer: A Biography*. (Boston: Houghton Mifflin Harcourt, 2000).

Dickstein, Morris. *Dancing in the Dark: A Cultural History of the Great Depression*. (New York: W. W. Norton & Co., 2009).

--------------. *Leopards in the Temple: The Transformation of American Fiction, 1945-1970*. (Cambridge, Massachusetts: Harvard University Press, 2002).

Didion, Joan. *The White Album*. (New York: Simon & Schuster, 1979).

--------------. *The Last Interview and Other Conversations*. (Brooklyn: Melville House, 2022).

Emerson, Ralph Waldo. "Self-Reliance," "The Over-Soul," and "Compensation" in *The World's Great Thinkers ~ Man and Man: The Social Philosophers*. (New York: Random House, 1947).

Fiedler, Leslie. *Collected Essays of Leslie Fiedler*. (New York: Stein and Day, 1971).

--------------. *An End to Innocence: Essays on Culture*. (Boston: Beacon Press, 1952).

Fussell, Paul. *Wartime: Understanding and Behavior in the Second World*

War. (New York: Oxford University Press, 1989).

Garrett, George. *James Jones*. (New York: Harcourt Brace Jovanovich, 1984).

Geismar, Maxwell. *American Moderns: From Rebellion to Conformity ~ A Mid-Century View of Contemporary Fiction*. (New York: Hill and Wang, 1958).

--------------. *Writers in Crisis ~ The American Novel Between Two Wars*. (Boston: Houghton Mifflin Company, 1942).

--------------. Review of *Never So Few*, by Tom T. Chamales. (*Saturday Review* 23 March 1957: 12-13).

Geismar, Maxwell (Ed.) *The Portable Thomas Wolfe*. (New York: Viking Press, 1950).

Giles, James R. *James Jones*. (Boston: Twayne, 1981).

"The Good Life of James Jones." *Life* (11 February 1957: 83+.)

Groom, Winston. *1942 ~ The Year That Tried Men's Souls*. (New York: Grove Press, 2006).

Gottlieb, Robert. "How Good Was James Jones?" (*New York Review of Books*, Nov. 8, 2012).

Handy, Lowney. Unpublished letters to James Jones, *et al.*, now archived at the University of Illinois at Springfield. See Thomas J. Wood and Meredith Keating, *James Jones in Illinois: A Guide to the Handy Writers' Colony Collection*. Selected letters by Lowney Handy excerpted in *Writings from the Handy Colony* (see below).

Hendrick, George (Ed.) *To Reach Eternity: The Letters of James Jones*. (New York: Random House, 1989).

Hendrick, George; Howe, Helen; Sackrider, Don. *James Jones and the Handy Writers' Colony*. (Carbondale, Illinois: Southern Illinois University Press, 2001).

--------------. (Eds.) *Writings from the Handy Colony*. (Urbana, Illinois: Tales Press, 2001).

"Housemother Knows Best." *Time* (12 November 1956: 128).

Jones, James. *From Here to Eternity*. (New York: Charles Scribner's Sons, 1951).

--------------. *Some Came Running*. (New York: Charles Scribner's Sons, 1957).

--------------. *The Pistol*. (New York: Charles Scribner's Sons, 1959).

--------------. *The Thin Red Line*. (New York: Charles Scribner's Sons, 1962).

--------------. *Go to the Widow-Maker*. (New York: Delacorte Press, 1967).

--------------. *The Ice-Cream Headache and Other Stories*. (New York: Delacorte Press, 1968).

--------------. *Viet Journal*. (New York: Delacorte Press, 1974).

--------------. *WWII: A Chronicle of Soldiering*. (New York: Grosset & Dunlap, 1975).

--------------. *Whistle* (New York: Delacorte Press, 1978).

Jones, Kaylie. *As Soon As It Rains ~ A Novel*. (New York: Doubleday & Co., 1986).

--------------. *Lies My Mother Never Told Me ~ A Memoir*. (New York: William Morrow, 2009).

Kash, Steve. "Interview of Kenny Snedeker: The Lowney Turner Handy Writers' Colony." *Tribune Star*, 10 October 2001.

Kennedy, David M. *Freedom from Fear: The American People in Depression and War, 1929–1945*. (New York: Oxford University Press, 2005).

Kido, Saburo. Review of *Lucky Come Hawaii*, by Jon Shirota. (*Honolulu Star Bulletin* 7 January 1966: 3).

King, Allan (Director). *The Private World of James Jones*. (Ottawa, Canada: Canadian Broadcasting Corporation, 1967). Television documentary film. (30 mins.)

Krim, Seymour. *Views of a Nearsighted Cannoneer*. (New York: Excelsior Press, 1961.)

--------------. *Shake It for the World, Smartass.* (New York: The Dial Press, 1970)

--------------. *You & Me: The Continuing One-on-One Odyssey of a Literary Gambler.* (New York: Holt, Rinehart and Winston, 1974).

--------------. "James Jones: Novelist of the Enlisted Man." (*Washington Post*, 1986)

LaGuardia, Robert. *Monty: A Biography*. (New York: Arbor House, 1977).

Leonard, William. "She Teaches Tough Guys to Write." *Chicago Sunday Tribune Magazine*, 14 July 1957.

Lennon, J. Michael. "Glimpses: James Jones 1921-1977." Paris Review 103 (Summer 1987): 205–36. Selected quotations from interviews first conducted for the 1985 documentary film *James Jones: Reveille to Taps*, produced by J. Michael Lennon and Jeffrey Van Davis.

--------------. *Norman Mailer: A Double Life.* (New York: Simon & Schuster, 2013).

--------------. (Ed.) *Selected Letters of Norman Mailer*. (New York: Random House, 2015).

--------------. (Ed.) "'The Wisdom of a Serious Redneck': Norman Mailer Remembers James Jones." (*James Jones Literary Society Newsletter* 10, no. 4, Fall 2001).

Linderman, Gerald F. *The World Within War: America's Combat Experience in World War II.* (Cambridge, Massachusetts: Harvard University Press, 1999).

Lumet, Sidney. *Making Movies.* (New York: Alfred A. Knopf, 1995).

MacShane, Frank. *Into Eternity: The Life of James Jones ~ American Writer.* (Boston: Houghton Mifflin Company, 1985).

Mailer, Susan. *In Another Place: With and Without My Father, Norman Mailer* (Northampton, Pennsylvania: Northampton House Press, 2019)

Mailer, Norman. *Advertisements for Myself.* (New York: G. P. Putnam's Sons, 1959).

Mangan, Pat. "Author Sells First Novel To Movies for $300,000" (*The Miami Herald*, January 25, 1957).

Maugham, W. Somerset. *The Razor's Edge* (New York: Doubleday & Co., Inc., 1944).

Mellow, James R. *Hemingway: A Life Without Consequences.* (Boston: Houghton Mifflin Company, 1992).

Mills, Hilary. *Mailer: A Biography.* (New York: Empire Books, 1982).

Mitchell, Burroughs. *The Education of an Editor.* (New York: Doubleday & Co., 1980).

Morris, Willie. *James Jones: A Friendship.* (New York: Doubleday & Co., 1978).

--------------. *New York Days.* (Boston; Little, Brown and Company, 1993).

Norton, James. Online review of *From Here to Eternity ~ The Complete Uncensored Edition* (From: http://www.flakmag.com/books/eternity.html, 2012).

Patterson, James T. *Grand Expectations: The United States ~ 1945-1974.* (Oxford and New York: Oxford University Press, 1996).

Puzo, Mario. *The Godfather Papers & Other Confessions.* (New York: Putnam, 1972).

Ray, David. "Mrs. Handy's Curious Colony," *Chicago Magazine,* September 1956.

----------------. *The Endless Search: A Memoir.* (New York: Soft Skull Press, 2003).

Rollyson, Carl. *The Lives of Norman Mailer ~ A Biography.* (New York: Paragon House Publishers, 1991).

Russell, Ross. *Bird Lives!* (Boston: Da Capo Press, 1996).

Samet, Elizabeth D. *Looking for the Good War: American Amnesia and the Violent Pursuit of Happiness.* (New York: Farrar, Straus and Giroux, 2021).

Sampas, Sebastian. Letter to Jack Kerouac, pg. 363 in Deluxe Paperback Edition of *The Sea Is My Brother: The Lost Novel.* (New York: Perseus/Da Capo Press, 2011). [Edited by Dawn M. Ward.]

Shapiro, Dawn Sinclair (Director). *Inside the Handy Writers' Colony.* (Chicago, Illinois: Woodlawn Avenue Productions, 2008). Documentary film. (55 mins.)

Shnayerson, Michael. *Irwin Shaw: A Biography.* (New York: Putnam, 1989).

Smyth, J. E. *Fred Zinnemann and the Cinema of Resistance.* (Jackson, Mississippi: University Press of Mississippi, 2015).

Stelzer, C. D. "Lowney's legacy ~ More than a love of writing drove the strange colony in Marshall, Ill." *Illinois Times* (Springfield, Illinois, Feb. 20, 2008).

Styron, Alexandra. *Reading My Father* (New York: Scribner, 2011).

Styron, William. *This Quiet Dust and Other Writings.* (New York: Random House, 1982).

Terkel, Studs. *"The Good War": An Oral History of World War II.* (New York: Pantheon, 1984).

UIS. Archives of the University of Illinois at Springfield. For details of the Handy collection, see Thomas J. Wood and Meredith Keating, *James Jones in Illinois: A Guide to the Handy Writers' Colony Collection.*

Uzzell, Thomas. *The Technique of the Novel: A Handbook on the Craft of the Long Narrative.* (New York: Citadel, 1959).

Van Davis, Jeffrey (Director/Producer) and Lennon, J. Michael (Producer). *James Jones: Reveille to Taps.* (Springfield, Illinois: Sangamon State University Foundation, 1985.) Documentary film.

Van Doren, Carl. *The American Novel.* (New York: Macmillan Company, 1940).

Vidal, Gore. *Rocking the Boat—A Political, Literary and Theatrical Commentary* (Boston: Little, Brown, 1962).

Wakefield, Dan. *Between the Lines* (New York: New American Library, 1966).

Waldoff, Leon. *Keats and the Silent Work of Imagination.* (Urbana, Illinois: University of Illinois Press, 1985).

Weatherby, W. J. *James Baldwin: Artist on Fire.* (New York: Donald I. Fine, 1989).

West, James L. W. (Ed.) *Conversations with William Styron.* (Jackson, Mississippi: University Press of Mississippi, 1985).

---------------. *William Styron: A Life.* (New York: Random House, 1998).

Wheelock, John Hall (Ed.) *Editor to Author: The Letters of Maxwell E. Perkins.* (New York: Charles Scribner's Sons, 1950).

Whipple, A. B. C. "James Jones and His Angel: His Talent Lay Buried Under Frustration and Rebellion Until an Illinois Housewife Made Him Write 'From Here to Eternity'." *Life* (7 May 1951: 142+).

Williams, Tony J. *James Jones: The Limits of Eternity.* (Lanham, Maryland: Rowman & Littlefield Publishers, 2016).

Wolfe, Thomas. *You Can't Go Home Again.* (New York: Harper & Brothers, 1940).

Wood, Thomas J. " 'Not following in the groove' ~ Lowney Handy, James Jones, and the Handy Colony for Writers." (*Illinois Historical Journal 90*, Summer 1997).

Wood, Thomas J., and Meredith Keating. *James Jones in Illinois: A Guide to the Handy Writers' Colony Collection.* (Springfield, Illinois: Sangamon State University, 1989).

"Writer's Colony." *Sepia* (December 1957: 36–40).

"Writers' Colony: Woman Who Trained James Jones is Tutoring Two Negro Authors." (*Ebony*, November 1957: 114+).

Zinnemann, Fred. *An Autobiography—A Life at the Movies.* (New York: Scribner, 1992).

ABOUT THE AUTHOR

M. J. Moore is the author of a biography (*Mario Puzo: An American Writer's Quest*) and a novel (*For Paris ~ With Love & Squalor*). Moore's writing has appeared in *The New York Daily News, Literary Hub, The International New York Times,* and *The Paris Review ~ Daily*. He lives in New York City.

photo©Dan Ross-Moore